LANGUAGE ACROSS THE CURRICULUM

Heinemann Organization in Schools Series

General Editor: Michael Marland

HEAD OF DEPARTMENT
Michael Marland

THE ENVIRONMENT OF LEARNING
Elizabeth Richardson

PASTORAL CARE
Michael Marland

THE TUTOR
Keith Blackburn

COMPREHENSIVE VALUES
Pat Daunt

ORGANIZING RESOURCES
Norman Beswick

LANGUAGE ACROSS THE CURRICULUM
Michael Marland

RESOURCED-BASED LEARNING
Norman Beswick

MIDDLE SCHOOLS
Tom Gannon and Alan Whalley

SCHOOL DECISION-MAKING
Cyril Poster

SIXTH-FORM COLLEGES
Eric Macfarlane

Language Across the Curriculum

the Implementation of the Bullock Report in the Secondary School

MICHAEL MARLAND C.B.E.
*Headmaster, Woodberry Down School, London
and a member of the Bullock Committee*

with specialist contributions by

Douglas Barnes

Lecturer in Education, the University of Leeds

Ann Dubs

Head of Reading Centre, Woodberry Down School

Colin Harrison and Keith Gardner

*Schools Council's Effective Use of
Reading Project, Nottingham University*

Dr W. A. Gatherer

Chief Adviser, Lothian

Nancy Martin

*Schools Council's Writing Across the
Curriculum Project, University of London*

Irene Robertson

*Schools Council's Language Across the
Curriculum (Case Studies) Project*

HEINEMANN EDUCATIONAL BOOKS

LONDON

Heinemann Educational Books Ltd
22 Bedford Square, London WC1B 3HH
LONDON EDINBURGH MELBOURNE AUCKLAND
HONG KONG SINGAPORE KUALA LUMPUR NEW DELHI
IBADAN LUSAKA NAIROBI JOHANNESBURG
EXETER (NH) KINGSTON PORT OF SPAIN

ISBN o 435 80578 9 (cased)
o 435 80631 9 (paper)

First published 1977
Reprinted 1977, 1978, 1979

Printed and bound in Great Britain by
Cox and Wyman Ltd, London, Fakenham and Reading

Contents

Acknowledgements

Although I must take full responsibility for any failings in this book, I should like to thank the many colleagues, writers, and speakers whose ideas and experiences I have found very helpful, and the members of some seventy 'Language Across the Curriculum' conferences run by schools, LEAs, and the DES which I have attended whilst writing this book, and whose questions and suggestions I have found so helpful.   **M.M.**

Nancy Martin wishes to acknowledge with thanks: Janice Drewry, Alderman Callorn Comprehensive School; M. Torbe, Elm Bank Teachers' Centre, Coventry; D. Allen, M. Halligan, A. Macalpine, R. Minovi, Westerhope Middle School. Irene Robertson wishes similarly to thank Mr G. Steward, Headmaster, A. Hoskyns, and the fourth-year physics group of Sir William Collins School, London.

The author and publishers wish to thank the following for permission to reproduce copyright material: The *Evening Gazette* (Cleveland) for 'Continuously, monotonously . . .' by Karen Robson, pupil at Marton Sixth Form College, Middlesbrough; Longman for the diagram from *Patterns of Language* by McIntosh and Halliday; Syndication International for the leading article 'The Courage of Jack Jones' from the *Daily Mirror*; H.M.S.O. for the extracts from *A Language for Life* (The Bullock Report); Macmillan, London and Basingstoke, for the extracts from *The Development of Writing Abilities* by Britton *et al.*; Prentice-Hall, Inc., Englewood Cliffs, N.J., USA, for the diagram from p. 52 of *Be a Better Reader* Book VI, second edition, by Nila Banton Smith © 1973 by Prentice-Hall Inc.; The Schools Council and Ward Lock Educational for material quoted in connection with the Writing Across the Curriculum project in Chapter 5, pp. 145–68.

We are grateful to R. Mitson, principal of Abraham Moss Centre, Manchester, for permission to use the worksheet 'Taking Part in Discussions'. The text was produced by the Humanities team in 1974, and the illustrations are by Pete Fricker.

We would also like to thank the Headmaster of Abbey Wood School, London S.E.2., for permission to reproduce Appendix 3; the Headmaster of Culverhay School, Bath, for Appendix 5; the Working Party members for Appendix 4; Ronald Hase for considerable help towards Appendix 1.

GENERAL NOTE

Throughout this book, *A Language for Life*, Report of the Committee of Inquiry appointed by the Secretary of State for Education and Science under the Chairmanship of Sir Alan Bullock, F.B.A., is referred to simply as 'the Report', and that committee as 'the Committee'. All quotations from it are identified by the chapter and paragraph number in brackets immediately after the quotation.

Preface

The Heinemann Series on Organization in Schools is a systematic attempt to help schools improve the quality of the secondary-school experience by a methodical study of the ways in which they can be organized. The series has been planned to cover the central philosophy and every aspect of the planning and running of schools. Each book has been written by a different author and from a different point of view, out of his or her own observation, experience, and conviction; thus there is inevitably some overlapping between volumes, as certain topics (such as the responsibilities of senior staff, or the provision of resources) need to be included in a number of books.

Language Across the Curriculum is not a summary of the Bullock Report. I have endeavoured, with the aid of a number of specialist contributors, to take the central challenging recommendation of the report, and try to help secondary schools make it operational. Essentially, therefore, this book accepts the Report's arguments for a language policy, and takes on the task of working out some of the details. The Report gave only six pages specifically to the subject of 'language across the curriculum', although in a sense a great deal of the rest of the report was directed to that idea. Schools anxious to consider the practical implications of that central recommendation have asked for more details to consider. In this book the contributors and I endeavour to take up and expand those six pages. The scope of this book's interest means, therefore, that very many major sections of the Report are ignored completely, or referred to only from the point of view of a secondary-school language policy; there is nothing in this book about the initial stages of reading, about drama, about initial training, the provision of advisory staff, or even very much reference to many aspects of the teaching of the English Department as such.

Learning, it is now clear, involves language not merely as a passive medium for receiving instruction, but as the essential means of forming and handling central concepts. Thus learning is not merely *through* language but *with* language. The task of devising a policy adequate for this is now laid on every school. There are, however, difficulties.

In the first place the huge bulk of research, thought, and reporting on language and learning has been concerned with the early years, with 'language acquisition'. The commendable ambition of bringing secondary and primary teachers into a closer working relationship, and the obvious truth that language development goes on across such organizational divisions, has led to some overlooking of the special problems faced in the secondary age-range. Schools looking for help in formulating a language policy have found that most of the literature and most of the examples apply to the young child.

Secondly, schools have found the array of specialists somewhat bewildering. They have also found polarized philosophies, frequently over-stated in public pronouncement, which have chosen to leave out the necessary truths of other points of view.

Those of us working with secondary-age pupils have got to find a way of bringing together what is known about language with special reference to this age range, and have to synthesize the separate insights into a workable policy. Clearly no one 'policy' can be drawn up, circulated, and implemented in a diversity of schools. A policy can not be 'bought in' from some central agency. Nor, however, can it be devised in a vacuum, without the knowledge and practice that has been tried out elsewhere. This book therefore aims to provide some of the knowledge, analysis, and range of examples that will make it easier for a school to plan for its own needs. There is no blueprint policy in these pages, nor does the book pretend to give all the answers; rather it tries to list the aspects which a school might consider, and to give details of the possibilities within them.

Each of the specialist contributors has written independently, and each speaks for himself or herself. Thus they would not necessarily agree completely with each other's points, nor those of my own text. Similarly none of us would wish to claim that what we write would be entirely approved of by the Bullock Committee were it still sitting. I believe that this book is within the spirit of the report, but in working onwards from the main recommendation each of us must develop individual methods.

This book is therefore designed to be a practical help to those in secondary schools developing their own 'language policy across the curriculum', especially heads of subject departments, senior staff responsible for organizational, staffing, pastoral, curriculum, and resource decisions, heads and deputy heads, and members of the many school working parties who are trying to make sure that language and learning work together.

PART I

Towards a Whole-School
Language Policy

1. The Need for a Language Policy

The bargain

138 In the secondary school, all subject teachers need to be aware of:
  (i) the linguistic processes by which their pupils acquire information and understanding, and the implications for the teacher's own use of language;
  (ii) the reading demands of their own subjects, and ways in which the pupils can be helped to meet them.

139 To bring about this understanding every secondary school should develop a policy for language across the curriculum. The responsibility for this policy should be embodied in the organizational structure of the school.

(Conclusions and Recommendations)

The central recommendation of the Bullock Report is a tough one, difficult to approach, complex to work out, and extremely taxing to implement. Yet despite its daunting challenge, comprehensive schools up and down the country have embarked upon an attempt to see what is in it for them. I have found a real enthusiasm and energy in many schools. There have been numerous conferences of representatives from schools and many one- or two-day closures when the entire staff of a school or a group of schools have come together to consider the challenge. Others have set up Working Parties or Committees to start a detailed examination of the problems of language and learning in their schools.

This vigorous reaction comes, it seems to me, from a clear realization that recommendations 138 and 139 are sound educational common sense. In a way the Committee has articulated, and supported with a careful scrutiny of a wide range of research, what experienced secondary teachers have long sensed: difficulties with language hamper understanding and growth in most areas of learning, and, conversely, those areas of learning could provide real contexts for language growth. The aim of a 'language across the curriculum policy' is simply to face that basic educational problem by endeavouring to create a 'virtuous circle': *if a school devotes thought and time to assisting language development, learning in all areas will be helped; if attention is given to language in the content and skill subjects, language development will be assisted powerfully by the context and-purpose of those subjects.* Indeed, because much of learning is possible only through the personal operation of language, unless the curriculum is planned so as to encourage a real communication and personal use of language, there will be considerably less learning. If, conversely, the opportunities for pupils to explore ideas through language in the curriculum are developed, language will grow with the learning. Thus the policy can be seen as shrewd bargaining between teachers for the mutual benefit of their subjects and their pupils.

The background

As the Report acknowledges, one major force in formulating ideas for the 'language across the curriculum' movement was the work of the London Association for the Teaching of English, a widely based movement drawing on a larger number of practising teachers, but centred on the Institute team, led by James (later Professor) Britton. The Association's 1968 annual conference provided the discussion document drafted by another member of the team, Harold Rosen, on behalf of the Association following the work of that conference. That document joined Douglas Barnes' now famous paper on talk in the classroom in the book published in 1969 *Language, the Learner, and the School.*[1] It was an influential book, important because its concern was language, especially talk, in *all* learning, and because it gave prominence to the secondary situation at a time when virtually all language development work was orientated to the younger child.

In 1966 the Schools Council had set up the Writing Research Team, also led by James Britton,[2] and in the revised edition of *Language, the Learner, and the School*, published in 1971, Harold Rosen included the theoretical model of discourse that the team had developed. That year the Schools Council started a continuation project to disseminate the findings and ideas of this research.[3] In all that work special tribute is due to Professor Britton, whose own study had come out the year before.[4] He represented the best of the British tradition of academic consideration rooted in a sympathetic understanding of classroom conditions.

Of course, the British climate was favourable in many ways. Indeed one needs to study the extraordinary separation of subject teachers in large American high schools to realize how favourable our tradition has been. George Sampson's famous dictum in his influential

[1] D. Barnes, J. Britton, H. Rosen, *Language, the Learner and the School*, Penguin, 1970; revised edition, 1971.

[2] J. Britton, A. Burgess, N. Martin, A. McLeod, H. Rosen, *The Development of Writing Abilities 11–18*, Macmillan, Research Series, 1975.

[3] Nancy Martin's two sections, pages 145 and 231, are based on this work.

[4] J. Britton, *Language and Learning*, Allen Lane, 1970.

English for the English ('Every teacher is a teacher of English') was widely known and quoted, even if its implications had not been properly explored. Further, the literary critics had helped by stressing the function of language. D. W. Harding had written:

> Utterances cast in the form of communication are at the same time a means of exploring one's experience and defining oneself. And they are not just a communication of the *results* of self-exploration; language processes themselves contribute to the act of discovery, leading the speaker on unexpectedly from what he intended saying to what he finds he has said.[1]

And the works of F. R. Leavis, which powerfully affected secondary school English after the war, were based on similar assumptions about the function of language.

By the end of the 'sixties the teaching of specialist English in the secondary school had been substantially if not completely rejuvenated. Despite the difficulties, confusions, and failures entailed, the new emphasis on language as a personal expression had revealed educational possibilities that would be of value outside English. The time was also propitious as psychologists, sociologists, and linguists had produced fundamental work and helpful insights that explained some at least of the difficulties educationalists were facing. Professor Britton and his team were able to synthesize these insights in the important theoretical work that provided the basis for Chapter 4 of the Report.

The Committee, as 'A unified approach' in the next chapter will make clear, drew also on an entirely different tradition, that of the students of reading. In this country reading has been thought of as something taught only to the young or the backward. In America, however, reading has long been seen as an activity that requires help and teaching, as they would say 'in the content areas'. The 'Reading Consultant' has school-wide responsibilities, and the theoretical understanding of the reading process has been developed widely. This is not surprising for, as Professor Lunzer has noted, 'Education in the USA has long been less élitist than in Britain. The teaching of "reading to learn" is an essential consequence of the democratization of Education'. The United Kingdom Reading Association worked hard to develop these ideas, and the introduction of a 'Reading Development' course in the Open University Post-Experience Course in 1972 can be taken as marking the acceptance of the need for understanding and teaching reading in the curriculum. Thus when the Bullock Committee came to consider its brief there were two strands of work available—language and learning, and reading—which related to all aspects of secondary education and were joined as the demand for a 'language across the curriculum policy'.

[1] I owe this quotation to the excellent introduction by that leader of English teachers, Denys Thompson, to his *Directions in the Teaching of English*, CUP, 1969.

Reading standards

One indication of the need for the policy is the findings of the Committee on reading needs and reading standards, and the education profession is inevitably and rightly concerned with the results of these findings. We must want to know whether we are doing the good at which we aim. Unfortunately, emotive reaction to the notion of 'standards' has made an objective consideration difficult. The Committee itself was set up at a time of national near-panic that 'standards' were declining. To some, any talk of standards is anti-educational, likely to be right-wing, anti-progressive, and élitist. However, a nation, an Authority, and an individual school must attempt to know what it is doing: it has a duty to establish its success both for educational and for financial reasons, that is to justify its mandate and to claim its funding. As we move towards a closer relationship with our local communities, indeed, we are likely to be held even more accountable, and now the expansionist and optimistic years are over, the call to reveal and explain is likely to be stronger than ever. We have barely started to evaluate, but we must, and a book in this series will be devoted to assisting schools with their own evaluation.[1]

The Report studied very carefully the available data on reading standards, mainly the NFER surveys of 1948 through to 1971. Chapter Two of the Report explores in detail the reasons why, contrary to public expectation, it is not possible to agree that standards in the early 'seventies were lower than earlier. In the first place there was considerable doubt about the statistical basis of the testing in 1971, and more significantly there was strong criticism of the validity of the tests, which had dated badly. A simple statistical point needs explanation: as standards *overall* increased in the post-war years, the mean naturally rose. As the test used remained the same, the tested population moved up towards the highest possible scores in the test, the 'ceiling' thus coming nearer to the mean. The more able fifteen-year-olds were by then already performing so well that they were unable to improve their scores: they had hit the 'ceiling'. This meant that the computed mean could no longer rise with the rising standards, as the superior scores, artificially held back, depressed the true mean. As the Report commented: 'Reading ability has outstripped the available tests' (2.34).

However, for secondary schools some of the findings on standards are important, provided that one remembers that these are national averages, and there are substantial local variations. The following conclusions are the relevant ones:

[1] Martin Shipman, *In-School Evaluation*, Heinemann Organization in Schools Series, forthcoming.

Definitions of the terms 'literate' and 'illiterate' vary to so great an extent
as to make them of little value as currently employed. (2.1–2.2)
The level of reading skill required for participation in the affairs of modern
society is far above that implied in earlier definitions of literacy. (2.2)
Comparability of levels of 'literacy' between countries is difficult to
determine. However, there is no evidence that standards in England are
lower than those of other developed countries. (2.3)
There is no firm statistical base for comparison of present-day standards
of reading with those of before the war; and in terms of today's problems
it is questionable whether there is anything to be gained from attempting
it. (2.11)
The tests at present in use in national surveys are inadequate measures
of reading ability, since they measure only a narrow aspect of silent comprehension. (2.13)
The changes in the last decade in the scores of 15-year-olds on both tests
are not statistically significant, and standards in this age group remained
the same over the period 1960/71. In the light of the limitations of the
tests this fact is not in itself disturbing. (2.19)
There is no evidence of a decline in attainment over the years in the lowest
achievers among 15-year-olds. Since national surveys were instituted in
1948 the standards of the poorest readers have risen, and the gap between
the most able and least able has narrowed. This reflects upon the capacity
of existing tests to measure the achievement of the most able readers.
(2.19; 2.29)
There was no significant change in the reading standards of 11-year-olds
over the decade 1960–1970, but such movement as took place after 1964
was in all probability slightly downwards. (2.20; 2.29)
There is evidence to suggest that this probable slight decline in the scores
of 11-year-olds may well be linked to a rising proportion of poor readers
among the children of unskilled and semi-skilled workers. (2.22–2.25;
2.29)
There is some evidence that children of seven are not as advanced as
formerly in those aspects of reading ability which are measured by tests.
(2.26–2.28)

Some of these points are worth pondering:
1. The evidence does support concern at possible lower reading
standards at eleven, and research subsequently published from the
ILEA literacy survey confirms this.[1] That the fall has been pulled
up by the age of fifteen as far as one can see should not be allowed to
mask the fact that the secondary experience is thus diminished by
the reading deficiency of the pupil during those years.
2. The composition of the group who are less able readers has
changed. It is now more homogeneously working-class. This
depressing fact was not noticed in press coverage, and has such
implications, after a quarter of a century of egalitarian education,
that it is worth emphasizing here. The report found:

> While reading standards at the lower end of the ability range have im-
> proved in most socio-economic groups, the poor readers among the

[1] ILEA, Research and Statistics.

children of the unskilled and semi-skilled have not improved their standards commensurately. The result is that the lower end of the ability range has an increased proportion of these children. (2.25)

Although we can be encouraged by the closing of the gap between the most and least able, and the overall improvement of the least able, we must surely be deeply concerned by this fact.
3. Whatever the overall effects, standards are not good enough for current cultural and social needs:

It is obvious that as society becomes more complex and makes higher demands in awareness and understanding of its members the criteria of literacy will rise. (2.2)

There is clearly no room for complacency, but a real need for strenuous effort. The effort required must be across the whole curriculum if it is to be effective.

Whole-school policies

This central idea is being considered at a suitable time, for, it seems to me, now that comprehensive schools have been established almost throughout the country, the first requirements of their establishment have been met, and the new organism is being evaluated and re-shaped. The great strength of the comprehensive school is variety— of pupils, families, staff, and learning activities. This variety is an exciting, heady educational brew, but it should not be allowed to disguise the crucial danger of the comprehensive school, which is the corollary of its variety: fragmentation. The sections of the school pull apart too easily, each looking inward to its own development and each Department becoming a separate power structure, offering pupils a separate unrelated experience. At the same time others in the school, overawed by the intense build-up of teacher talent and committed expertise in various areas, pull back to their own specialism, leaving language to the English teachers. An Art Department becomes a centre of visual stimulus whilst the rest of the school is a visual desert;[1] the English Department becomes the 'sensitive centre of feeling and expression'; the craft department the only area where workmanship is admired, and so on. This tendency towards fragmentation is often more noticeable to the careful visitor than to the permanent member of staff, who has learnt to take it for granted. In these schools there is little dialogue across the school, meetings

[1] cf. The description of the Art Department in *The Creighton Report* by Hunter Davies, Hamish Hamilton, 1976.

are only in Departmental teams, and the pupil is on a package tour from subject to subject.

In facing this degree of fragmentation, it is important to see that so-called 'integration' is not necessarily a solution, indeed my observation is that whatever merits there may be in bringing a group of subjects together,[1] fragmentation, far from being overcome, is actually often made more intense: some of the fragments will have become larger and internally more coherent, but the isolation between them may be even greater. The Humanities faculty may be sharply cut off from the Creative Arts faculty, even more than used to be the case with a gaggle of small Departments in a crowded staff room.

If the strength of the comprehensive school is variety, the challenge is to avoid fragmentation, retain that variety, and achieve coherence. Coherence in a school does not necessarily mean integrated areas; it certainly does not mean that every, or even some, parts of the work should be moulded to feel the same, so that Housecraft, social studies, and English are interchangeable. It means instead that, whilst each aspect of work in the comprehensive school should be encouraged to be different, to retain its special contribution, there should be properly worked out agreements amongst the staff on a number of 'whole-school policies'. There would be agreements on overall aims, and a precise understanding of what is contributed by all and what is contributed by certain specialisms. For these agreements I prefer the phrase 'whole-school policies' for the obvious but important reason that the *whole* school, including its pastoral work, central approaches to pupils, and relations with parents, must be involved.

There are a number of important aims for whole-school policies: moral education, preparation for work, visual literacy, and social education are among them. The theme of this book is that in achieving coherence whilst retaining variety, the building of a whole-school language policy could be the most important and the most valuable.

Disseminated and specialized approaches

In considering whole-school policies, I find it helpful to think of two approaches to the curriculum, that is two approaches to helping pupils learn any desired skill or aspect of knowledge. It is possible to consider any of our curriculum aims against these two approaches:

(a) *Disseminated*. This approach argues that a particular activity is too important to be left to specialists. To leave it to a timetabled slot

[1] I discuss the grouping of learning activities in detail in *The Curriculum and Timetable of the Secondary School*, forthcoming in this series.

would be to risk artificial isolation. 'We must all join in!' is the battle cry. Thus a Head teacher may say 'Preparation for work is too important to be limited to a specialist "careers" lesson. It permeates our curriculum, so that we all contribute'.

(b) *Specialized*. The opposite approach fears that if specific provision with a specialist at a fixed time is not made, the aspect under consideration will at best be mishandled by under-prepared teachers, and at worst disappear altogether. A Head teacher of this persuasion will declare 'Preparation for work is too important to be left to anyone when he or she feels like it. We make sure it's properly taught by teachers who've got some knowledge and training'.

The pros and cons of both the disseminated and the specialized approaches are clear:

Disseminated	*Specialized*
possibility of linking to other concerns	risk isolation
pupils sense importance through variety of staff involved	pupils sense importance through focus of staff involved
risk of no one having sufficient expertise and experience	security of known specialists
risk of activity being ignored	certainty of pupils meeting 'proper' tuition

It is interesting to see where a school stands on any aspect of the curriculum:

Moral Education   usually Disseminated, but not always. The Schools Council's Moral Education Project is often used as specialized material.

Sexual Education   specialized

Careers   usually specialized, though I argue for disseminated

—and so on. Careful curriculum planning involves judging which combination of these two approaches suits the aim. A whole-school language policy is likely to demand *both* approaches.

The diagram attempts to show the activities a school might encourage its pupils to engage in. The vertical axis indicates any subject, with pure exposition and exercise at the top. As you move *down* the subject axis, you move to learning situations in which there is a demand for pupil activity: projects, practical group-work, visits, etc. Similarly, the horizontal axis indicates pure language work, with sheer de-contextualized instruction at the farthest point, and language used in an activity on the left. At the extremes, language and subjects are far away from each other, neither bearing on each other. In the

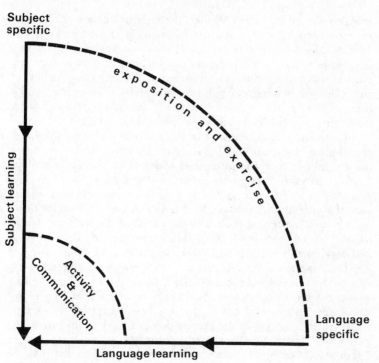

centre they converge, and it becomes impossible to divide subject from language, for the two are fused in the activity. It is here that the most valuable learning probably takes place, but the experience must include the ends of each line; a pupil will not usually make the centre without the experience of the ends.

Teaching and using language

The ultimate aim is always use. Understanding normally comes best when use is possible. We know now from extensive research that learning *about* language rarely improves *use* of language. However, we cannot learn merely by use without reflection, explanation, and theorizing.

It has been well said by the American Harold L. Herber, who has carefully analysed the relationship between the specific teaching and the *use* of skills: 'Independence should be looked upon, not as a means, but as the end product of skills and content instruction'.[1] He goes on to make the basic point that those who wish for independent

[1] Harold L. Herber, *Teaching Reading in Content Areas*, Prentice-Hall, 1970, p. 30.

learning should consider the idea that: 'If independent activity is expected and students have not been *shown how* to perform that activity, this is *assumptive* teaching.'[1] I draw the conclusion that specific preparation for independent learning is always required, both in short straightforward assignments like a reading homework and in lengthy sequences like a project activity. This preparation is best offered in two forms: specifically in isolation, and taught simultaneously within the context of other subjects.

Assumptive teaching *assumes* that skills have already been mastered, or will grow in the course of the activity. There is a tendency to push the assumptive teaching lower and lower down the age groups as teachers of each year-group progressively consider that the best preparation for the independence of the following year is independence *this* year also. A whole-school policy in any field would never assume such mastery of skills. It would analyse the skills and knowledge required, endeavour to establish how they are best acquired and developed, and plan contexts and activities so that they provided the best opportunities for practice and use, with the necessary specific teaching when required. In a whole-school policy the link would not be left to chance, but would be articulated in a policy document, and carried out by the teacher in the activity context when teaching occurs at the precise point of need, according to the policy, and drawing on the shared knowledge.

For a fully coherent curriculum policy, two approaches must be closely interrelated. The entire teaching staff must know that specific tuition is given in certain skills by known teachers and at agreed stages. And all those giving specific tuition must know that context and purpose will be created in a variety of other situations by their colleagues, and that these situations will call on the pupils' memories of the specific teaching. One without the other, or both without an overall plan, is to leave the learning to chance or to restrict it to isolated exercises.

Using language

I sometimes think of the secondary school and its work as a complex organization to *increase* the differentiation in language skills. Those who come to us weak are increasingly offered less stretching challenges (especially when we have multi-task mixed-ability groups) and are allowed in all subjects to find ways around language difficulties. They may in mid-schooling then opt for the strikingly less language-orientated subjects. Thus they arrive weak, and go out

[1] ibid.

hardly any more experienced, whilst the more linguistically able are constantly confronted with language demands and with experiences that generate further language development. The two extremes pull farther apart.

Within the classroom there is a similar process. This results from the ingenuity of many teachers in by-passing language. We circum-navigate print, we reduce writing to gap-filling, we cut down teacher talk, and we lower our expectation of pupil talk. Half knowledge about socio-linguistics, and myths about the class bias of language encourage this further. In a misguided attempt to take pupils 'direct' to knowledge and skills, without losing them in a fog of verbal prob-lems, we dramatically reduce their opportunity to develop language, and deny them the greatest tool to knowledge. At its simplest the pedagogical question at the heart of this book is whether to *use* language or avoid it. What does the teacher do when a pupil baulks at a language situation? That is the core of a language across the curriculum policy. Those who help him *round* it, will also cut down the number and importance of such situations. Those who would help him *through* it would also wish to plan those language situations carefully. All teachers need to be concerned about pupils' use of language. While pupils having difficulty with language must have the unhampered opportunity to flourish in those subjects in which reading and writing play a lesser part, the teachers of those subjects still have a language responsibility. It is unfair to ask the English teachers to carry the entire burden, bad psychology to encourage the pupils to think that good writing matters only in English, and a pity to miss the opportunity to help pupils learn language use in other contexts.

Building a whole-school language policy will help all members of staff devise suitable language situations and indicate strategies to help them through those situations. Some of these, no doubt the easier to agree upon, will be small technicalities, useful common approaches to skills. Such details must not be seen as beneath our linguistic ambitions. On the other hand a policy will never be built merely on such details.

If we are to lead the pupils *into* language, and not devote our ingenuity to helping them *around* it, we must consider the language very carefully. Thus a language policy will be partly concerned with what kind of language we use to explore our subjects, what kind of reading material we offer, and what kind of writing we expect from the pupils. We should not avoid using language, but we should ensure that for the pupil it is usable language that we offer.

True use of language requires something to be expressed, a context, and an audience—someone whose response matters to the writer or speaker. These conditions are simple enough to understand, but difficult to create in mass education. The 'exercise' is very nearly at the opposite extreme: it consumes words without allowing the essential ingredients of a language context. 'Correction' similarly denies the pupil the essential function of a responsive audience, offering only an error filter. Yet the school situation is not as gloomy as that may suggest. The heart of a whole-school language policy is finding and cherishing 'language contexts'. This can be done, and not only by the laborious devising of unusual schemes involving elaborate planning. Indeed it could be argued that only if the 'exercises' in 'the classes' can be converted to fill this need is there any hope for a language policy, for in schools we work in and with groups.

2. The Bullock Report and the Policy

The Bullock Report considered, in relation to schools:

(a) all aspects of teaching the use of English, including reading, writing, and speech;

(b) how present practice might be improved and the role that initial and in-service training might play;

(c) to what extent arrangements for monitoring the general level of attainment in these skills can be introduced or improved;

(page xxxi)

For the purposes of the secondary-school language policy, it is important to sense what kind of report it is, and to see how it bears on our concerns. In this section I shall highlight eight *aspects* of the report which seem to me to help focus our concerns. These are not specific recommendations from Bullock, but are themes which run through the Report, and which bear centrally on the idea of a whole-school language policy.

The importance of language

It has become a fashionable half-truth to declare that we live in a visual age, that with the dominance of the visual image and its cheap availability in newspaper, magazine, hoarding, and screen, the word has become less important, virtually a thing of the past. Such arguments point to the vividness of the news photographs, the way advertising communicates most of its message by a picture, the diagram which so effectively replaces written instructions, the flow-chart and pictogram, even the international wordless toilet signs throughout the world. Half-remembered extracts from Marshall Macluhan confirm this version of reality. Even if the word is still admitted as useful, so this argument goes, it is virtually only the spoken word, for the telephone, the radio, and the television have replaced writing and reading for all but a few specialists. For too long schools have concentrated remorselessly on the archaic and alien (i.e. exclusively middle-class) culture of print. We have not prepared people for the aural world of spoken communication, so vital in an economy of service industries and personal communication.

There is much truth in this argument. However, it gets the elements wrong; it confuses the relationship between the uses of language; and it oversimplifies the relationship between education and subsequent skills.

The truth is that communication media are in competition with each other to only a limited extent. It is perfectly possible for there to have been the expansion in visual and spoken communication without the written word declining. The evidence in fact shows clearly that the use of the written word has increased. As society has changed and the manufacturing and mining industries have given way to various forms of 'service' industry the written word has become considerably more important:

> The changing pattern of employment is making more widespread demands on reading and writing skills and therefore exposing deficiencies that may have escaped attention in the past. (1.2)

This is true across most of the employment ranges. The manager of a group of National Health Service dental clinics, for instance, has told me of the horror the recruits have of the desk, because it involves paperwork, where young employees find difficulties. In higher, but still widespread job levels the demands are greater:

> The expansion in Junior Management has been considerable, and one dimension of competence at this level is the ability to produce a written report. (1.2)

Of course a considerably larger proportion of an age group aim for Further or Higher Education after school, and even in the most practical or vocationally orientated courses, print remains a substantial, indeed the dominant, source of learning. It shows no signs of reducing, and every sign of increasing.

Outside education and employment the ordinary demands of life still expect an easy ability to cope with print. The simplest daily newspaper requires a reading age of thirteen for a reasonable level of comprehension. My experience of recent class teaching is that very many older secondary pupils cannot get much of the sense from most sections of a newspaper. The editorial of *The Sun* or the *Daily Mirror* is really baffling to many. As we offer more participation to a wider spectrum of society, print-needs increase. Even claiming one's rights and finding one's way around society require the ability to read. The Report noted that 34 per cent of Americans tested in a 1971 survey by the US National Reading Council were unable to read an application for medical aid. There is no doubt that in reading alone 'the level required for participation in the affairs of modern society is far above that implied in earlier definitions. It is obvious that as society becomes more complex and makes higher demands in awareness and understanding of its members the criteria of literacy will rise' (2.2). This is true also beyond reading. Whilst it may be true that the telephone has decreased the amount of letter writing amongst those who were likely to have been the frequent and lengthy letter writers of previous eras, the need to put pen to paper has become greater across the population as a whole. The rise in the importance of speech is similarly frequently misunderstood. We have moved away from the oral tradition, and now the purposes for which speech is required and the mode necessary for many of these purposes seems to me to require the sustenance of a wider literacy. There is no returning to the oral tradition of rural areas, nor is it honest to claim that the average person today feels at ease with fluent speech if he or she cannot read and write to a similar level of competence.

Language, thought, and learning

If literacy in its widest sense is necessary for modern society, it is also necessary for the educational process that lasts until pupils are sixteen, or in many cases seventeen or eighteen. As the report comments: 'The one feature shared by all educational institutions is that they make heavy demands on the language of those who learn and those who teach'. It is curious that we have worked so vigorously on the great post-war dream of secondary education for all without realizing that it requires the underpinning of literacy: 'The success of the secondary school can be said to depend very considerably on the level of achievement in reading and language. Unless the pupil can read, write, and talk competently he cannot benefit from the range of learning which the secondary school provides' (15.31). Curiously many of the movements in secondary education require more reading, or if not more quantitively, the reading is more important: Nuffield Science, SMP Maths, the Humanities Curriculum Project, and much that is now the commonplace of the Crafts and the Humanities. As 'chalk and talk' has been replaced by source materials, worksheets, topic books, resource-based learning, and the extensive use of libraries, literacy has been made functionally essential to education, especially with older pupils. Even a teacher intending to place discussion work at the focus of the attention finds that for all except a few contribution to the discussion is severely limited by literacy problems. The non-reader who can talk really coherently will be found, but is rare in our society and especially in our schools. Language is vital to learning to provide access to the source materials and the learning experiences.

This dependence of schooling on language is no mere useless stumbling block put in the way of the young as self-protection by the middle-class, middle-aged, formally educated. It can be shown, as Dr Gatherer points out in the next chapter, that the process of thought itself is dependent on language, and growth in the first depends on growth in the second. It is by verbalizing experiences that a young person can generalize them, and thus 'work on' them. Only through language can we hypothesize, and the ability to hypothesize is the central ability of developed thought:

> The effort to formulate a hypothesis, to put into words some possibility we have envisaged, results in a 'spelling out' to which we may then return, in the light of further experience and in search of further possibilities. By a kind of spiral, the formulation itself becomes a source from which we draw further questions, fresh hypotheses. The statement we have made becomes an object of our own contemplation and a spur to further thinking. It is probably true to say that *the higher* thought processes become possible to the child or adolescent who in this way learns to turn his linguistic activities back upon his own formulations. (4.7)

Professor Jerome Bruner sees the development of analytic thinking as one of the major contributions of secondary schooling, but he stresses that it is through strenuous pressure on language development that this capacity is gained:[1]

> What is significant about the growth of mind in the child is to what degree it depends not upon capacity but upon the unlocking of capacity by techniques that come from exposure to the specialized environment of culture[2]

The report sees language not merely as a dressing for thought, a way of making previously achieved knowledge clear. It sees the process of thinking as part of the process of developing language, and, again, the virtuous circle needs to be set up by the teacher so that the one helps the other. The two sides to this are illustrated in these two points:

> Language has a heuristic function: that is to say a child can learn by talking and writing as certainly as he can by listening and reading. To exploit the process of discovery through language in all uses is the surest way of enabling a child to master his mother tongue. (4.10)

Thus language helps learning and learning helps language, and the more closely the two are related the more effective the total process.

Reading and language

There is a tendency in schools to think of reading as a separate activity, requiring separate tuition. Indeed, as the setting up of the

[1] cf. 'Language as an Instrument of Thought', in A. Davies (ed.), *Problems of Language and Learning*, Heinemann Educational Books, 1975.

[2] J. S. Bruner, *The Course of Cognitive Growth* (1964), reprinted in A. Cashadan, *et al.*, *Language in Education*, Routledge & Kegan Paul, for the Open University Press, 1972, p. 166.

Committee was accompanied by public speculation about a possible decline in 'reading standards', the Committee was labelled by many as 'the reading committee'. From the first, however, it was clear to members that this was an unhelpful limitation: it is impossible to consider reading as an isolated educational activity.

On the one hand, ability to read depends on and grows out of language ability. Indeed, reading of a passage that is too far beyond the reader's verbal experience is virtually impossible. As reading is *not* simply a matter of decoding word by word in left-to-right sequence, but of a continuous speculation and checking, if a reader has to spend too long on an individual word, he loses the overall sense. Similarly, the guessing ahead is eased if the reader is familiar with many of the word collocations. On the other hand, writing and talking skills grow out of reading. Not only are individual words picked up from the 'passive' skills of reading (and listening), but whole possibilities of how words can be put together are absorbed, ready to be called on in the 'active' uses.

Some language skills are patently common to all uses. For instance, one of the highest and most difficult language skills is the ability to *reorganize* information. A good reader, like a good writer or a good speaker, has. to be able to absorb a sequence of points, and re-create these to meet a specific need. The reader who can take the points made only in the order in which they are given, is limited in the same way as the writer who can list his points only in narrative order.

Thus although, as I shall discuss later, *specific* attention to reading is also required, a major theme of the report is the importance of conceiving the reading curriculum as an interwoven part of the total language curriculum.

The continuity of reading

If my last point can be thought of as 'horizontal', that is that learning to read takes its place across a variety of activities, there is an even less well understood point to be stressed which could be called vertical: learning to read, and thus being taught to read, takes place in all years of the secondary school. The Report quotes a simple but telling axiom of I. A. Richards: 'We are all of us learning to read all the time'. The Report sees the teaching of reading as a continuous process, certainly throughout the years of the secondary school.

Popular phraseology, even that in use amongst teachers, encourages a 'threshold' view of reading: 'Can he read yet?' 'He's learnt to read.' 'Do you have many non-readers?' These and similar phrases only too clearly suggest there is a single step called 'learning to read'; it is easily identified; and when reached, well, that's that, and we can all sigh with relief. Parents have the greatest temptation to view learning to read in this episodic way—one of the childhood milestones that it is a mercy to be able to stop worrying about because there's change of school and all that adolescent turbulence ahead. But teachers fall into the over-simplification also; many teachers of older junior pupils too readily expect their pupils to be able to read, and certainly most secondary teachers expect it of all their pupils, identifying 'backward readers' who fall below a certain criterion. This label gains the pupils the help of a remedial teacher, but it also allows the rest of us to leave the teaching of reading to those teachers. They handle the 'non-readers' and therefore know about teaching reading, while we handle the 'readers' (although some seem a trifle ropey), and obviously there's no need for us to know about how to teach reading. This is to commit two related fallacies:

1. *The fallacy of the threshold,* which presumes a clear cut-off between reading and not reading. Even if certain tests at certain times arbitrarily define a certain standard as the threshold below which a pupil is a 'non-reader', in practice we know that there is an infinite gradation from the first recognition of the meaningful shapes of letters to the complex ability of an educated adult to be able to reconstruct the author's intentions from the printed page. Certainly there are moments on that gradation that are especially significant: the first de-coding of a word; achieving a reading age of nine; and the age of thirteen is also perhaps an important threshold, marking the start of the ability to cope with a free range of self-chosen unedited texts. There is probably, it seems to me, an unmeasured step, not reached by many, which allows free access to the bulk of complex adult prose. Despite these rough stages, it is important to realize that pupils need help with their basic primary skills in reading well beyond these early thresholds, and there is no huge single step called 'learning to read'.

2. *The fallacy of basic skills.* The attitude that learning to read, once done, can be left behind, fails to recognize that word recognition is merely the primary skill, inadequate on its own. There is a hierarchy of reading skills, through the intermediate skills of sequences of words, to the comprehension skills. When it can be shown that as many as one third of the adult population cannot adequately comprehend popular news items and the like, it is easy to accept the arguments for the teaching of reading continued beyond word recognition to the real grappling with the sense. Too many of us—indeed most of the nation's secondary teachers—have presumed that once word recognition was roughly mastered all else would follow, that basic skills *were* 'reading'.

The report thus suggests a thread of reading tuition (discussed in Chapter 5) stretching from the earliest years to the end of formal education, *for all pupils*. It is worth knowing in the secondary school that the Report also pushes this back to the earliest stages. Whilst it accepts the concept of 'reading readiness', it substantially modifies the passive acceptance of this:

> It cannot be emphasised too strongly that the teacher has to help the children towards readiness to read. There is no question of waiting for readiness to occur; for with many children it does not come 'naturally' and must be brought about by the teacher's positive measures to induce it. (7.11)

Not only are the beginnings to be thus pushed back, but considerable encouragement is given to achieving satisfactory skills by the time of change from first or Junior schools. Although no fixed levels can be given for any age it is vital to keep the encouragement going:

> Delay beyond the age of seven in beginning to read puts a child at educational risk. There is evidence to show that many children who have made little progress in reading on entering the junior school are even further behind at eleven and that this deficiency continues to the end of their statutory school life. (Conclusions & Recommendations 212, 18.4)

The thread, though, continues right through the secondary stage, for there will be some pupils still needing substantial help with word recognition skills during these years; almost all the pupils will also need help when facing a new word or a sentence with a teasing word order. Immediately it is agreed that 'basic skills' are not mastered once and for all, it is obvious that every secondary teacher must be able and willing to give help at basic skills. It also means that the intermediate and higher skills *need teaching*.

The corollary of this is that the hierarchy of reading skills should not be thought of as something through which the pupil passes, leaving earlier stages behind. *Teaching must be available for all stages simultaneously*. Thus the seven-year-old should be faced with inference, reorganization, evaluation, and appreciation, much as word recognition, word attack skills, and the intermediate skills of sentence construing should not be thought of as left behind in the secondary school:

> The development of reading skills is a progressive one, and there are no staging points to which one can attach any particular ages. We cannot therefore speak of kinds of reading ability as being specific to the middle years and as something essentially different from those used in the upper forms of the secondary school. The primary skills of the early years mature into the understanding of word structure and spelling patterns. The intermediate skills, so essential in word attack in the early stages, are at work in skimming, scanning, and the extraction of meaning in the more complex reading tasks of the later stages. The comprehension skills themselves do not change; it is in the increasing complexity of the purpose to which they are put as the pupils grow older that the difference lies. (8.1)

If 'we are all of us learning to read all the time', and if we accept that pupils in the secondary school, of all abilities and all ages, have a range of reading difficulties, then those of us working in secondary schools must 'all of us be teaching reading all the time' also.

The need for intervention

In all work with language there is a tension, which can be creative, between two approaches, the contextual and the didactic. (These models are analogous to the disseminated and the specialized approaches to the curriculum, which I outlined in general terms on pages 9–11.) The first quite rightly stresses the need to create interest in the pupil, to motivate by an end product, and to offer stimulus and encouragement. It hopes that the skills will be *required* by the context and thus that the need to learn them will engender the actual learning. The second quite rightly stresses the importance of actually explaining things, on giving practice in skills, of 'teaching'. Contextual learning suggests that specific tuition will be meaningless without purpose and context. Didactic learning fears that without clear explanation the context will be insufficient to give real learning opportunities.

In practice, no teacher has a strategy which entirely ignores one or the other. In theory many teachers, however, do over-stress one or the other, fashionably the contextual. The Report holds a careful balance between the two, recognizing essentially that *purpose* is required for language growth, and therefore that the teacher must always look for ways of creating contexts, but also that *intervention* is essential. I should say, therefore, that it is an interventionist report. This conclusion indicates the balance: 'Language competence grows incrementally, through an interaction of writing, talk, reading, and experience, and the best teaching deliberately influences the nature and quality of this growth' (C & R 3). This 'deliberate influence' is more specifically defined elsewhere as intervention, and the balance is carefully put:

> The handling of language is a complex ability, and one that will not be developed simply by working through a series of textbook exercises. If we regard this approach as inadequate we have equal lack of sympathy with the notion that forms of language can be left to look after themselves. On the contrary, *we believe the teacher should intervene, should constantly be looking for opportunities to improve the quality of the utterance.* (1.10)

My italics there point the theme of this book: to help a school find ways in which all its teachers can intervene positively, but within a real language context.

There is a growing body of thought that it is precisely the less favoured pupils who require the most, but also the most careful, intervention. Douglas Pidgeon, for instance, has argued[1] persuasively that in the initial stages of reading it is children who have not experienced in their homes the 'specific expectancies of what reading was going to be like, of what the activity consisted of, of the purpose and use of it' who need pre-reading help with phonics before word recognition is possible. Those experienced in teaching less able secondary-age pupils similarly find that more help must be given, more specific intervention is necessary. It is important to stress, however, that there is no suggestion that the less favoured children do not require a rich context in which to use language. Of course, they do, but this will be insufficient without appropriate intervention. In his anxiety not to be over-dominant and in his wish to allow the pupil the opportunity for self-motivated growth, the teacher must not slip into the opposite failure, which is 'assumptive teaching'—assuming that points are understood.

A variety of solutions

A consistent theme of the Report is that there is no single, simple, magic solution to any aspect of language education. This conclusion was not arrived at lightly. It did not please the journalists, who would undoubtedly have preferred a strong recommendation for this that or the other 'technique', nor some of the witnesses who gave their evidence—for some were pushing single solutions. The hope of agreeing that some method of organizational approach would offer certainty of success probably lay in many people's minds. The Report found that each teaching situation requires a different combination of approaches. Thus, on the initial stages of learning to read: 'There is no one method, medium, approach, device, or philosophy that holds the key to the process of learning to read' (C & R 56), and a similar refusal to offer 'the key' will be found in the sections on curriculum organization (15.3–15.4) and pupil grouping (15.10–15.11).

A careful questioning of the experts, who appeared at first to be overwhelmingly stressing one approach, revealed that their own convictions were not in fact overwhelming: the self-styled National Council for Educational Standards did not in fact recommend a full diet of clause analysis, nor did the proponents of an 'imaginative, creative' approach actually imply that there should be no specialized technical teaching. Time and again it became clear that although popular educational articles and talks tend to peddle polarities, a

[1] Douglas Pidgeon, *Logical Steps in the Process of Learning to Read*, Educational Research, Volume 18, Number 3, NFER, June, 1976.

careful observation of actual teaching and research reveals no support for the extreme positions. It seems that it is not the system that matters, but being systematic; it is not the method that matters, but being methodical. Indeed it is one of the hard facts of educational decision-making that when a decision is made to choose one course or another it is important to realize that there is some virtue in the course rejected, and a compensation has to be built into the decision for that which has been lost.

There is no place for superficial polarities, presuming that the truth of one point of view means there is no truth in another. This is specially so of the pseudo-polarities of 'progressive' and 'traditional'. Neville Bennett's now famous research[1] followed the Report, and despite its inevitable limitations of methodological completeness in measuring language, showed in detail that primary teaching cannot always be so divided. My own review of the studies of language in the secondary school lead me to stress that success in most of the supposedly 'progressive' aims involves a marked 'traditional' component. This is especially true of independent study, the use of multiple learning sources, and of the pupil's ability to question and think for himself.

From the point of view of a secondary pupil's language development, it is clear that there is no single policy that will provide the magic solution. Neither a teaching method, an organizational procedure, nor a particular line in learning materials will itself make a sufficiently strong impact. In rejecting the efficacy of any method in itself, the Committee was not endeavouring to compromise—it is the *easy* way out in educational discussion to plump for one 'method' as totally hopeful, and the Committee chose the harder course. It came to realize that the *total* pattern of the educational process needs attention. The ingredients must be right, but the overall pattern cannot be left to tradition or chance.

School management

This central recommendation of the Report has major implications for school management. Indeed the Report is deeply concerned with overall school management, for only if the whole school can be mobilized is there a possibility of a substantial move forward. The first decade of comprehensive schools developed through the power and intensity of their subject departments. It was in these teams, vigorously led and finding new strength from the number of specialists brought together, that the curriculum was extended. But it was extended patchily, and in a disconnected way. Indeed the

[1] Neville Bennett, *Teaching Styles and Pupil Progress*, Open Books, 1976.

force towards 'Integration' was a reaction to this divisiveness. I argue elsewhere[1] that this is not the only or the necessary reaction to the less happy effects of Departmental strength and separateness. One essential series of strands in this coherence is whole-school curriculum policies. These are the deliberate planning of curriculum aims that are to be achieved not merely via one subject or range of activity, but in a number, or indeed all. This way of looking at the curriculum implies that there is central planning in the school, and that this central planning can cope with detail. For the sake of this discussion the mode of such planning is not important. Whether it is fully democratic, centred in one person, or uses some combination of approaches, is not vital to the point that coherence is possible only if there is central oversight and control. Implementation of the Report requires an overall agreement and central oversight and control in the school. It must be agreed and published what specific teaching is given on all aspects of language. Then all teachers must agree on the complementary approaches that they will use. In its support of this view, the report can be seen as a treatise on school management: to be concerned about literacy is to be concerned about school management.

A unified approach

Above all it is a unified report. Too much of the writing about aspects of English teaching throughout the 'fifties and 'sixties was fragmentary. That was the period of 'English through this' and 'English through that'. It was the period of polarities, when creativity became set against accuracy, and the imagination against technical control. Those working in linguistics were felt to be in a different camp to those educated in literature. The teaching of reading was seen as a technicality quite separate from imaginative response to literature. English specialists vied with each other, and departments within schools were often engaged in internecine disputes, or if the department was unified then it was as likely to be at odds with the school, claiming a sensitivity and responsiveness to pupil needs beyond the rest of the staff. Astoundingly good work was done in patches, but at the price of overlooking the entire range of language needs of a pupil, and at the expense of failing to mobilize the total strength of a school.

The journals, the records of conferences, teachers' books, and pupils' books all stand witness to this fragmentation, in which the passion of adherents to an approach drove teachers with a different emphasis to feel that they were in conflict. This split was seen at its strongest

[1] *Comprehensive Schools*, forthcoming in this series.

in the United States, where the teachers of 'English' felt themselves
to be in a virtually different profession to the teachers of 'Reading'.
Indeed they belonged to different professional associations, with little
in common. As the separate teaching of reading has continued right
through the High School years, the two professions confront each
other in a way which is avoided by the tapering off of the separate
(remedial) teaching of reading here. In confrontation the typical
abusive epithets indicate the polarity: the teachers of English call the
teachers of Reading 'skilly', and the teachers of Reading hurl back
in return the criticism 'woolly'! It is difficult to sense which is the
worst abuse, but easy to realize that the polarities have been institutionalized. Thus, on the whole, the teacher of English expects the
pupil to be able to read, which means his job is to teach *about* literature.
Hence an emphasis on genre, authors' biographies, and literary
history. Conversely, the teacher of Reading merely 'uses' literature.
This was well illustrated at a large conference of the New England
Reading Association, where after stand after stand of schemes, kits,
spirit masters, and charts to help the pupil learn to read, one salesman
was loudly declaiming the value of the 'supplementary material'
which his firm offered. This supplementary material proved to be
boxes of books!

The report considers the possibility of recommending separate
reading specialists, 'Reading Consultants', and 'Reading Departments' (paras 8.6 and 8.7). Indeed it goes as far as to say that 'some
aspects of this concentrated attention were impressive'. However,
the Committee pulled back with horror at the implications of the
specialism, pointing out that: 'the disadvantages out-weighed the
benefits. Although there was no "horizontal split" in the teaching of
reading, there was a very sharp "vertical" split between reading and
English' (8.7). In refusing this split, the report refused all others,
linking the imaginative with the practical, the personal with the
technical, the literary with the factual, and, indeed, all kinds of
reading, even discipline and class control: 'the subtle aims we have
outlined in the Report cannot be achieved unless there is peace in
the classrooms' (15.27).

This final characteristic of the Report, a unity of approach, is the
central force behind the whole-school language policy, growing out
of what the Report calls 'the organic relationship between the various
aspects of English, and . . . the need for continuity in their development throughout school life' (Plan, p. XXXV). This unity of the
report has four perspectives. It is a call for interrelationship:

1. between the modes of language: talk, writing, listening, and
reading;
2. between the uses of language: imaginative and practical;
3. between the different learning activities across the curriculum;
4. through the ages of schooling.

Unfortunately we are a long way from this unity in professional work. Those who have studied reading in this country are considerably less interested in talk. Those who have devoted professional concern to problems of pupils' writing are often notably uninterested in problems of reading. Those who have specialized in literature are frequently badly read in linguistics. Indeed the bibliographies of key works for teachers in each of these fields barely overlap at all. Yet those of us working to help actual pupils term after term must produce a unity of all these aspects. The Report seems to me the first comprehensive and unified approach to language development.

Even post-Bullock there is a real risk of fragmentation within the language effort. In some schools the 'language policy' is mainly directed to 'correcting' writing, in others, seemingly more knowledgeable, talking and writing are the focus. Reading beyond the initial stages is given a high priority in some other, though fewer, schools. (This lower priority comes, I suspect, from the fact that much work on reading has been American.) It is rarer and difficult to find a truly integrated approach, just as it is rare to find a truly integrated approach from conference, speaker, or specialist writer. This is a pity, and surprising in view of the close integration of the report.

The task of school leadership, then, is to develop this unity within the school, so that all teachers can draw upon the insights and techniques of the various specialists.

3. Language and Education

Dr W. A. Gatherer

The nature of language

We do not know how language came into existence. For thousands of years, civilized man has pondered the nature of language, and from earliest times there have been theories as to its origins and characteristics. Modern scholars have tended to discount speculation about the historical origins of language, on the grounds that we simply do not have sufficient evidence to make useful hypotheses. While the development of particular languages is still studied by historical linguists, the main emphasis of modern linguistic scholarship lies in the study of language as it is observed in the actual world.

Attempts have been made to infer the origin of language from studies of speech-acquisition by infants. But children learn their mother tongue in an environment which is entirely different from that of primitive man; they acquire a language which is already established and in use; and in any case we are far from having a natural history of language acquisition to draw upon for data. Another way which has been attempted is to try to infer from so-called 'primitive' languages some of the features which may have characterized man's early language activity. But there are no primitive languages. However primitive may be the economies or cultures of aboriginals, their languages are fully developed. Their vocabularies and grammars are no less complex or systematic than the languages of the most highly civilized peoples. Another field of study which has been used to try to throw light on the origins of language is zoology. The communication systems of animals, however—even of apes, which are physiologically nearer to man—are so different from human language that there would seem to be no possibility of comparing them in any illuminating way. What we must do, modern scholars have concluded, is examine language as we find it, as it is used as an important aspect of human behaviour.

There have been hundreds of attempts to define language, and different schools of linguistic scholarship have approached it in different ways. Usually, however, you can look at language in either one of two ways: as a system of signs, or as a kind of social behaviour. These are equally valid viewpoints and your choice of approach will normally depend on your particular interest—that is, whether you are interested in the *analysis* of language or whether your main concern is with the *uses* of language. Modern scholars generally take the view that language is too complex a phenomenon to be defined in brief, and in any case the word *language* has undergone such a semantic spread or radiation of meaning as to preclude any really worthwhile definition. It is preferable to *describe* the characteristics of language. Thus we can work towards a description of the structure of language and then consider the functions of language.

When we think of language as a set of signs, we must be clear that the *signs* are distinguishable from *symbols*. A sign is a token, a mark or device with a special meaning attached to it—for example, animal noises, such as a cat's purring or a dog's bark, are signs of the animal's feelings. But they are not symbols, for symbols represent things because they are selected to do so. Symbols are conventional signs, like the shapes on maps which signify railways, churches, and golf courses. Language uses arbitrary symbols; that is, a word or a phrase cannot be thought of as a 'natural' or 'inevitable' embodiment of a meaning. Many people are unaware that words are wholly conventional signs which convey nothing of their meaning in their sound or shape. An illustration of this is the old joke about the Italian who invented a pasta and was asked why he called it *spaghetti*: he said 'Because it looks like spaghetti, it feels like spaghetti and it tastes like spaghetti'. Like Aldous Huxley's character who, looking at some pigs, said 'Rightly is they called *pigs*', people tend to confuse the linguistic symbol with the thing it symbolizes. A moment's thought, however, about the linguistic symbols used by different languages to represent the same thing will prove this point: the term *horse* in English denotes the same thing as is denoted by the very different words *hippos*, *equus*, *Pferd*, and *cheval*. Onomatopoetic words like *tick*, *cuckoo*, *dingdong* are partial exceptions to the rule, for they do to some extent imitate actual noises; but even with this type of word the arbitrariness of linguistic symbolism can be shown by the fact that different word-sounds are used for similar noises in different languages: for example a French cat goes *ron-ron*, not *purr-purr*; in German the sound of a bell is *Bim-Bam* and a door banging is represented by *knapps*.

The symbols of which language consists are primarily the sounds of speech. M. A. K. Halliday suggests that language can be thought of as *organized noise*, and most linguists agree that speech should be regarded as the primary substance of language. Speech comes first, in the history of man as a species and in the development of the individual. Some linguists point out that to speak of 'written language' is misleading, for writing is merely a record of language; but most modern scholars now regard writing as another form or mode of language. The sound substance or phonology of a language consists of a finite number of units which linguists call phonemes. A phoneme is a minimum significant sound used by a particular language— significant because the phoneme marks the difference between the meaning of a word as against any other word. For example, it is the initial phoneme which contrasts the meaning of *bin* and *pin*, *tin* and *chin*. The linguist recognizes the sounds /b/, /p/, /t/ and /ch/ as distinctive features; of course, the /i/ sound and the /n/ sound are also phonemes. Note that in the sound of the word *bib*, the initial /b/ is a different *sound* from the final /b/; but the linguist recognizes both instances as manifestations of the same phoneme. Because the initial phoneme is different in its actual sound from the end-phoneme, we class both sounds as *allophones* of the phoneme /b/. (The diagonal lines are used to 'mark off' a phoneme.) All languages use a range of between 20 and 50 phonemes, but different languages will, of course, use different sets of the phonemes available to the human voice. English uses about 46 phonemes: the precise number cannot be stated because it will depend on the dialect you speak. It will also depend on the way you define a phoneme, for linguists are by no means unanimous as to what a phoneme really is: the term has been called a 'logical fiction' because linguists do not agree as to its definition; but they do agree that it is a useful and meaningful term.

The phoneme is thus the 'atom' or smallest unit of language. But it has no distinctive meaning: that is, by itself, a phoneme cannot carry what we would normally recognize as a meaning. The smallest unit of language which bears meaning is the *morpheme*. Like the phoneme, the morpheme is not a universally agreed concept, but it is another very useful term in linguistic analysis. The morpheme is the smallest individually meaningful unit in an utterance. The word *uneatable*, for example, can be divided into the morphemes *un*, *eat* and *able*. Every word can be analysed into one or more morphemes. A *free* morpheme is one that can constitute a word by itself, and a *bound* morpheme is one which never occurs alone, being always found along with at least one other morpheme. In the word *uneatable*, for example, *un-* is a bound morpheme. In this particular word, *-able* is actually a bound morpheme, though it may appear at first sight to be a free morpheme: but it is not the same morpheme as the free form *able* in such an utterance as *He's able*. Morphemes can also be divided into *roots* and *affixes*, an affix being a bound morpheme used to extend or modify the meaning of a word, and a root being a bound or free morpheme which remains when all affixes have been removed. For example, in *uneatable*, *un-* and *-able* are affixes, and *eat* is the root. Every word 'contains' a root, many words consisting of a single root.

The word *word* has been used frequently in preceding paragraphs without definition. It is, in fact, difficult to define a word. Aristotle defined the word as 'the smallest significant unit of speech'. But linguists have reserved that role for the morpheme. And what does 'significant' mean? Does *to* have a meaning in itself? Leonard Bloomfield, the father of 'structural' linguistics, gives the classic definition of a word as a *minimum free form*, that is a unit which can have meaning when used alone. But as Otto Jespersen, the great Danish grammarian, points out, there are many forms which are not free but which are given the status of word (for example, the French *je* or the Russian *K* [towards]) and others which normally do not occur as free forms, such as the English *the* and *a*. Bloomfield also suggests that a word can be characterized as a form which cannot be 'interrupted' by another form. For instance a phrase such as *Look here* can be interrupted by the insertion of a preposition—*Look over here, Look under here*. But *Look* cannot have another form intelligibly inserted in it—you cannot say *L-over-ook* or *o-look-ver* or *l-here-ook* or *he-over-re*. (It is true that in certain English styles you can jokingly embed one form in another— for example, *Abso-blooming-lutely!*—but this is an abnormal occurrence.)

The academic difficulty in defining a word emerges from linguists' preoccupation with language as speech and their insistent search for 'linguistic universals', that is characteristic features of all languages. In spoken utterance we do not normally separate off 'words' except perhaps when speaking very slowly as when dictating—and even then we may separate off forms which we would not accept as words: for example: *I'm go-ing to Jugo-slavia*. At the same time, we have all been trained to space out the forms we call words when we write. The recognition of the word as a unit is a universally held ability in users of human language. The very fact that we normally think of a word as the unit we separate off by white spaces on the page indicates that we have an intuitional awareness of 'wordness', even though we can recognize that it is difficult to be precise about what *word* means. To think of a word as *the smallest unit of language which can stand alone and still have meaning in itself* is good enough for all practical purposes.

Morphology, the relationships of morphemes, has been called 'the grammar within words'.[1] The combining of words into larger structures is syntax. Both morphology and syntax are included in the domain of grammar. Before we consider grammar, however, it will be worthwhile to discuss the relationship between grammar and *lexis*, the vocabulary of a language.

Lexicology is the study of words and their relationships with one another, where these relationships are outside grammar. Thus the associative habits of a word—their likelihood of appearing in a sequence along with other words—is called *collocation*. A *lexical set* is a set of words that generally collocate with one another: for example, *wine, water, beer* and *milk* form a lexical set which will usually collocate with such words as *bottle, drink, spill* and so on. The *thesaurus* of a language is a collection of words in lexical sets; thus the thesaurus tells us a number of words that can usually be substituted for a given word without excessive loss of meaning. The dictionary of a language is a list of the words used by the language, the number of words included being limited by the lexicographer's editorial strategy (the size or price etc.) and the state of his current knowledge.

[1] H. A. L. Gleason, Jr, *Linguistics and English Grammar*, Holt, Rinehart & Winston, 1965, p. 164.

Some words form a closed system: there is a finite and identifiable number of them used in a language. Examples in English are the prepositions, the articles *a, an, the*, and the pronouns. Most words, however, are members of an *open set*: there can be no end to the number of words which can be substituted for them in a grammatical utterance. For example, in the sentence frame

$$///\, \text{The} //\qquad\qquad //\, \text{is} //\qquad\qquad ///$$

the blank spaces can be filled by an infinite number of possibilities. (Even if one could exhaust all the known words ever invented, one could carry on inventing words which grammatically fit the space.)

Returning to Halliday's suggestion that language can be thought of as 'organized noise', we can see how the phonemic and morphemic organization of vocal sound gives language form. For a complete description of language we must account for the *substance*—that is, the sound and the writing—and the *form*. Also, as will be seen, we must describe the ways in which linguistic forms are used in human intercourse. The study of linguistic sound substance is phonology.

LINGUISTIC SCIENCES				
Phonetics - - - - - - - - -				
Linguistics - - - - - - - - - - - - - - -				
SUBSTANCE		FORM		SITUATION (environment)
phonic	phonology	grammar lexis	context	extra-textual features

I

The study of linguistic form involves examining the grammar and the vocabulary of languages—how the units of form are related together in words and sentences. What language means in human situations is the concern of semantic studies. Thus the form we impose upon the substance of language is seen to consist of grammar and lexis.

Before we discuss the nature of grammar it is important to consider the different schools of thought which have contributed to our knowledge of language in modern times. The so-called Prague School has influenced our thinking on the relationship between the structure of

[1] M. A. K. Halliday, in *Patterns of Language*, Longman, 1966.

language and the uses to which it is put in social intercourse. Their interest in the functional aspects of language has been paralleled to some extent by the British School, of which Firth is the acknowledged founder. Firth's interest in 'the context of situation' and the ways in which language interacts with social and cultural influences inspired much of the most important linguistic scholarship of our time. In America there have been two extremely influential schools, the 'structuralists' or Bloomfieldians and the 'transformationalists' or Chomskyans.

Structuralism may be said to be a preoccupation with the classification of the elements of language. Structural linguistics as a discipline owes most to the work of Leonard Bloomfield (1887–1949) whose book, *Language* (1933) established the notion that linguistic scholarship should confine its attention to the 'observable facts' of language as it is spoken, its aim being to classify the 'corpus' of linguistic data at different levels: first the phonemes, then the morphemes, then the words and word classes, then the sentences and sentence-types. Bloomfield argued that this was a rigorous scientific process, and that it should exclude aspects of language which could not be treated with precision and objectivity, such as the analysis of meaning or the intuitions of the native speaker. The discovery procedures employed by structuralist linguists were used with great effect in their descriptions of American Indian languages, and they have thrown much light on the nature of the phonological, morphological, and syntactical process by which language operates.

Noam Chomsky's first book, *Syntactic Structures* (1957), and the many works by him and his followers published since then, represent an entirely different view of the purposes of linguistics. Chomsky's training was in structural linguistics, but he found that the methods which had worked so effectively in the analysis of phonemic and morphemic forms did not satisfactorily apply to sentences. The lists of phonemes and morphemes in a given language are finite (though a list of morphemes would be very long) but it is impossible to list the sentences of any natural language. There can be no limit to the number of sentences that can be produced by a speaker of any language. It is infinite. Language therefore has a 'generative' or 'creative' or 'open-ended' character which cannot be accounted for by the methodology of structuralist linguistics. A language consists of an indefinitely large corpus of utterances, and no grammatical description of language can be adequate unless it accounts for the grammar's capability of generating sentences. An acceptable grammar must be seen as a 'device' of some sort (the term *device* is an abstraction, having nothing to do with physical or mechanical processes) for producing the sentences of a language. Further, the grammar must be capable of generating all the *grammatical* sentences of a language and none of the *ungrammatical* ones which speakers can produce on occasions owing to slips of memory or some psychophysical defect. Chomsky's work, and that of the Chomskyan school generally, has been largely devoted to difficult and often abstruse attempts to produce a 'scientific' grammar of English that satisfies these conditions.

Chomsky's influence on linguistic scholarship has been deep and pervasive. Every linguistic scholar of note who has published work in the last decade has had to take Chomskyan ideas into account. The most important non-Chomskyan grammatical models, such as Halliday's 'scale and category' grammar and Sydney Lamb's 'stratificational' grammar, are *generative* in the sense that they attempt to fulfil the same objectives as Chomsky prescribed for grammars, even though they employ quite different procedures and conceptual frameworks.

When we think of language as a kind of social behaviour, we must look to the disciplines of anthropology and sociology in combination with general linguistics. Edward Sapir (1884–1939) reminds us that 'language is a cultural or social product, and must be understood as such'.[1] Anthropological linguistics has thrown much light on the nature of language, particularly by demonstrating that language is a means of categorizing and ordering human experience. The linguistic habits of people who are members of a particular society contribute to the formation of a 'world-view' which is to some extent peculiar to themselves. As Benjamin Lee Whorf put it: 'We dissect nature along lines laid down by our native languages'.[2] According to this school of thought, the way we think about or perceive our environment is deeply affected (not to say distorted) by the language we have acquired as native speakers. But the 'Whorfian hypothesis' cannot be accepted unreservedly: it is difficult for members of very different cultures to form reliable insights to one another's ways of thinking, and the kinds of relations between language and thought upon which the theory rests are by no means well established. At the same time, studies of the role of language habits in the enculturation of the young in different societies continue to illuminate our linguistic knowledge. It seems unquestionable that there are close perceptible relationships between the way we learn to speak and the way we learn to think. Just as we use language to rationalize our environment, so the environment in which we live influences our language and language habits.

The association of linguistics and sociology has become extremely close and important in recent years. Sociolinguistics may be said to be the study of language as a 'mode of action', to use a phrase of the great anthropologist, Malinowski; but although there has been a great deal of recent work in this field scholars are reluctant to claim it as a specific discipline. Halliday has said that he has been 'doing socio-

[1] E. Sapir, in *Culture, Language and Personality*, D. G. Mandelbaum (ed.), University of California Press, 1961.

[2] B. L. Whorf, in *The Psychology of Language, Thought and Instruction*, J. P. De Cecco (ed.), Holt, Rinehart & Winston, 1969.

linguistics' all his life but has always called it linguistics.[1] All the great linguists have been concerned with the relationship between language and social interaction. The social functions of language, how it transmits cultural ideas and attitudes, how it relates to the social structure, how it helps or hinders the socialization of the young, are all current preoccupations of linguists, and their studies have contributed valuably to our understanding of language and how it works.

To sum up our present position in man's ceaseless effort to describe the nature of language, a few generalizations may be found useful. Some of these represent accounts that have been made briefly in preceding pages, and others will indicate topics which will be dealt with in following sections.

1. *Language is primarily speech.* All the written language that ever existed is but the froth on an ocean of speech. Man is *homo loquens*, and it is speech that makes him human.

2. *Language is systemic.* However confusing and amorphous language may appear as we contemplate it as a human activity, language can be described systematically and scientifically. Rules can be discerned which govern its patterning and its cohesion.

3. *Language is dynamic.* It is constantly changing, never static. Its rules are never rigid and immutable.

4. *Language is social.* Every speaker speaks as a member of a particular community, and his language is partially a result of its traditions, values and social attitudes. Language cannot be wholly understood except in relation to the other human institutions with which it interacts.

5. *Language is personal.* Every speaker directs, modifies and regulates every act of speech according to the personal intentions with which he utters, according also to the purposes that lie behind his utterance, and according also to the state of emotions in which he happens to be when he makes an utterance.

6. *Language is meaningful.* Language expresses thought, and arouses thought in others. The symbolism of language enables both speaker and hearer to discern meaning, often of a different kind from that intended.

Acquisition and development

The relationship of language and thought has occupied the minds of scholars for centuries, and the growth of psychology and linguistics

[1] M. A. K. Halliday, in *Problems of Language and Learning*, A. Davies (ed.), Heinemann Educational, 1975.

has produced a massive literature on the subject. For the educational-
ist it is important to examine the various theories and conceptual
frameworks adduced to explain the manner in which children develop
their linguistic competence, since our teaching strategies will rely on
the theoretical validity and practical effectiveness of our conceptions
of language acquisition and development. An understanding of how
children learn should underlie our decisions about how we should
teach them. The most influential learning theories in the modern
educational scene are those propounded by the behaviourist psychologists and those of the Piagetian or developmental psychologists.
Chomskyan linguists have contributed certain notions about the
nature of language learning which must also be taken into account;
and the work of J. S. Bruner and his associates must also be given
attention.

Behaviourists develop their theory of language learning from their
observation of the visible behaviour of animals and children. The
fullest account of this learning theory was given by B. F. Skinner in
his book *Verbal Behaviour* (1957), but the theory has been developed
and explicated since then by many psychologists and psycholinguists.
The theory has been labelled S-R (Stimulus-Response) because it
stipulates that effective behaviour consists of producing satisfactory
responses to satisfactory stimuli. It states, to put it simply, that if a
child produces a linguistic response which the mother or other care-
taker accepts as appropriate he will be rewarded with some indicator
of approval. Consequently the child will tend to produce the same
response to the same stimulus in similar circumstances. The response
is reinforced by the reward. If the response is not satisfactory the
mother will not reinforce it and it will tend not to recur. This account
can be held to explain how it is that a child produces speech and also
how he learns to understand speech. It does not, however, tell us
anything about how the child's utterances (responses) came to be
made; this is accounted for by learning theorists in terms of imitation:
the mother's behaviour is a secondary means of reinforcement because
the child finds it satisfying to imitate her. According to Skinner, the
mother will reinforce responses which at first only approximate to
the desired response, and by a series of such reinforcements gradually
'shapes' the child's behaviour towards the behaviour she recognizes
to be 'correct' or 'appropriate'.

The Russian psychologist, I. P. Pavlov, argued that a response to
one stimulus can be elicited by another, associated, stimulus. Pavlov's
classic example of the dog's salivating in response to the ringing of
a bell in place of the sight of food is still the best illustration of this
'contiguity theory'. Learning theorists have adapted this notion to
language acquisition: thus we have the theory of mediation, which
states that a word can operate as a mediating stimulus, producing
a response in the absence of the original physical stimulus. Thus
through the mediation of language all kinds of associations can be

built between objects. Children learn what words mean by associating the meanings of known words with new words they are used alongside: for example, if a child is told that a library is a house for holding books he will connect *house* and *holding* and *books* to form an idea of the meaning of library. Mediation theory can also account for the way a child acquires the ability to produce sentences he has never heard before. The explanation is that different sets of words are classified grammatically in the child's mind by occurring in the same place in the framework of an utterance: thus by hearing the strings 'See the book', 'See the man', 'See the train', and so on the child learns to produce a new utterance by inserting a known word in the place previously occupied by other known words.

It has become fashionable to reject learning theory outright because it fails to account adequately for various known facts about language development. But it must be conceded that learning theorists are still actively investigating language activity, and our knowledge is continuously being increased. It would be wrong to dismiss the theory on the grounds that its explanatory power is weak, since further and more refined explanations are still being produced. Moreover the theory should not be rejected on the grounds that it is mechanistic and takes no account of the innate capacity for learning that some psychologists have shown children to possess, for behaviourist theories do not preclude the existence of innateness of various kinds. Educationists must not ignore learning theory, for it has given us valuable insights and suggested teaching strategies of great importance, for example in the teaching of basal reading and number.

The most notable critic of behaviourist learning theory is Chomsky, who approaches language acquisition in an entirely different way. Chomsky argues that a child must be born with some kind of knowledge of language programmed into his brain. Without this postulate of a 'Language Acquisition Device' it is impossible to account for children's ability to achieve linguistic competence. The linguistic 'input' the child gets from adults is necessarily limited and deficient, fragmented and full of irregularities. The child cannot learn the language from the utterances he hears unless he possesses some innate 'universal grammar' which enables him to perceive the 'grammaticality' or acceptability of a sentence and to utter grammatically correct sentences which he has never heard before. Chomsky supports this argument by pointing out that children learn to speak at an early age, before the development of general cognitive faculties: that their ability to acquire their mother tongue has little to do with general intelligence (after all, stupid children learn to speak)—or motivation (lazy children learn to speak): and that formal language teaching is unnecessary for the acquisition process.

The *faculté de langage* postulated by Chomsky has no demonstrable psychological reality, but it is a powerful concept, particularly in its general relationship with pedagogical theory. Although Chomsky's theories have no direct application to teaching, since they involve highly technical linguistic and philosophical hypotheses, they have affected many educationalists' attitudes to language learning. W. B. Currie has stated the case: 'Native speakers seem to show at the initial stage of language learning that they have underlying faculties which make learning possible. This also makes language learning personal and . . . "creative".' Currie suggests that the 'universal ideas of language' which lie behind learning processes are best thought of as 'underlying semantic notions from which the child organizes the deep dependencies and relationships of his language'.[1] He argues that the most effective teaching relies upon 'inductive methods' which ally the child's intuitions and 'native experience' with material—speech of writing in the case of language work—which offers him opportunities for hypothetizing and discussing and ultimately 'discovering' for himself the principle to be learned.

Chomsky insists on the existence of a genetically inherited capacity which is specifically linguistic. Many psychologists, on the other hand, base their view of language learning on Piaget's theory of innate cognitive mechanisms. Piaget sees learning as resulting from the intellectual processes of assimilation and accommodation, both of which are functions of the organism's need for adaptation. The child is born with certain *schemes* and *schemata* or behaviour patterns which act on environmental stimuli: for example, because he instinctively sucks the nipple he will suck someone's finger using the same scheme of actions. This is the process of assimilation. As a result of interaction with a new feature of the environment the schemata are changed to cope with the new situation: for example, the assimilatory behaviour involved in picking up something within reach will be changed when he crawls along the floor to pick the object up. This is the process of accommodation. More and more complex schemata are developed as the child matures. The child's development proceeds through a continuous process of generalizations and differentiations, each phase involving a repetition of the previous processes but moving towards a higher level of organization. The developmental continuum can be divided into three major phases: the sensori-motor phase (age 0 to 2); the phase during which there is a preparation for conceptual thought (roughly ages 2 to 11); and the phase of cognitive thinking (ages 11 to 12 upwards).

Applied to language acquisition, Piaget's theory of cognitive development provides powerful new insights. When new stimuli are presented, the child's reaction is governed by the structures he can currently command. He interprets and applies new linguistic information in terms of what he already knows. He assimilates and accommodates language substance as he encounters it. Piaget himself has not been directly concerned with language development, and research by psycholinguists using the Piagetian conceptual framework is still

[1] W. B. Currie, *New Directions in Teaching English Language*, Longman, 1973.

at an early stage. Nevertheless a valuable conception of language development is emerging—that it proceeds through the interaction of active experimentation by the child and the internalized cognitive structures he possesses at a given stage.

The Russian school of psycholinguistic studies, founded by Vygotsky in the 1920s and extensively publicized by Luria, regards language as an essential factor in mental growth. Vygotsky and Luria do not accept the Piagetian notion of inevitable development: it is the interaction of language and situation in a social context, the Russians believe, which gives the child the capacity to organize his mental activities. Language therefore plays a crucial role in mental development. Since rational, intentional communication between minds is impossible without speech, says Vygotsky, the growth of a child's thinking ability and the growth of his linguistic competence are concomitant with and closely related to his social development. The internalization of speech, at about the age of seven, leads to the development of higher forms of intellectual capability. Interaction with adults encourages mental development.

The work of Jerome S. Bruner has also been of great importance in developing our understanding of the relationship of language and mental development. As an educational psychologist, Bruner holds that mental development passes through three main stages of readiness, the enactive, the iconic, and the symbolic. These stages, reminiscent of Piaget's stages of pre-operational, concrete-operational and formal-operational, are accompanied by appropriate stages of mental need. In his eloquent and influential expositions of the nature of 'discovery learning', Bruner argues that learning depends on the opportunities provided to allow the pupil to explore his environment in terms of his own needs and capacities: 'Discovery teaching generally involves not so much the process of leading students to discover what is "out there", but, rather, their discovering what is in their own heads.'[1] Teachers must let pupils use what they know. Bruner uses the notion of *compatibility* (which appears to contain echoes of Piaget's notions of assimilation and accommodation): new knowledge will only be truly possessed by a child when it has been connected with his existing repertoire of ideas and knowledge.[2] He urges educators to appreciate the need to give pupils training in such processes as 'pushing an idea to its limits'—for 'going beyond the information given' is the most important characteristic of man as a thinker. He argues the need to encourage a pupil to reflect upon and evaluate his or her own thinking processes. Language, Bruner points out, makes this 'self-loop' easier, as when the child realizes that the same concept can be expressed by completely different words.

Bruner believes that the 'channelling capacity' (the ability to

[1] J. S. Bruner, 'Some elements of discovery', in *Learning by Discovery: A Critical Approach*, L. S. Shulman and G. R. Keislar, Rand McNally, 1966.

[2] This idea is echoed by the Bullock Report, 4.9.

handle information) can be improved when information is organized in suitable ways appropriate to particular situations. The main advantage of discovery learning is that it increases the pupil's intellectual potency: he develops the ability to devise strategies of approach and effective learning structures. The way in which he structures his learning in a given lesson will help his understanding of regularities and relationships at other times. Bruner conceives this structuring process as an ability to 'code' information. Language enables us to codify the input of our senses, and thus to organize and make sense of our experience. The coding ability of the human mind allows us to create and to comprehend meaningful language out of all the raw linguistic substance available to us.

In a recently published paper[1] Bruner outlines some of his recent thinking on language and cognition. He proposes the term 'species minimum' to connote the basic linguistic competence postulated by Chomsky and others who claim the existence of innate language capability possessed by all speakers of all natural languages. Beyond this linguistic competence there is another kind called 'communicative competence' which includes the ability to make and understand utterances in accordance with the circumstances in which they are made. Bruner suggests that this kind of competence is also 'species minimum' in the sense that every normal person can be expected to achieve it without special training. Communicative competence, says Bruner, can be taken to involve the achievement of the 'concrete operations' described by Piagetian psychologists. Beyond this innate, species-minimum competence, however, there is what Bruner calls 'analytic competence' which, as with Piaget's 'formal operations', involves 'the prolonged operation of thought processes exclusively on linguistic representations, on propositional structures, accompanied by strategies of thought and problem-solving appropriate not to direct experience with objects and events but with ensembles of propositions.'

In this view, language is seen as an instrument of thought. If we set aside the highly technical arguments adduced by Bruner to explicate his conception of the psychological relationships between language and cognition, we may regard his postulate of analytic competence as the ability to use language *for* thinking. Analytic competence is not acquired 'naturally', as is communicative competence, but is acquired through formal education by means of being engaged in intellectual pursuits. In school, knowledge is 'decontextualized', made abstract, and schooling demands analytic competence for the pursuits it requires of the students.[2]

[1] J. S. Bruner, 'Language as an Instrument of Thought', in A. Davies (ed.), *Problems of Language and Learning*, Heinemann Educational Books, 1975.

[2] This latter elaboration of the theory is based on a revised paper by Bruner and Karen L. Peterson which is summarized by Alan Davies, *op. cit.*

That the mental skills involved in the higher-order uses of language are not acquired without the intervention of the educator is a fundamental assumption in modern research and development. Much effort is being expended on attempts to identify these higher-order skills, and at every stage in the educational process there are strategies now being proposed to facilitate their development. The nursery school curriculum is being profoundly influenced by the work of Dr Joan Tough and her associates in the Schools Council project, 'Communication Skills in Early Childhood'. Tough takes the view that the most productive activity in early childhood education is the child–adult dialogue, carefully devised by a trained adult to give the child experience of 'thinking strategies' which will become internalized through practice. She has described a range of such strategies and her project is concerned with developing teachers' awareness of the skills of thinking and language-use that children can achieve and giving teachers training in the use of dialogue to promote the growth of these skills.[1]

For older primary pupils similar programmes relating language-use and thinking are being produced: *Concept 7–9*, for example, provides children with problems which have to be discussed in group work, so that they explore their own linguistic resources, and share those of others, to find the means to arrive at practical solutions and decisions. For an older age-group, such programmes as *Man A Course of Study* provide pupils with the techniques of acquiring data about their environment and lead them into 'thinking strategies' which are their own rather than externally imposed routines. The Schools Council project, 'Writing Across the Curriculum', carries the study of the relationship between language and thinking into the secondary school stage, and is producing some interesting studies of the learning process at work in the classroom.

In their descriptions of the processes of thinking, psychologists have accorded an important role to concept formation. The young child forms concepts of objects, sounds and feelings which are internalized representations of categories of experience. With the acquisition of language many of these concepts are verbally labelled and recognized. Concepts may be acquired easily by means of hearing or reading verbal formulations of their content, but some are so complex that they cannot be grasped without a preliminary sequence of 'leading up' concepts or a series of experiences which offer instances (and noninstances) of the concept. In school, the two most common methods of presenting concepts to pupils are to offer verbal formulations and to offer 'practical' experiences which exemplify the concepts. Almost all teaching is a process of presenting concepts in these ways.

The role of verbal formulation is obviously of great importance in the teaching of all subjects in the secondary school. Much of the

[1] Bullock Report, 5–8, and forthcoming papers.

teacher's skill in communicating concepts relies on the language he chooses to convey his meanings. Similarly, much of the pupil's success in understanding what is being taught lies in his ability to transmute the teacher's language into concepts. Most teachers know that the copious presentation of examples facilitates understanding; but many appear to show less appreciation of the role of the language used. Barnes and others have pointed out that many teachers tend in expounding their subject to use language which some pupils fail to understand.[1] If the pupil's access to technical terms is limited he will not acquire the prerequisite concepts which lead to understanding.

Specialist teachers may use a specialist language containing forms with which the pupil is not acquainted, or of which he is only vaguely aware; and even when the teacher is very well aware of the important role played by language he may simply not know how best to communicate, in effective linguistic interchange, the concepts whose verbal formulations are so familiar to himself. Such concepts in mathematics as *oppositeness* and *magnitude* may be quite difficult for a child to attain without extensive experience of instances, but may be very difficult for the teacher to exemplify in a short space of time. Teachers of history may freely use such terms as *state* and *government* without being fully aware of the inchoateness of the pupils' understanding of the concepts. There is, moreover, a 'language of secondary education', which, apart from technical terminology, may constitute a barrier to comprehension. This is the 'textbook' style of discourse teachers tend to use in their exposition of a subject. The complexity of the sentence structure, the unfamiliarity of the vocabulary, the abstractness of the concepts may all obscure the meaning for the pupils.

For the educator, then, the most important thing about language is that it is essential for thinking. Although we do not know what the precise relationship between language and thinking is, it is evident that language enables us to communicate our thought. If some form of thinking is possible without language, it is nevertheless language which gives our thinking form, sequence and coherence, and it is by means of language that we give substance to our thought. We may think of language as a *clothing* of thought, but it is more satisfactory to think of it as the embodiment of thought in the way that a melody is the embodiment of the sounds of music. Thus we think *in* language; and effective thinking is not possible unless we possess linguistic competencies adequate enough to realize and express our ideas.

The pupil who, being told to 'Think before you speak' says, 'How do I know what I think till I hear what I say?' is expressing an important idea for teachers. 'Speaking one's thoughts' is in a real sense the very act of thinking. It is in the verbal teasing out of one's thinking that one learns to think effectively. Speech is therefore the primary instrument of thought and there is a process of 'talking one's way

[1] D. Barnes, 'Language in the Secondary Classroom', in *Language, the Learner and the School*, Penguin, 1971.

through' ideas which is essential to learning. Teachers of all subjects should be sensitively aware of the potentiality of this process. Pupils will not learn the thinking process of an academic discipline merely by listening or taking notes. They must *engage* in the language of the subject if they are to grasp its concepts. Learning physics is as much a process of learning to *talk physics* as anything else; and the teacher who merely insists on silence—or who fails to incite talk about his subject—fails to perceive the necessary connection between speech, thought and learning.

It is not enough, moreover, to expect pupils to engage in formal academic talk in the process of learning. Speech is a social activity and the speech which induces learning must not be divorced from the social situation in which it occurs. Pupils should freely express their thoughts, feelings and needs in the process of teacher–pupil interaction, so that they, the learners, can control their own learning. It is curious that many teachers who recognize the value of the 'Ah-hah! experience' in learning would greet spontaneously uttered 'Ah-hahs!' with disapproval, yet this kind of verbal recognition of understanding is a natural aid to learning, even in the privacy of the study. More importantly, learning requires the verbal marks of questioning. In every classroom pupils should be free to express their lack of comprehension, or to express their guesses or tentative formulations of a solution to a problem. Again, learning is a two-way process: when a pupil feels that the teacher should repeat or rephrase a statement he should be free to regulate the teacher's behaviour to accommodate his own thought processes; yet most teachers would object to being told to do this by a pupil.

Where a teacher is engaged in conveying the content and discipline of an academic subject, then, the process should involve the functional use of speech in various ways. Teacher and pupils should be caught up in a continuous dialogue in which ideas are assimilated by means of talk and listening, questioning and answering, *on the pupils' part* and on the pupils' initiative so far as this is consonant with the requirements of the classroom. A one-to-one tutorial, in which the student plays an active role, is often the ideal learning situation; but schools can seldom provide it. To obtain the benefits of closely personalized learning within the limitations of the institutionalized classroom is one of the principal objectives of good teaching.

Wittgenstein pointed out that one can think with a pen in one's hand as well as in one's head. The verbal teasing out of one's thought which is characterized by 'thinking aloud' can also be achieved by means of expressive writing: that is, by writing for oneself, for one's own benefit. This would seem to be a little-used pedagogical technique outside the English classroom. Most teachers expect their pupils to have acquired the skills of written communication independently and seem to consider that it is only the English teacher who need feel responsible for the teaching of composition. But writing is language, and though it has its own conventions and patterns it is dependent, for its efficacy as communication, on the same cognitive–linguistic skills as speech. To be able to write well on scientific or historical or technical matters it is necessary to be able to *think* well in the language of the subject. Expressive writing should therefore become a normal practice within the subject; for this promotes good thinking in the subject.

The ultimate sign of understanding a subject is the ability to convey one's knowledge in effective representational or transactional language. Most teachers expect a well-formed piece of exposition as an indication that something has been learned. Yet this is the most sophisticated of the language skills most of us acquire in life. It is not a part of learning to be able thus to convey information and ideas— rather it is the end-product of learning. It is unrealistic in teachers to look for this skill as if it were a natural acquisition, or something acquired somewhere other than in their own classrooms. Every teacher should attempt to teach the language skills essential to his or her own subjects.

Every teacher, furthermore, should be trained to be sensitive to the role of language in learning. This requires that every teacher should have a comprehensive knowledge of the nature of language, language-acquisition, and language learning. Successful teaching requires an awareness by the teacher of the linguistic processes involved in concept attainment and the reinforcement of what is comprehended. The teacher of history or science, as the Bullock Report puts it, must 'understand the process by which his pupils take possession of the historical or scientific information that is offered them'.

Language in the social context

Most natural languages exhibit degrees of variation in the patterns of lexical, grammatical and phonological choices which are habitually made by native speakers. One form of variation which assumes importance to the educator is *dialect*, which may be crudely defined as the form of a language identified as being peculiar to a particular geographical area or distinct community. A widely established language, such as English, German or French, will consist of a number of dialects, the 'language' itself being indefinable except as a set of dialects. The study of dialects (dialectology) has preoccupied amateur scholars for centuries; the identification of a dialect, however, is a highly technical process and the status of a dialect can only be established by painstaking and comprehensive descriptions of the differences in vocabulary, grammar and pronunciation between one linguistic community and all the others comprising the major language community.

In many languages, there are also 'cultural' linguistic variations discernible, so that the existence of social or subcultural dialects can be claimed. In English, French and other major languages a special status can be claimed for the language used commonly by educated people: thus 'standard English' may be regarded as a prestigious dialect of English, which carries the importance of mandarin Chinese as a universally accepted form of language. With respect to the grammar, Standard English (SE) is largely uniform among educated speakers all over the world (though there are minor differences). The same applies to the vocabulary, though again there are many words in common use in, say, the USA which are not familiar to speakers of SE in other parts of the English-speaking world. With respect to pronunciation, and particularly to accent, there are considerable variations, so that the nationality of different native English speakers can easily be heard: but these national differences are seldom great enough to prevent easy communication. The phonological variety of SE which has been used by British linguists to represent the standard is that of London and the English 'Public Schools'. Known as RP (Received Pronunciation) this variety of speech is used technically to provide norms for the purpose of making phonetic analyses of English speech. But RP must not be confused with SE: it does not represent the phonology of SE in any other part of the English-speaking world. It may be that there is a Welsh or Australian or Californian equivalent of RP.

Understandably the grammar of SE has come to be regarded as the 'correct' forms, and deviations appearing in subcultural 'nonstandard' dialects are widely considered to be incorrect. To say *I seen him* is incorrect, is equivalent to saying that the SE speaker would not use that form, preferring *I saw him*. But *I seen him, I haven't done nothing*, and many other non-standard forms are characteristics of certain dialects whose lineage is at least as ancient as that of SE, and linguists are naturally averse to making value judgements which do not concern them as scientists. The structural linguists of the Bloomfieldian school were particularly insistent that their approach to language was objective and that consequently they could not regard any one form of language as intrinsically inferior or superior to any other form. Further, it has been cogently argued by Labov and others that non-standard English dialects are not radically different systems but are in fact closely related to SE.[1]

This objectivity, however, has led many writers to assert that it is improper to apply prescriptions of any kind to language use. Robert A. Hall Jr's book, *Leave Your Language Alone*, is a good example of this extreme attitude. Some of Hall's assertions, which he calls

[1] W. Labov, *The Study of Nonstandard English*, NCTE, 1969.

'basic principles', have become familiar shibboleths in educational discussion:

> There is no such thing as good and bad (or correct and incorrect, grammatical and ungrammatical, right and wrong) in language.
> All languages and dialects are of equal merit, each in its own way.
> 'Correct' can only mean 'socially acceptable' and apart from this has no meaning as applied to language.[1]

This attitude results from a confusion between the scientific aim of objectivity which is proper for the linguist to sustain in his studies and the educational aim of intervention with children's language for the purpose of increasing its range and power. Hall's assertions are also representative of the imprecision of language which causes so much confusion in teachers' minds when confronted with statements that naturally seem to contradict their own common sense.

As it reads, the statement that 'there is no such thing as correct and incorrect, grammatical and ungrammatical etc.' is manifestly nonsense: no linguist would hesitate to say that *The balls boys the kicks* is ungrammatical and therefore incorrect. What Hall really means, of course, is that the linguist is not concerned with telling people how they *ought* to speak but is equally interested in studying all language, whether it is socially acceptable or not. The educator cannot afford to take this lofty stance. To teachers, all languages and dialects are *not* of equal merit, since for various reasons they are obliged to aim at making the standard forms accessible to their pupils. It is true that *correctness* is usually equated with social acceptability in the popular mind: this is the case with all forms of behaviour, and it is not surprising (nor is it in any real sense pernicious) that it should be so with language. Using language is a rule-governed activity at various levels. Just as we learn the 'rules of use' in social situations, we have to learn the 'rules of effectiveness' in communication if we are to achieve any degree of mastery. It is just as foolish to abjure all notions of correctness as it is to adopt intolerant and snobbish attitudes towards any deviation from the subjectively established standard of propriety which exists only in the mind of the individual.

It is true that many people do adopt invalid notions of correctness with regard to dialectal usage. The tendency is to conflate deviations in grammar and lexis and pronunciation and to condemn the whole 'speech package' of a dialect speaker as being socially inferior and therefore 'incorrect'. It is important for the educator to be able to distinguish between deviations which are functional for learning and those which are merely matters of social prestige. Variations in accent are seldom of any educational significance: teachers who criticize the use of 'glottal stops' in Cockney speech, for example, are clearly unaware that this is a speech characteristic, in different forms, of *all* speakers of English. Variations in pronunciation *can* be

[1] Revised as *Linguistics and Your Language*, Doubleday, 1960.

of marginal importance: the Scots pupil must learn to use the SSE (Standard Scots English) pronunciation of such words as *mouse, rough, floor* if he wishes to be understood beyond the borders of his own community. Variations in lexis can be educationally significant in a different way: knowing and enjoying the differences can be a real aid to linguistic maturity. Variations in grammar tend to be educationally significant only in the later stages of schooling, when it becomes important for pupils to master the subtler rules of rhetoric and style.

Linguists are at pains to point out that there is nothing intrinsically (linguistically) inferior about dialectal forms. In grammar, especially, there can be no appeal to the superior logicality or consistence of standard forms. The use of double or multiple negatives, for example, is quite common in many languages and was widely used in Shakespeare's time; this habit still survives among 'élite' speakers in such idioms as *I shouldn't wonder if it didn't rain* which is not grammatically different from *I didn't never hit nobody*. Again, the use of a plural form of *you* (*youse*) in some dialects is manifestly more consistent than the SE usage since SE uses plural forms for all the other personal pronouns.

It is, of course, quite proper to call these dialect forms 'wrong' when they are used within the norms of SE: when we speak SE we ought to conform with its established grammar, lexis and phonology. By the same token, it would be 'wrong' to use SE forms when speaking any other dialect where there are forms in the dialect which are 'proper' to that dialect. In dramatic dialogue, for example, the playwright uses his 'ear' for language to produce the forms which conform to and so mark the dialect of each speaker. And dialect speakers are just as sensitive as SE speakers to the required conventions of their own speechways: indeed they may be able to switch from one speech package to another. (Very few bidialectals, however, have equally good command of both the dialects they speak.)

The role of language in educational underachievement has been much debated in recent years, and indeed our interest in this subject has generated much valuable research into language development. The most notable theorist in this field is Basil Bernstein, whose work in studying the relationship between social structure and language-use has had a world-wide influence on educational thinking. In an early paper Bernstein distinguished between what he called 'public' language and 'formal' language, public language being characterized by restricted syntax and 'implicit' meanings, formal language being characterized by more explicit meanings, more elaborate syntax, and a more discriminative selection from a wider range of words. He makes it clear that both lower-class and middle-class people can make use of either public or formal language patterns; but he suggests that lower-class persons tend to make relatively little use of formal language while middle-class persons can make flexible use of both types. In later papers Bernstein substituted the term *restricted code* for 'public language' and *elaborated code* for 'formal language', and considerably developed his theoretical accounts of the social-class differences in the use of language. Despite the strenuous efforts of Bernstein and his associates to prevent educators from drawing crude inferences from their work, it soon became a widespread belief that lower-class children suffered educationally because the language they possessed was demonstrably inadequate. This led to the notion that socially deprived children should be treated as if they 'had no language at all' and required special programmes of structured lessons on vocabulary and sentence production.[1] This 'deficit hypothesis', as it was called by Bruner and others, has been attacked by many linguists who deny that non-standard dialects lack the formal properties necessary for the expression and communication of thought. All natural languages are equally capable of conveying ideas of great complexity. The work of William Labov with Black American children in New York has sharply confirmed this view: as Labov demonstrated, lower-class speakers do not have such a strong control of certain 'school language' features, but there is no evidence that their language, *as language*, is functionally unsuitable for learning.[2] Whatever may be the disadvantage suffered by lower-class children at school, it is not a necessary or intrinsic quality in their language. This general conclusion has been confirmed by R. K. S. Macaulay's work on language and education in Glasgow.[3]

One of the important distinctions to be made is the difference between competence and performance. Language ability tests measure pupils' actual productions at a given time in given circumstances. This does not necessarily coincide with their competence, what they are capable of doing with language. Children, like all other users of language, vary their linguistic performance with different situations, reacting in accordance with their emotional and purposive reading of each particular situation. Labov found that children who were seen to be inarticulate in a formal interview situation could behave quite differently in situations that were more congenial to them. Bernstein's more recent work makes it clear that the concept of 'restricted code' must not be equated with 'linguistic deprivation'.[4] It is not the case that lower-class children do not have

---

[1] See for example, C. Bereiter and S. Engelman, *Teaching Disadvantaged Children in the Preschool*, Prentice-Hall, 1966; F. M. Hechinger (ed.), *Pre-School Education Today*, Doubleday, 1966.

[2] W. Labov, *The Study of Nonstandard English*, NCTE, 1969.

[3] R. K. S. Macaulay and G. D. Trevelyan, *Language, Education and Employment in Glasgow*, pub. in typescript by the Scottish Council for Research in Education, 1973.

[4] B. Bernstein, 'A Critique of the Concept of Compensatory Education', in *Education for Democracy*, D. Rubinstein and C. Stoneman (eds), Penguin, 1969.

the linguistic forms in their possession; what seems to handicap them is that they have learned fewer strategies for the use of language. It is a socially specific disadvantage. The school is concerned with making explicit principles and operations in science and the arts, and the lower-class child, unlike the more advantaged middle-class child, has not had the social experience which would make him sensitive to the 'symbolic orders of the school'. Here, perhaps, Bernstein has come together with Bruner in suggesting that it is analytic competence which is required for successful learning in school—particularly at the secondary stage—and that the social circumstances of lower-class families tend to deprive the children of the kind of experience which makes for competence in thinking and language use. It is widely believed that socially (and 'culturally') deprived children do not have adequate language and social experience in their homes to enable them to cope with the demands made on them by the school. How these disadvantages can be compensated for is the concern of many recent and current educational projects, such as the Headstart programmes in the USA, the EPA programmes in Britain, home visitor schemes and such projects as the 'Talk Reform' project by the Gahagans, the Schools Council Swansea project, and Dr Joan Tough's project at Leeds. All of these projects represent what the Report (5.30) calls 'planned intervention in the child's language development'.

It has been argued, however, that it is simply social convention that requires the 'elaborated code' in school, and that children who do not use it suffer educationally because they fail to reach up to their teachers' expectations.[1] If this is the case, it is in the teacher that change should be effected: teachers should avoid basing their evaluation of pupils' competence solely on the basis of their speech patterns. Much more powerfully, it can be suggested that lower-class children can, in the right circumstances, manipulate concepts very skilfully even in the 'restricted code' and in their 'subcultural' dialect. The 'language deficit' view may therefore owe something to middle-class social bias. The linguistic differences described by Bernstein may simply be differences of *style* or *register* within dialects. Lower-class children are less accustomed to using the more formal registers employed in school.

Registers are varieties of language used in different social contexts. They can be characterized in various ways. In *The Five Clocks* Joos[2] employs a five-point scale of style: frozen—formal—consultative—casual—intimate. More recently, scholars have distinguished between formal and colloquial registers, casual and ceremonial, personal and impersonal, simple and complex.[3] A particular register can be described for any field of discourse: thus it is possible to distinguish

[1] Peter Trudgill, *Sociolinguistics*, Penguin, 1975.
[2] M. Joos, *The Five Clocks*, Bloomington, Indiana, 1962.
[3] Geoffrey Leech, *English in Advertising*, Longman, 1966.

the linguistic features of, for example, a 'scientific' register, or a 'legal' register, or the register of the classroom. Clearly effective discourse requires the selection of the most suitable register features for a given situation. Similarly, in successful writing we adopt the stylistic conventions which best suit our intentions and the various criteria we set up for particular purposes.

Children who have access to a narrow range of stylistic options will suffer educational disadvantage, and so long as the more formal styles are the only ones accepted in the classroom, lower-class children will be penalized. A similar penalty is meted out to speakers of non-SE dialects. There is a widespread belief that SE contains a God-given code of rules and that any variation from it represents an intrinsically inferior form of the language. Linguists have demonstrated that this is not true. No variety of English is *linguistically* inferior to any other in the sense that it is less effective in carrying meaning, or less beautiful or less complex or less consistent in its rules of grammar, lexis and style. Teachers who condemn the non-standard speech of the West Indian or Glaswegian or Cockney child are merely confusing their social or racial bias with their linguistic misconceptions.[1]

Language functions

In a brilliant and influential paper written for educators, M. A. K. Halliday suggests that the child who, in Bernstein's terms, uses a 'restricted code' is one who has failed to master the operation of certain language functions. 'The "restriction" is a restriction on the range of uses of language'.[2] In this and subsequent works, Halliday has provided us with a comprehensive view of the relationships between language and the social situations in which language is used. Each situation in which linguistic interaction occurs can be described structurally in terms of the general categories of *field, tenor,* and *mode. Field* is the type of activity going on—the social 'subject-matter' as it were. *Tenor* is the role relationships, how the participants are interacting with one another. *Mode* is the rhetorical function assigned to language in a particular type of situation—for example, whether spoken or written, whether the speech is informal or not, and so on. An utterance or text is linguistically determined by the field, tenor and mode of the situation: that is, the choice of meanings,

---

[1] P. Trudgill, *op. cit.*, p. 57ff.

[2] M. A. K. Halliday, 'Relevant Models of Language', in *The State of Language*, Univ. of Birmingham, 1969.

and hence the lexical and grammatical properties of the utterance or text are called upon to fit the situation.[1]

Halliday suggests that children internalize 'models' of language as a result of their experience of using language in different situations. 'The determining elements in the young child's experience are the successful demands on language that he himself has made. . . . Language is, for the child, a rich and adaptable instrument for the realization of his intentions; there is hardly any limit to what he can do with it'.[2] He proposes the following typology of the language models with which normal children are endowed:

INSTRUMENTAL. This is the simplest model, the use of language as 'a means of getting things done', for the satisfaction of personal material needs: serving the 'I want' function.

REGULATORY. The use of language as a means of regulating the behaviour of others, serving the function of 'Do as I tell you'.

INTERACTIONAL. This model refers to the use of language for maintaining and mediating one's relationships with others: serving the 'me and him' (or 'me and Mummy') function.

PERSONAL. This is the model which enables the child to express his own individuality: serving the 'Here I come' function.

HEURISTIC. This model refers to language as a means of finding out, questioning: serving the function 'Tell me why'.

IMAGINATIVE. This model enables the child to project himself into an environment of his own making, to create a world of make-believe: serving the 'Let's pretend' function.

REPRESENTATIONAL. This is the use of language as a means of conveying information and expressing propositions: serving the function of 'I've got something to tell you'.

These are not models of language acquisition, nor are they psychological or pedagogical categories; they are merely some of the functions language can perform, ways in which children can be seen to operate with language. In another sense, they are illustrations of the great variety of the uses of language, and for the educator this is the chief importance of Halliday's analysis. Teachers ought to be aware of the many ways in which language is used in social intercourse and in the course of the individual's life. Again, recalling the work of Piaget and Bruner, we must realize the importance of founding teaching procedures on the child's existing knowledge and experience, enabling him to make new experience compatible with what he already knows. Also, we must as educators be sensitive to the *unnatural* as well as the *natural* varieties of language-use: that is, the fact that some capabilities cannot be left to maturational processes. Halliday's *personal* and *heuristic* functions, both crucial to educational success, will only become familiar through planned experience and training.

[1] M. A. K. Halliday, 'Talking One's Way In: A Sociolinguistic Perspective on Language and Learning', in *Problems of Language and Learning*, Davies, A. (ed.), Heinemann Educational, 1975.
[2] 'Relevant Models of Language', *op. cit.*

Piaget's concept of 'formal operations', Bruner's concept of 'analytic competence', Bernstein's concept of 'elaborated code' and Halliday's concept of language models are all separately conceived entities of different theoretical frameworks, and we ought not to confuse or equate them: at the same time, they constitute powerful demonstrations from different disciplines of the existence of a way of using thought processes and language which must be the ultimate goal set for every pupil.

Another approach to the study of language functions arises from the interest of scholars such as J. L. Austin[1] and J. R. Searle[2] in discourse analysis. This is based upon a consideration of the *speech act*. An utterance is never merely a sentence: saying something purposively is an action, the intention being to produce some effect on the person addressed. For example, to say 'I promise (something)' is not merely to tell the hearer something: it *is promising*. Such *performative* utterances have meaning related to the speech situation as well as the meaning of their propositional content. Austin points out that an utterance has an 'illocutionary force' over and above its locutionary content. If I am trying to tell you something, I have succeeded in telling it as soon as you have perceived what it is I am trying to tell you. There are 'rules of use' which relate *what is said* to *what is performed*. The theory of discourse analysis is relatively new, and it is as much a philosophical concern as a linguistic one; but it has provided valuable insights into the functioning of language.

The way language is used in the classroom has become an important study for a number of educators.[3] Douglas Barnes, for example, has analysed classroom interaction in terms of the types of questions asked and answers elicited, the types of responses made to different initiating utterances and instructions, the relationship between the teacher's instructional language and the pupils' understanding and so on. Clearly children in the classroom have to learn the 'rules of use' to enable them to cope with their learning tasks. Sinclair and his associates have produced an elaborate analysis of classroom discourse, which has resulted from a fruitful combination of discourse analysis and interaction analysis (that is, the classification of verbal interchanges between teacher and pupils).

Sinclair establishes a hierarchy of discourse units: the *lesson*, the *transaction*, the *exchange*, the *move*, and the *act*, each unit consisting of combinations of the smaller units. The units are described linguistically in terms of Halliday's scale and category grammar. The units

[1] J. L. Austin, *How to Do Things with Words*, Clarendon Press, 1962.

[2] J. R. Searle, *Speech Acts*, OUP, 1969.

[3] See, for example, D. Barnes, J. Britton and H. Rosen, *Language, the Learner and the School*, Penguin, 1971; J. W. P. Creber, *Lost for Words: Language and Educational Failure*, Penguin, 1972; C. Rosen and H. Rosen, *The Language of Primary School Children*, Penguin, 1973; J. Sinclair, *et al.*, *The English Used by Teachers and Pupils*, Univ. of Birmingham, 1972.

at the lowest rank of discourse are called *acts*, which have functional properties and would seem to resemble what Austin means by 'speech acts'. This analysis makes available, for the first time, a descriptive framework for further research into how language operates in teaching and learning.

Usage

It has been said that using language is rule-governed behaviour. But many people tend to confuse the rules of grammar with the conventions of style. The rules and conventions of linguistic usage have preoccupied rhetoricians and grammarians for centuries; but recent studies have revealed that many widely held notions of what is 'correct' in usage are confused and confusing.

W. H. Mittins has pointed out various kinds of 'rule' invoked by various 'authorities'. There is the 'ipsedixitism': the rule that something is so because someone has said so with authority. Examples of this are the *shall/will* convention pronounced by Wallis in the seventeenth century; and Bishop Lowth's decision that *than* was always a conjunction and not a preposition and so must be followed by a nominative pronoun. Then there is the appeal to Latin. Latin was used as a model for the grammatical description of English, and seventeenth- and eighteenth-century grammarians also derived 'rules' for English usage from Latin. Thus Dryden condemned the use of a preposition as the last word in a sentence because in Latin prepositions are preposed. Then there is the appeal to '*logic*'; for example by those who deplore the use of *aggravate* for *annoy* because the word incorporates the Latin *gravis* and must therefore always mean 'make worse'.[1] The truth is that in usage there is no single standard of acceptability available to us; there are multiple standards.[2] What may be adjudged 'wrong' at one time may be widely accepted at another; what may be pronounced 'barbarous' or 'inelegant' by a self-styled authority may be universally used and tolerated in everyday practice; what may be urged as 'correct' in one part of the English-speaking world may be wholly ignored in another.

Some teachers are prone to confuse 'correctness' with 'desirableness': to lay down prescriptions as to what is proper in speech or writing, and to emphasize prescriptive 'rules'. *Don't's* often predominate over *do's* in traditional course books, and pupils are expected to be able to rationalize the cause of 'error' in terms of the 'rules'.

[1] W. H. Mittin, 'What is Correctness?', in *The State of Language*, A. Wilkinson (ed.), Univ. of Birmingham, 1969.
[2] See R. Quirk (ed.), *The Use of English*, Longman, 1962.

Many of these proscribed forms are common in the everyday speech of SE speakers: such forms, for example, as *It's me, Each of them have taken one, Who did you say you gave it to?* are universally employed in informal SE. It is absurd to suggest that they are erroneous in ordinary speech, though they would not normally occur in formal written English. The 'Correction of Errors' exercises characteristic of many old-fashioned textbooks exemplify this confusion between what is 'correct' in formal composition and what is normal in informal conversation. To require a pupil to 'correct' such sentences as 'Excuse me being late', 'I rose late so I had to hurry', 'The man only died yesterday', and 'Who did you come with?' is to misunderstand the difference between the uses of language in different situations.[1] These sentences are colloquial; they would seldom occur in the kind of prose in which the 'rules' they are thought to err against are relevant. The truth is that different styles of English require different conventions, not only of phonology and grammar and lexis, but also of meaning. There is no sense in setting pupils to 'correct' such sentences as those cited here, since they are all correct enough in appropriate contexts. They might be 'translated' into different registers or styles, but in the process of translation they will probably take on different meanings. It is worth remembering, too, that a number of so-called solecisms—such as the split infinitive, and the use of a terminal preposition—are quite frequent in the writing of our best authors. Taking liberties with conventions is a well-known characteristic of literary writing.

There is, then, no ineluctable or transcendental measure of correctness in any form of language. What is 'right' in any situation or task is what is most appropriate. The idea of correctness must yield to that of appropriateness, of suitability, as the most useful basis for judgements of the quality of effectiveness of language. The language that best fits the needs of the speaker or writer, the situation, the subject at hand, is the 'right' language. This is not to say that there is never a right–wrong opposition. Of course there are many occasions when it is possible to say, unreservedly, that one form is wrong and another is right. But it is necessary to distinguish between different levels of subjectivity in judgement making, with different ranges of acceptability. In the technical sense 'grammaticality' affords yes/no judgements which few native speakers would question. Where situational criteria operate a form can only be judged suitable by reference to the context. In matters of style our judgements are made by reference to our notions of what is 'adequate' or 'effective' or 'acceptable'. In questions of usage the only recourse we have is to what is generally deemed to be 'acceptable'.

---

[1] A. M. Philp, *Attitudes to Correctness in English*, Longman, 1968.

Grammar and education

The word *grammar* has several different connotations. Historically, *grammar* has meant the whole linguistic apparatus of a people, their speech and mainly their writings. To the modern linguistics scholar the grammar of a language is the organization of its words in sentences, its morphology and syntax. In education *grammar* has often been taken to indicate what is 'right' and 'wrong' in the use of language. Finally, a *grammar* can be taken to indicate a statement of how a language works. In modern educational circles distinctions are made between *traditional grammar*, *structural grammar*, Hallidayan or *scale and category grammar*, and Chomskyan or *transformational–generative grammar*.

Traditional grammar developed from the study of Greek and Latin grammars by such scholars as Aelius Donatus, whose fourth-century *Ars Grammatica* described Latin in terms of the eight parts of speech. A long scholarly tradition of grammatical studies, from the sixteenth to the early twentieth centuries, applied Latin grammatical concepts such as *tense*, *case*, and *voice* to the European languages, and a large number of reference grammars was produced for English, French, German and other European languages. Grammars of 'newly discovered' African and Asian languages were compiled, and by the beginning of this century a massive volume of technical information had been gathered for most of the known languages. Early in the century three great grammars were produced within this scholarly tradition: Henrik Poutsma's *Grammar of Late Modern English*, Etsko Kruisinga's *Handbook of Present-day English*, and Otto Jespersen's *Modern English Grammar on Historical Principles*.[1]

The school grammar drawn from this traditional corpus tended to concentrate on the parsing of words (*parsing* derives from *pars*, 'part' of speech), the analysis of complex sentences into clause-types and of 'simple' or one-clause sentences into Subject–Predicate–Object/Complement parts. Each part of speech was defined on a notional basis, according to its generalized 'meaning' and 'function'. Thus a *noun* was 'the name of an object, person or thing', a verb was a 'doing word', an adjective a 'describing word' and so on. Sentences were classified as simple, compound, complex, and compound-complex, and clause-types were categorized as independent and subordinate, each subordinate clause being defined functionally as adjectival, adverbial, nominal and so on. The rationale of the teaching of grammar in this way was largely utilitarian, since it was believed that an understanding of sentence structure would lead to more competent writing; but there was an idealistic aspect, too, as many educators firmly believed that the study of grammar developed a mental discipline which would transfer to other learning activities.

[1] H. A. Gleason, Jr, *Linguistics and English Grammar*, Holt, Rinehart & Winston, 1965.

There were many pedagogical objections to school grammar teaching during the 1920s and 1930s, and by the end of the Second World War most progressive educators were convinced that it was largely a waste of time. Research was demonstrating that there was little or no transfer of training to the pupils' productive language, either in speech or writing.[1] Much of the so-called 'grammar' in text books, moreover, consisted of dull and unprofitable exercises, such as the correction of 'Common Errors' and prescriptive 'rules' of composition and prosody.

At this time, too, structural linguists in America were criticizing traditional grammar from a linguistic viewpoint. They argued that a grammar based on Latin could not be valid for English, since the two languages are 'essentially, basically, radically different'.[2] The languages are certainly dissimilar in their methods of organizing linguistic substance: Latin is highly inflectional while English is mainly distributive (that is, the English sentence relies more on word-order than on the inflection of words). The linguists criticized traditional grammarians' reliance on notional categories for defining the elements of the sentence, and demonstrated that it often fails. (For instance, if a noun is 'the name of something' and a verb 'denotes an action', is *dictation* a noun or a verb or both?) They criticized the traditional scholars' exclusive interest in the written language—this itself as a term is a misnomer to the structuralist, who equates language with speech and regards writing as 'speech written down'. They also criticized the prevalent school grammar for being preoccupied by false notions of correctness and by prescriptive and proscriptive rules.

Structural linguistics produced a 'new grammar' of English and other languages. This was scientifically worked out as an analysis of the sentence into 'immediate constituents' (ICs) or 'pattern parts'. For example, the sentence *The three old ladies upstairs own a boxer dog with a mean temper* can be broken down into various pairs of constituents, each pair consisting of lesser parts until the minimal meaningful linguistic elements are reached.[3] Thus the sentence can be cut into two ICs:

The three old ladies upstairs	**own a boxer dog with a mean temper**
NOMINAL GROUP	VERBAL GROUP

The verbal group can be cut into

own	**a boxer dog with a mean temper**

[1] See, for example, W. J. Macaulay, 'The difficulty of grammar', in *British Journal of Educational Psychology*, 1947, 17, pp. 153–162.

[2] Charlton Laird, *Thinking About Language*, Holt, Rinehart & Winston, 1961.

[3] This example is taken from Gleason, *op. cit.*, Chapter 7.

All the constituents of the sentence can be shown by means of a 'tree diagram' thus:

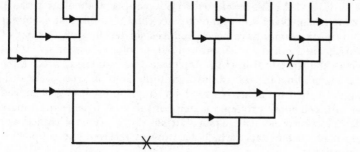

Grammatical descriptions of a structuralist type were produced by C. C. Fries, Harold Whitehall, Paul Roberts and others in the USA and by Randolph Quirk, Barbara Strang and W. H. Mittins in Britain.[1] Apart from the sentence analyses which the 'new linguistics' offered there was also a considerable revision of the grammatical terminology of the traditionalists, and some educational grammarians (for instance, Whitehall and Roberts) proposed a quite novel set of terms for use in schools. Although some of the grammatical work of the structuralist school has been superseded during the last decade, much of the writing contained important scholarship and some of the books, in particular those of Fries, Quirk and Strang, are still to be highly recommended for their valuable insights into the nature of the English language.

M. A. K. Halliday's 'scale and category grammar', now developed into a full-scale systemic grammar of English, has been much studied by British educators. Halliday proposes a taxonomy of units: *sentence, clause, phrase* (or *group*), *word* and *morpheme*. Thus a sentence can be shown to consist of one or more clauses, a clause of one or more phrases, a phrase of one or more words, and a word of one or more morphemes. This is the *rank scale*, and a unit can be seen at times to operate at a different rank from its usual one. Thus in the sentence *The man I saw ran away* the noun phrase *The man I saw* contains a *rank-shifted* clause, *I saw*: that is to say, *I saw* would normally be a clause but in this sentence it is part of a noun phrase, the unit below it in the rank scale. The notion of rank-shift is an illuminating one,

[1] C. C. Fries, *The Structure of English*, Harcourt Brace, 1952; H. Whitehall, *Structural Essentials of English*, Longman, 1958; P. Roberts, *Patterns of English*, Harcourt Brace, 1956; *ibid., English Sentences*, Harcourt Brace, 1962; R. Quirk, *The Use of English*, Longman, 1962; B. Strang, *Modern English Structure*, Arnold, 1962; W. H. Mittins, *A Grammar of Modern English*, Methuen, 1962.

particularly for deepening our understanding of the relationship between syntax and logical meaning.

Halliday also proposes a category of *structure* which enables us to identify the structural elements of a sentence. The structural labels S, P, C, and A, can be glossed as Subject-place, Predicator-place, Complement-place and Adjunct-place, and a number of grammar study programmes have been produced for teachers on this basis.[1] This is an 'Immediate Constituents' type of sentence analysis, but where the structural linguist employs a binary-division process the Hallidayan linguist will employ a multiple-division process. According to Currie, the 'many ICs model is simple to use in class, can lead on to much more profound statements about language than mere identification of elements in places; it can also form part of a functional approach to language, which has always received the support of education'.[2]

Chomsky's transformational-generative (known as TG) grammar presupposes, as we have seen, that a grammar must be able to account for all the grammatical sentences possible to produce in a language. His grammatical model therefore specifies the grammatical rules required for constructing sentences. The words and morphemes of a sentence are arranged in functional constituents such as subject, predicate, object and so on, and a speaker's knowledge of this internal structure can be represented (in part, at least) by means of 'phrase structure' rules.

The first of these rules is simply that a sentence can consist of a noun phrase followed by a verb phrase, and the rule is represented thus:

$$S \longrightarrow NP + VP$$

(The arrow is an instruction to 'rewrite' the left-hand symbol as the string of symbols which follow it.)

Other rules tell us that *NP* can be rewritten as *Art*+*N* (since a noun phrase can be rewritten as *boy, table, Johnson* etc; that *Art* can be rewritten *as a, an,* or *the*; that *VP* can be rewritten as *Aux*+*V* (since a verb phrase can consist of an auxiliary and a main verb); that *Aux* can be rewritten as *can, may, will, should,* etc., and so on. Thus we can list some grammatical rules:

1	S	NP+VP
2	NP	Art+N
3	VP	Aux+V+NP
4	Aux	(can, may, will, should, etc.)

[1] See W. B. Currie, *New Directions in Teaching English Language*, Longman, 1973. This is an excellent short account of current school grammars and their development.

[2] W. B. Currie, *op. cit.*, 45.

5	V	(walk, hit, kick, explain, etc.)
6	Art	(a, an, the)
7	N	(boy, table, Johnson, ball, etc.)

We can now construct a *derivation* of a sentence by rewriting the left-hand symbol with the elements on the right-hand. For example, the sentence *The boy will kick the ball* yields the following derivation:

S
NP+VP (by rule 1)
Art+N+VP (by rule 2)
Art+N+Aux+V+NP (by rule 3)
Art+N+Aux+V+art+N (by rule 2)
the+boy+will+kick+the+ball (by rules 4, 5, 6, 7)

This derivation can be represented by a *tree diagram*:

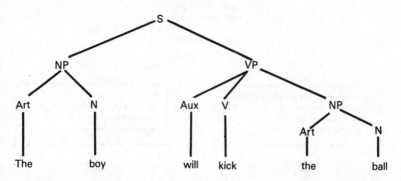

This 'phrase marker' is the TG representation of the syntax of one sentence. (Chomsky is not, of course, suggesting that a speaker consciously or unconsciously applies these rules in his mind. The rules merely represent 'internalized' rules that are implicit in the grammar.)

Phrase structure rules can be shown to underlie the *kernel* or basic sentences in English. Chomsky points out, however, that phrase structure rules can only generate a partial grammar to cater for a mere fragment of English. In addition to these rules, the grammar requires *transformational* rules which transform phrase markers into other phrase markers by adding or deleting or rearranging elements. The basic rules generate the 'deep structure' of a sentence; the transformational rules change the deep structure into the 'surface structure'. There are many transformational rules: for converting active to passive, or singular to plural, for rearranging the elements of a sentence, and so on. It is the transformational rules which account for the ambiguity of such a sentence as *I like her cooking*. It can be shown that several different basic sentences yield this same phrase marker: for example, *I like what she cooks*, *I like the way she cooks*,

I like the fact that she cooks etc. Different transformational rules convert the different basic sentences into the same 'surface' sentence.[1]

In addition to transformational rules, a TG grammar employs *morphographemic* rules, which convert the various morphemes into the form of written words, and *morphophonetic* rules, which convert the morphemes into their phonological representations. The Chomskyan theory can be graphically described by a simplified model:

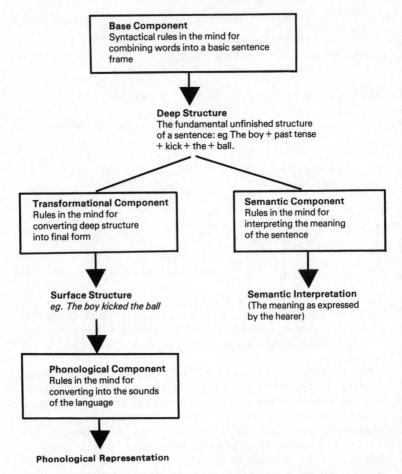

Base Component
Syntactical rules in the mind for combining words into a basic sentence frame

Deep Structure
The fundamental unfinished structure of a sentence: eg The boy + past tense + kick + the + ball.

Transformational Component
Rules in the mind for converting deep structure into final form

Semantic Component
Rules in the mind for interpreting the meaning of the sentence

Surface Structure
eg. The boy kicked the ball

Semantic Interpretation
(The meaning as expressed by the hearer)

Phonological Component
Rules in the mind for converting into the sounds of the language

Phonological Representation

Chomsky's preoccupation with syntax has been attacked by a new school of 'generative semanticists' who argue that meaning and syntax are intertwined: the grammar starts with a description of the meaning of a sentence, and then generates the syntactical

---

[1] This example is taken from an article by John Searle in a Special Supplement of the *New York Review*, 29 June, 1972.

structure by means of syntactical and lexical rules. They postulate a 'semantic component': rules in the mind for generating the structural frame of a sentence and its meaning simultaneously. The theory of generative semantics is relatively new, but the growing modern interest in the relation between syntax and semantics may well have implications of some importance for our understanding of how a grammar works.

The concept of deep and surface grammar is present also in Halliday's consideration of *system*. This category concerns the options which operate in the selection of the forms realized in a particular structure. Three systems operate on the clause. The system of *transitivity* concerns the 'actor', the 'process' and the 'goal' as functions in a clause. Thus in the sentence, *Sir Christopher Wren built this gazebo*, the 'actor' function is realized by *Sir Christopher Wren*, the 'process' function by *built* and the 'goal' function by *this gazebo*. The system of *Mood* concerns the speech functions of the clause, and the options which allow a speaker to vary his role in communicating with others in social interaction. Such speech functions as making statements, asking questions, uttering orders and making exclamations are expressed grammatically by the *mood* system. The system of *Theme* concerns the organization of the clause as a message. The English clause consists of a 'theme'—the 'psychological subject', the peg on which the message is hung—and a 'rheme', which is the 'new' information. Thus in *I don't know*, *I* is the theme and *don't know* is the rheme; in *Suddenly the rope gave way*, *Suddenly* is the theme and the rest of the utterance is the rheme.[1]

It will be obvious from this very brief and simplified account of modern grammars that we now have a comprehensive body of descriptive matter for discussing the structures of sentences, and educationalists have not been slow in attempting to make use of it for teaching purposes. Both Chomsky and Halliday have exerted great influence on educational thinking, not only by providing sources for pedagogical grammars but also by providing insights into the operation of language in thinking and communication. In America, Chomsky's work has been extensively misapplied. The term 'generative' has been widely misinterpreted and associated erroneously with educational notions like 'creative writing' and 'productive learning' and Chomsky has himself warned educators that he sees little direct relevance to schooling in his TG grammar. In Britain, Halliday has openly interested himself in education, and has written several seminal papers on the educational implications of his work, particularly in the sociolinguistic field. As W. B. Currie puts it: 'Bloomfield took a destructive and even a vicious attitude to school language work; Chomsky has been marked by a studied agnosticism on the question of application. Halliday has maintained a steady and

[1] M. A. K. Halliday, 'Language Structure and Language Function', in *New Horizons in Linguistics*, J. Lyons (ed.), Penguin, 1970.

fruitful contact with educational programmes for over a decade'.[1]

The place of grammar in the classroom has been diminished during the last half-century because the traditional pedagogical grammar was thought to be deficient, but also because teachers lost faith in grammar work as a source of training in the use of language. Modern English teaching begins with the belief that you best learn English through using it, and our concentration on the productive involvement of children in practical language-using situations is unquestionably justified. The language-acquisition paradigm described by modern psycholinguistics suggests that the development of linguistic skills as children mature will best occur if they are continuously experimenting with language in live or simulated interaction with other users of language: that is, by engaging in talk, reading and writing in contexts which motivate the active interchange of ideas. The importance of such practice is so great that efficient teachers rightly resist any activity which may compete for the time required, especially when they cannot fully accept that the activity is genuinely useful.

At the same time, all pupils must acquire a set of linguistic concepts and terms. Whether he wants to or not, every teacher is engaged in transmitting notions about language all the time he is teaching. The teacher is rightly concerned with language production and the systematic teaching of a pedagogical grammar, however modern, however 'respectable' in its linguistic conception, cannot be regarded as productive in this sense. Since native speakers of English acquire a grammatical competence intuitively, the methodical description of grammar, along with the procedures of analysis, cannot be justified in terms of results, and the time given to it would be better employed in other language activities.[2]

With children in the primary school, grammatical terminology of a minimal kind may be occasionally useful, for example in advising pupils about their writing of sentences and so on; but in practice teachers need do little more than draw attention to generalizations emerging from the children's own knowledge.[3] With older pupils in the secondary school, the teacher should, however, be prepared to use grammatical knowledge more explicitly, since the discussion of texts, whether in reading or the pupils' own writing, requires descriptive terms—what linguists call a 'metalanguage'—for talking about language. This implies that teachers—of all subjects—should be sufficiently familiar with the terms and concepts of modern linguistic analysis to enable them to speak usefully about the language used in pupils' work. That there is no room for formal grammar

---

[1] W. B. Currie, *op. cit.*, p. 52.

[2] *The Teaching of English Language*, Bulletin No. 5 of the (Scottish) Central Committee on English, HMSO, 1972.

[3] *Children and Their Primary Schools* (Plowden Report), HMSO, 1967, p. 222.

teaching does not mean that there is no need for teachers to know something about grammar. There is a good case for the acquisition of grammatical knowledge by all teachers, so that they can convey to their pupils the linguistic insights which improve efficiency in the use of language at all stages and for all purposes.

It is of course, the teacher of English to whom we look for the major contribution in language teaching. Even in the English classroom, however, formal grammar has little justification. The English teacher must, of course, pay particular attention to his pupils' use of language, devising the means to promote competence and to motivate study and practice. English teachers should know a great deal about grammars and grammatical theory. They should be able, when they see the need, to give their pupils illustrated explanations to show the value of particular applications of rules and conventions —thus they should be capable of giving lessons on grammar in order to explicate a point of style, or to show how common errors can be understood and avoided, or to give the pupils guidance as to how they can construct more effective sentences. All of these activities are better thought of as *rhetoric*, the art of composition; but they require grammatical analysis to be properly appreciated. And since the metalanguage cannot be learned by pupils in the course of a systematized programme of grammar work, the teacher should take every opportunity that arises to use the terms which facilitate reference to linguistic features. This is the process of 'mention'; the gradual conveying of a body of terminology as the need for terms arises. Through 'mention', which of course involves much sophisticated knowledge and skill in the teacher, the pupils will in time acquire a vocabulary for talking about language which will enable them to work with language at a mature level.

The teacher of foreign languages requires a thorough knowledge of the grammar of the languages he teaches, and his competence will be greater if his operational knowledge is founded on a good understanding of grammatical theory. Traditionally, modern language teachers have looked to their English colleagues to give pupils a 'grounding' in English grammar on which they can work. This is not now a legitimate expectation, since it is not necessary for pupils to have formal grammar in the English classroom. Modern linguists have turned, of course, to oral methods, but even so many feel it desirable to employ some grammatical description. Where this is the case, the foreign language teacher must provide the information himself; and it is to be hoped that he will be able to make use of the work of linguistics scholars. Almost everything that Chomsky, Halliday and others say about English applies to French, German, Russian and other modern languages. The process of 'mention' and the spot lesson to illustrate a process or a construction, can be as effective in foreign language teaching as in English.

The teacher of Latin can also benefit from a knowledge of modern grammatical theory. New Latin pedagogical grammars have been produced, some of which purport to introduce patterns more systematically than the traditional textbooks did. More importantly, perhaps, the very dissimilarity between the grammars of Latin and English suggests that secondary school pupils with an academic turn of mind could benefit from a specially devised course of grammatical study designed to give them an understanding of 'universal' grammar. Taught properly, a course in Latin could lead to knowledge of the systems and categories of grammar which, besides being interesting in its own right, could provide a good basis for the study of modern languages.

PART II

The Components of a Policy

4. The Teachers' Approach

An attitude to language

Because access to so much learning is through language, and because the very process of understanding involves verbalizing, that is because learning is operating with language, it is clearly important that all teachers have an outline idea of the fundamentals of how language works. Whatever our specialist function in education we work with language, and we must, as individuals and as a school team, have a common attitude towards our most precious skill. And yet this is not easy for a number of reasons.

In the first place many people's ideas about language, what it is and how it works, are folk lore with very little basis in truth; indeed frequently they are misleading. This is not surprising as most of the research studies into the nature of language, which Dr Gatherer outlined in Chapter 3, are fairly recent. The findings of the linguists from the 'twenties onwards have not yet filtered down into everyday educated knowledge. Most professional people know far more about economics, sociology, or the internal combustion engine than they do about language.

Further, language is very personal, and it is difficult for all but the linguistic specialist to find ways of talking about language, which, of course, means talking about *oneself*, without becoming personal, embarrassed, touchy, or upset. It is easier for us to talk about the technicalities of, say, teaching with audio-visual aids than our use of language in the classroom. I fear that this aspect of a suggested language policy may seem daunting: if linguistics is such a deep, difficult, and disputable study, what can the ordinary teacher usefully learn of it? Yet Dr Gatherer has shown the agreed central truths, and his six generalizations on page 35 are the foundations of a teacher's and a school's approach to working with language. I would suggest that a school could use those six statements as a basis for considering language in the school.

Perhaps the most fundamental linguistic point for educators is that language 'is a means of categorizing and ordering human experience' (Dr Gatherer's phrase). Therefore people who teach those subject areas concerned with the analysis and categorization of experience need to realize that they are not merely using language as an expository device: the pupil must re-use it to achieve the categorizing and ordering that is the intellectual heart of the sciences, the humanities, and even mathematics.

For the teacher the 'arbitrary', 'selected', 'conventional' nature of the symbols of language means that attention and the establishment of criteria for helping pupils must be directed at how language is used in the society we are preparing our pupils for. Attempts to establish 'natural or inevitable' meanings are artificial. A knowledgeable and reasonably sensitive attitude to language is, I suspect, likely to encourage the school to teach specific skills, rather than to attempt to make the pupil into the teacher's own image.

Dr Gatherer's point about language and thought should permeate the pastoral and curricular life of the school: he points out that the idea of language as the 'clothing of thought', is less useful than considering it as the 'embodiment of thought'. That being so, we cannot offer language forms ('Energy is ...', 'A ritual is ...', 'Symmetry is ...') 'off the peg' for the pupil to don and use. The pupil must come to the understanding through exploratory language.

I shall take four aspects of thinking about language, and show how teaching practices might be affected by this attitude.

English as a distributive language

Perhaps the central technical point about our language is that it is essentially a *distributive* language; that is, sense comes out of the connections between words. In an inflected language the connections are shown by changes in the actual words; in an uninflected language by the word order, or distribution.

The normal English word order is very deeply embedded in our minds:

The man hit the boy.

We all know exactly what this means, and if 'boy' and 'man' are transposed the meaning alters. In an inflected language, word order is far less important for sense because it is obvious whether the boy did the hitting or the man according to the inflected ending. Thus the distributive nature of our language, and its consequent dependence on word order, is far more important than inflection.

Yet schools tend to be more interested in the more easily noted, and thus 'corrected' inflectional oddities of a pupil than in helping pupils towards making more of word order. A school pondering this might consider scrutinizing examples of pupil's talk and writing to establish if word order could be profitably worked on.

The vocabulary

Both a strength and a difficulty of our language is its immense and immensely varied vocabulary. 'The vernacular of vernaculars', as Robert Graves called it, has grown from 'the lingo used between the

Norman-French conquerors and their Anglo-Saxon serfs', and kept the resulting diversity of vocabulary. We have, for instance, an unusually wide choice of prefixes of different origins. We have also a number of near alternative words, but each with particular associations and uses. Never watched over by an academy, constantly added to as we borrowed from other languages, our vocabulary allows a richly personal use, but only to those who are at ease with it. Spelling conventions are particularly difficult, a problem which goes back to the post-conquest time when there was a long period during which spelling patterns did not settle down. The spelling difficulties which trouble pupils should be seen not merely as requiring surface tidying, but as a problem central to their gradual exploration of this large vocabulary.

If we ponder the nature of our vocabulary and its system, we realize that a school as a whole must have a conscious plan to help pupils throughout their school years, a plan which will be both specific and contextual. Much of Chapter 6 will be devoted to the kinds of practical policies that might grow from this consideration.

Notions of appropriateness

In our anxiety not to be sloppy, and in our own nervousness about language, we sometimes push rules which are inappropriate for the occasion, are too early for the pupils' growing approximations, or are even entirely wrong: that is, they just do not exist. I am not alleging that because on an off day in a casual piece of writing a well-known writer uses a particular form that it is acceptable. I am suggesting that some rules exist only in schoolrooms. Dr Gatherer has nicely balanced the necessary objectivity with the equally necessary need to learn ' "rules of use" in social situations' and ' "rules of effectiveness" in communication'.

In establishing a language policy, a staff might need to explore the difference between accepting everything and giving positive help. Some teachers in a rash of conscientiousness endeavour to prune and shape pupils' language into what they take to be acceptable. Let us consider some of the wrong-headed reasons which are sometimes advanced by teachers, and which a language policy should clarify.

'Laziness' is one of the commonest explanations, as well as criticisms, of socially less prestigious pronunciations. A moment's thought, however, challenges this. The 'dropped' 't' in 'butter' can be dubbed 'lazy' only by those who forget that it is acceptable, indeed even 'correct', to leave out the 't' in 'often'. (Fowler criticizes those who pronounce the 't' in 'often' by the label of 'spelling pronunciation'.) Labov looked carefully at stigmatized pronunciation forms and concluded:

> Some of the extreme developments of vernacular vowel shifts in New York City, Detroit, or Chicago are tense vowels which seem to involve a great deal of muscular effort compared to the standard. . . . The usual response is to cite laziness, lack of concern, or isolation from the prestige norm. But

there is no foundation for the notion that stigmatised vernacular forms are easier to pronounce.[1]

'Illogical' or 'ungrammatical', are other justifications for attacking pupils' speech. Teachers who themselves fought to change their grammatical patterns, who learnt the rules of, e.g., subject–verb agreement or of the subjective and objective forms of pronouns, often mis-apply those rules, dubbing alternative *forms* as 'illogical'. It can be, for instance, that the subject form is different from that in standard English. It is not that there are no rules, but that in different forms of speech the rules are met in different ways.

Suffolk speech, for instance, like many other British regional dialects, has different forms for pronouns:

Us don't want t' play wi' he.
Oi don't think much o' they.
Oi went out a-walkin' wi' she.

or in the lovely description of a new schoolmistress by an old Suffolk woman:

O, har be a buptious botty bitch, har oon't speak t' th' loikes o' we.[2]

There is, of course, perfect language *logic* in the pronoun forms used. It is a consistent pattern, and readily understood. There is certainly no inferiority, still less any confusion or illogicality. The speakers have learnt a grammar which differs from standard English, but which is every bit as grammatical. The school concerned, as it rightly would be, with helping the older pupil cope with the more widely used pronoun patterns would be ill advised, and indeed would be inaccurate, to dub 'he', 'they', 'she', and 'we' as wrong, and to label them nominative forms in objective positions. They are *objective forms* in this grammar, but different objective forms. It ill becomes the teacher to be incorrect in his reason and method of 'correction'.

It is best, I feel, to consider, for instance, West Indian speech only after having given that kind of attention to a mainland dialect. The same points apply: the usual forms are not irregularities; the common phrases, indeed, are not bad grammar. Certainly it is intellectually impossible to analyse the speech as slipshod or illogical. For instance, there will always be subject–verb agreement, and there will always be a consistent use of the appropriate case for pronouns. However, the *form* of verb will differ, as will the form of the pronoun. Here is a West Indian talking:

I had was to let she think I wouldn't tell he, but, after all, Big Joe and me is friends, and anything I hear 'bout I does tell he, despite the way he does treat me sometimes.

[1] William Labov, 'The Study of Language in its Social Context', in *Studium Generale*, Volume 23, 1970, reprinted in J. B. Pride and Janet Holmes (eds), *Sociolinguistics*, Penguin, 1972.
[2] The examples are all taken from A. O. D. Claxton, *The Suffolk Dialect of the Twentieth Century*, Norman Adlard and Company, 1968, p. 11.

The use of 'she' and 'he' is entirely consistent, as is the verbal form 'I does tell', 'he does trust me'.

There is some etymological wrong-headedness amongst teachers who complain about language being spoilt by neologisms, barbarisms, or Americanisms. Too frequently the grounds for the objection are inaccurate. Underlying the whole concern is a false attitude to the language of the past, assuming it to have been a pure one which is being corrupted today. Many of the words being objected to have far more respectable antecedents than the objectors realize. Phrases like 'to meet up with' or 'to make out', which have enjoyed a new lease of life in recent years, in fact started life in this country, in perfectly respectable use, before exportation to America, and a subsequent return home. An example of a usage that has had the full attack of schoolmasterly scorn is the suffix '-wise'. There are many respectable antecedents for this: for example, Bunyan uses 'double-wise' and Coleridge 'maidenwise'.

Of course, this is not to say that we should not be sensitive to usage, and should not have preferences. Nor is the acceptability of a usage in the past evidence of its suitability now. However, we must not (a) attack with inaccurate weapons, substituting fallacious linguistic history for personal taste or for current inappropriateness, and (b) we should consider whether the effort is anyway worth it when the tide of language will take its channels whether individuals try to block it or not. Should we not be using our efforts more positively? As I said in another context, 'the basis of our teaching must be adding, enriching, and encouraging—not deleting, criticizing, inhibiting.'[1]

The 'two languages' theory is another dubious piece of popular linguistic folklore. Its popularity seems to depend on the advocacy of those who have moved socially and economically from less favoured settings and like to feel they still have social and linguistic roots to which they can return. Investigations show that their version of the language they left behind, however warm a feeling it gives them in the bar, is *not* the original, but is nearer their current speech pattern with the insertion of the cruder signals to mark its origin. Labov's careful research makes this quite clear:

> We have not encountered any non-standard speakers who gained good control of a standard language, and still retained control of the non-standard vernacular. . . . Although the speaker may indeed appear to be speaking the vernacular, close examination of his speech shows that his grammar has been heavily influenced by the standard. He may succeed in convincing his listeners that he is speaking the vernacular, but this impression seems to depend upon a number of unsystematic and heavily marked signals.[2]

[1] In an essay 'Mainstream', in Denys Thompson (ed.), *Directions in the Teaching of English*, CUP, 1969, p. 56.
[2] William Labov, *op. cit.*, p. 187.

The class and the locality

Perhaps central to a school's attitude to language will be a consideration of the implications for the secondary school of the theories of
language acquisition and class variations in language. An individual
grows by developing successive approximations to the models he
needs and wishes to acquire. His present language cannot usefully be
regarded as deficient: this would be to encourage the wholly inappropriate beliefs that there are gaps to be filled by offering prepared units
to add to the present form. We know how much harm is done both by
denigrating and over-romanticizing non-standard languages. We
must respect the language the pupil brings with him, and the
language of his home. Our tradition is favourable to the socially less
acceptable forms of speech. Synge listening with relish to the peasants
in the Arran Isles, whose speech was 'like a nut or an apple', is part of
our tradition, as is the peasant poet John Clare. The plays of Shakespeare, are nearer to the vernacular tradition than those of Racine or
Corneille. When these great truths have been in danger of being lost
there has always been someone to remind us. David Holbrook, for
instance in *English for Maturity* and *English for the Rejected*, spoke
eloquently for the power and effectiveness of ordinary speech. His
pleas were absorbed into our system. We may need reminders, but
our educational and cultural tradition, respects the vernacular.

There is an opposite danger: to accept any forms of speech (and
some teachers extend this to obscenities) on all occasions comes from
a mistaken idea that we are thus going out to meet the pupils on their
own ground. A school must relate to its community in a way which
is very subtle, as far as language is concerned. Bullock does stress
that: 'We believe that a child's accent should be accepted, and that
to attempt to suppress it is   ational and neither humane nor necessary.' (10.5) Speaking of 'acceptable standards of grammar and
diction' the Report similarly stresses that: 'The aim is not to alienate
the child from a form of language with which he has grown up.' (10.6)
It is very easy to jump rapidly from these, surely by now unconten-
tious, linguistic recommendations to a simplistic 'anything goes'
approach. From that it is easy to presume that because the local
community does not *use* the speech patterns of standard English,
for local people too 'anything goes'. *The opposite is true*, and a school
that at best wishes to relate to its community and at worst at least
wishes not to offend it must develop a sophisticated understanding of
the local community's expectations. Labov has demonstrated from
careful research evidence[1] that the 'upwardly socially mobile' are
highly sensitive to the sounds of the speakers to whose way of life they
are aspiring. Elsewhere he points out that 'the pattern of subjective
reaction tests shows that those who use the highest percentage of

[1] William Labov, 'Phonological Correlates of Social Stratification', in
American Anthropology, **66**, No. 6 (2), 1964.

stigmatised forms are quickest to stigmatise them in the speech of others'.[1] Labov's work has shown that an urban speech community is not so much a community of people who *speak* in the same way, but one which shares the same prejudice about how others speak. 'Social attitudes are extremely uniform throughout a speech community. . . . In fact it seems plausible to define a speech community as a group of speakers who share a set of social attitudes towards language.'[2] This notion must be respected, incorporated into the school's policy: social *attitudes* are part of the language pattern of the community. Yet educationalists with a great regard for the speech patterns of an area, and a genuine wish to act on that regard, easily become superior and patronizing about the area attitude *towards* speech (and thus to the variations in speech which a speech community has). This is unreal, and indeed dangerous, for it can lead to real breaches with the parent body and with the community.

Conclusion

Underlying any language policy must be some knowledge of language. A school must work out a functional pedagogical understanding of language, and establish an attitude to it. Such an understanding is likely to contain ideas about:

The function of language in life;

How language develops in the young child;

What human beings *do* with language;

The special characteristics of our language, including its vocabulary;

The social context of language;

Notions of appropriateness.

The hardest task is to find ways of working with the pupil's own language, and yet to help him to be able to make his own ideas and ways of thinking which lie outside the scope of that language.

The language of school

I now come to the special question of the language demands of each subject area. Every teaching situation uses language to a considerable extent. Even PE depends on the teacher's explanations, instructions, commands, and encouragement, and the pupils' response to these

---

[1] William Labov, *op. cit.*, p. 180.
[2] *ibid.*, p. 196.

words. Science, despite all the emphasis on manipulative skills, is essentially based on language. The most obvious way it is used is to carry the subject-teaching of the ostensible curriculum, but *at the same time* there is a hidden curriculum, that in which language itself is being taught. For pupils, knowledge lies out there in shadowy phrases used by the teacher or in dense language printed in books. it is not just that so many of the words are unfamiliar; the way they go together is different too: 'When he tells us to do something, it's OK; I can do it. But when he asks us *about* something, I can't make it out.'

The first problem at school is the sheer quantity of new words and new ways of putting things. As the pupil gets older this accelerates— indeed some attempts to lighten the load for the immediate post-primary years have the effect of making the mid-secondary language incline so steep as to be insurmountable by many. Either way the vocabulary expectations of the new specialized curriculum are very heavy. There also can be devastating language strictures, tight regulations that prevent natural, thoughtful reactions. The English teacher criticizes the use of 'nice' ('Has no meaning. Choose a better description'); the geography teacher will not allow you to describe anywhere as 'beautiful' ('Not the point; you're writing about the land form and the population pattern'); the science teach gets very cross if you say 'I' ('Scientists are objective and impersonal'); the craft teacher is upset if you ask for 'one of those' or 'that' ('You must use the right names; everything's got a name').

The reading material in different subjects is startlingly different, each subject from the other and all from fiction. It is not only the vocabularies that are different. The predominant paragraph patterns are quite different. Mathematics is a startling example. In the last twenty years there has been an increase in the amount of reading offered by and expected by textbooks. (Earlier ones were merely the examples to use after the teacher's explanation.) The language is quite different not only in the use of special terms, but also in the limited and special meanings of ordinary words, such as 'if', 'only', 'all, 'except', 'lot'. The vital difference though, is the almost totally non-redundant and relatively unambiguous language in mathematics. It is arguably the hardest language used in the schools.[1] Other subjects offer other difficulties, where again the problems are terminology, special use of normal words, and density. The logical relationships are tightly packed and difficult to disentangle.

In this passage from a Nuffield reader for middle-secondary school pupils, there are the following difficulties: terminology; sentence structure (three compound adjectives plus 'light' between 'the' and

[1] Considerable research into this has been published in the USA. A readily available and clear analysis by Regine Baron Brunner has been published in this country: 'Reading Mathematical Exposition', in *Educational Research*, Volume 18, No. 3, NFER, June 1976, p. 208.

'bulb'); logical pattern ('Although . . . unfortunately'); important concept differences embodied in similar words ('effective', 'efficiency'); postponed meaning ('You have only . . . to').

Efficiency

Although the tungsten-filament coiled-coil gas-filled light bulb is effective, unfortunately it is not very efficient. A high proportion of the electrical energy that goes into it is transformed into heat. You have only to place your hand close to it after it has been on for a little while to convince yourself of this. Then place your hand close to a fluorescent tube which has been switched on for the same time and judge for yourself how little heat is being wasted. The difference between the incandescent lamp and the fluorescent tube will then be obvious. The fluorescent tube has a greater efficiency—about three times as great.

Even passages that apparently use no difficult terminology actually offer problems. The concept in the following is quite difficult. The structure of the last sentence is very difficult, and loses most pupil readers:

Your experiments have shown that energy very often gets changed into heat, and that it is possible to change heat into other forms of energy, or at any rate, to change some of it. The essential thing in any machine that changes heat into some other form of energy is that some part of the machine is hotter than all other parts.

In order to grasp the meaning of the second sentence one has to understand the complement ('that some part of the machine is hotter than all other parts'), which occurs at the end of the sentence. The subject ('The essential thing') is separated from the verb ('is') and the complement by a long descriptive phrase. I call this 'postponed meaning', a frequent device of expository writing, but very unfamiliar to the pupil. Teachers often use it in speaking, and I noted the following start to a sentence said in a classroom:

Another thing we ought to do if we're going to have the folders ready by the time we've planned (and we need to keep to that so that I can look through them in time) is . . .

By which time sense is lost to most listeners!

Other science reading is like that in crafts in that it demands two things at once—reading and doing. At other times, especially in biological aspects, science books offer a pattern of enumeration or classification. This can be quite difficult to read. And, of course, all science writing has a compactness not far short of that in mathematics. Then there is a range of newly introduced written forms, each fresh, each abruptly started, and each demanding special conventions: notes, observations, paragraph answers, essays, which are studied by Nancy Martin in Chapter 5.

In the classroom there can be a dominance of impersonal language, so that the linguistic material of the child and his home are thrown out, and even a false middle-class delicacy introduced. Even more often, the conventions of a certain form of language are insisted on too completely and too early. In too many language transactions there is a closed expectation, in which the pupils learn narrowly the kind of expected answer. On other occasions the language is designed primarily to gain group control. Of course, control is necessary in schools, and public language will have to be used in various ways for that control, but care is needed if the control element in language is not to seep into other situations. For instance, a girl was once so conditioned by the control function of language that when the teacher quite genuinely enquired in an English class 'What are you laughing at, Jane?', she automatically responded 'Oh, nothing, Miss' even though the lesson was on a piece of literature in which there was humour and the teacher really wished to discuss what was funny in it.[1] In all these ways there is a real possibility of creating a linguistically alien territory, one in which many of the pupils are continuously baffled. If there is a sink-or-swim attitude, most pupils will, if not sink, at least only just keep afloat.

Analysis shows that the language expectation of some subject specialists is difficult and linguistically remote, and that the reading demands of those subjects are sharply differentiated from experience gained in Primary Schools. This needs to be understood, and the question for staff debate is: what should be done as a response to this knowledge?

The 'left-wing' approach is to solve the problems by dramatically adjusting the language requirements of each subject area: producing simpler reading material, removing special language forms, and trying to make the language experience as like ordinary talk as possible. The 'right-wing' approach is to attempt to teach the pupils how to cope.

Each school must establish its own position. The first is to risk losing real language growth in a variety of valuable extending contexts. The second is to risk total learning failure. Something of each is required —so that the language environment of the subject is not hopelessly daunting and so that the pupil is specifically helped to cope: this is doubly valuable in that it makes the subject learning more effective and gives a fresh language context. A school searching towards a policy is likely to want first to examine the language environment that it has created. To do this a seminar or working party will want to bring together examples of the language presented to pupils at various levels: textbook, worksheets, blackboard transcriptions, tapes of teacher talks. It will then want to discuss and analyse these. Secondly, it will want to consider a similar sample of the language expectations put to the pupils: what are they asked to say and write? (Sections of Chapter 5 discuss these in detail.) This analysis should lead to action of two complementary kinds:

[1] I own this anecdote to Anthony Adams of the Cambridge Institute of Education, together with many good ideas, although, of course, I may have done him an injustice in the recording of them.

1. Alteration of the language environment, either by simplification or by postponement of certain difficulties.
2. Specific help in facing the problems it is agreed to leave in the curriculum. (Most of Chapters 5 and 6 are devoted to suggesting ways.)

Neither course on its own is adequate. Certainly it would be abdication to rely entirely on the first. It would not be possible to educate intellectually without developing the language forms necessary to those skills studied. Learning and language benefit if the two processes are considered together. It should be possible to consider the entire language environment of the school, including the letters to parents, the circulars, and the notice boards. Even more important are the ways in which children are talked to in formal and informal situations, in playground, corridor, and assembly. It should then be possible to start monitoring, as Douglas Barnes suggests in Chapter 5, and then adjusting and teaching simultaneously. If the pupil is to grow intellectually, emotionally, and socially, he must feel at home in the school language environment. If this is to happen, that environment must not be too remote, and he must not be left unintroduced to it.

Teacher talk

At its worst the secondary classroom is mostly teacher talk: some figures show 70 per cent of the talk is by the teacher. Research in one case showed an average of one question every thirteen seconds! This gives barely time for a reply. Yet the voice of the teacher is not to be despised for that reason—it is one of the main modes of educating and there are other classrooms where it is heard too rarely. However, a whole-school language policy is likely to consider the use teachers make of their own talk. This will range from informal private chat on the one hand to careful exposition and reading aloud on the other. From another point of view it will range from communication with individuals, through small groups, full classes, and even such larger groupings as team-teaching gatherings, or school assemblies.

Such an enquiry is readily possible with the portable tape-recorder. The first step is to find out what is happening—that is, the proportion of one activity to another, and the extent of interaction with the pupils. The next step is to judge how well it is happening. It is rarely that any of us have had any attention paid to our own use of our voice from any point of view: indeed, it appears that most training courses give no specific tuition or consideration to teacher talk.

Considerable help is now available from Douglas Barnes, writing in the two books noted in the reading list, and later in this book he has contributed a consideration of how a school, a department, or a teacher can monitor success in communication. I should like to suggest here the various kinds of teacher talk that could be considered.[1]

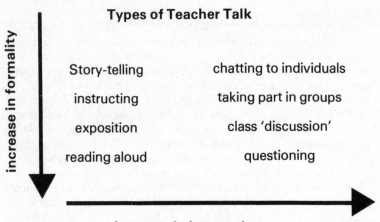

Types of Teacher Talk

increase in formality		
Story-telling	chatting to individuals
instructing	taking part in groups
exposition	class 'discussion'
reading aloud	questioning

increase in interaction

In considering each type shown in the diagram, a policy is likely to give some advice based on group analysis of recordings of actual events. It will be seen that the teacher requires a flexibility to take him from his occasional role as 'performer' (most of the left-hand column have a performing aspect), to his person as, at one extreme, equal converser, and of course the more usual middle role of 'sympathetic adult'. It is fashionable now to play down the first. A science teacher, for instance, will insist that his subject works through small-group practicals, and he will refuse to believe he is ever a verbal performer. However, an observer will note full-class exposition, instructions, even reading aloud. The move to remind the teacher not to talk at the class the whole time must not mask the number of occasions when he must talk to them all, and talk well.

The art of giving a clear instruction, telling a vivid story (scientists, mathematicians, historians, and geographers all need to do this occasionally), and giving a clear exposition can be worked on. For instance, the sentence I quoted earlier as an instance of postponed meaning is an example of a common difficulty. In general, the pattern of a sentence should ensure that the point being made is emphasized by grammar, word order, and stress, so that the listener does not have to un-scramble, rearrange, and put together the elements of the remark before he can make sense of it. For instance, I once heard a

[1] I have also paid some attention to the *techniques* of instructions and questioning in *The Craft of the Classroom*, Heinemann Educational Books, 1975.

teacher briefing a group who were about to go on a small field trip. He had issued a folder, and was explaining its function:

> Each of you will have a folder.
> It *gives* you a map of the walk
> It *gives* you a check list of points to look out for
> It *gives* you . . .

The repetitive use of the first phrase and the stress on each 'gives' with a falling mumble after each one subordinated the items he wished to highlight. For questioning, whether of individuals, small groups, or full classes, a great deal of study is required. There is too much use of questions to which we already know the answer, too much rejection of other possible answers, too many gap-filling questions, and so on. The art of questioning deserves study.

It is unlikely that experienced teachers will be willing to practise their reading aloud, yet not only is good reading aloud an asset to any teacher in a school for appetite-whetting, highlighting of key passages, and putting across vivid material which is not to be read by the class, but the aural articulation of a passage is valuable in helping pupils learn the vocal patterns necessary for inner articulation. We should all be more willing to work at this skill.

Finally, there is the more informal but even more important role of the teacher in discussion. He must adopt a way of speaking which is readily acceptable and comprehensible, and yet he needs constantly to be aware of the pupil growth which comes from their interaction with his responses, questions, suggestions. His knowledge of language theory is vital here: it is wrong to think that help is given by stopping and 'correcting'. In fact it is by involved response with the substance of what is being said that he will help the pupil towards richer and more meaningful discussion.

How to talk as a teacher can be an ongoing study for any serious whole-school learning policy.

5. Pupils' Use of Language

The place of reading

Colin Harrison and Keith Gardner

Reading is the most heavily researched single area of the whole curriculum, and yet, paradoxically, it remains a field in which a good deal of fundamental work has yet to be approached, and one of which a great many teachers would claim to be almost wholly ignorant. If this is true of teachers at the primary level, where for many an understanding of reading was founded on a single lecture in a three-year college course, how much more does it describe the position of teachers in secondary schools, who have generally had no training at all related to reading but nevertheless feel conscious that the ability to read fluently is the basis for most school learning, and one of the surest predictors of academic attainment. The Report has made it clear that only a continuously developing in-service framework can ameliorate this situation, but the report itself does provide a more than adequate introduction to current thinking on reading for someone new to the field. The report has certainly stimulated the thinking of many secondary heads of English and senior teachers, and led them to review the situation in their own schools; many are now concerned that they feel ill-equipped to interpret data on reading performance from feeder primary schools, especially when each school seems to have used a different test instrument. In many schools the part played by the remedial department is being reappraised, and senior teachers may feel vaguely uneasy about the *status quo*, but are conscious that the remedial specialists are the only staff members with any claim to an understanding of the problems of poorer readers.

The present section explains briefly something of the reading process, and then identifies some of the ways in which a secondary school wanting to develop the reading of all children, and not simply those who are poorer readers, could set about the task. The intention is not to prescribe, but to point out possibilities and alternatives in what is a relatively new area of enquiry.

The reading process

What happens when a person reads? The simplest answer might be: meanings are extracted from a set of printed symbols. This kind of definition does nothing to explain how a series of blobs of ink come to be interpreted as a message, but it serves to emphasize a crucial point in contemporary thinking about reading, which is that even from the very earliest stages reading is concerned with meaning. The implied distinction here is between two views of reading: the first for convenience we shall call the 'card-reader' model; the second is already well known by Professor Kenneth Goodman's phrase 'psycholinguistic guessing game'.

When a computer card-reader scans a punched card, the combination of holes representing each alphabetic character is read in serial order across eighty columns and the information converted into a string of binary digits. Three crucial aspects of this reading process are: every letter of every word is scanned; each letter is read in strict serial order; the reading process itself is not influenced by text content. Until fairly recently this mechanistic view was accepted or implied in most descriptions of reading. It was assumed that the fluent reader scanned each word, converted the letter-strings into sounds or sound-images, and then matched the sound images with those in memory store; in other words, meaning was something added *after* the word had been phonically decoded, or turned into a sound-image. There is now a good deal of evidence[1] to show that this is by no means a satisfactory account of what happens. A fairly dramatic experiment conducted by Graham Rawlinson[2] will serve as illustration. Rawlinson asked subjects to read aloud a number of increasingly taxing passages from a standard test, the Neale Analysis of Reading Ability. He did not tell his subjects that the final passage had been rewritten so that in every word of six or more letters all except the first two and final two letters were in random order. The following is an extract from one of the partial anagram texts:

> Each April, at the re-apapnarece of the
> cukcoo in its faimilar hanuts, bird-wachetrs
> must mavrel at the acracute flghits
> with which birds span the dinstcaes beetwen
> their sesnaoal abdoes.

The unsuspecting subjects found such passages surprisingly easy to read, and hardly slowed their reading down at all. Furthermore, they grossly underestimated the number of errors in the text, sometimes reporting that they had noticed only 'a few misprints'. Rawlinson concluded that any definition of reading as a letter-by-letter scanning and matching system was ruled out by what his subjects were able to do. Similarly, it could hardly be the case that subjects were splitting

[1] Some of this evidence is found in E. A. Lunzer and C. Harrison's contribution to G. Steiner (ed.), *Psychology of the Twentieth Century*, Kindler, Zürich, 1976.

[2] G. Rawlinson, 'How Do We Recognise Words?', in *New Behaviour*, **1**, 1975, pp. 336–338.

words up into phonemes before searching for meaning, since the words in the transformed text are made up of highly irregular phonemes which often produce words which sound very unlike the original. No-one would deny that most of us sub-vocalize while reading; what seems to be the case is that in fluent readers this usually follows rather than precedes the grasping of meaning. Similarly, although one would accept that the ability to break a word down into its phonetic components can be valuable when one encounters a new or unfamiliar word, it would appear to be a strategy which a fluent reader uses comparatively rarely.

The computer card-reader, therefore, does not offer a very close parallel with a person's reading; the reading process is infinitely more flexible and can cope with missing information, misprints, anagrams, handwriting styles and type fonts never encountered before, any of which would confuse a computer. Much of this ability to grasp meaning is explained by Goodman's description[1] of reading as a psycholinguistic guessing game: reading is seen essentially as a matter of prediction of what will come next, and it works within a dual framework of rules, one set related to thought and the other to language. Goodman stresses that reading is not a precise process, but one in which intelligent guesswork based on partial information is the modal strategy, with recourse to deeper reflection and re-reading if semantic or syntactic anomalies occur. This description of the reading process is supported by a good deal of recent research, and although Goodman's own work on the analysis of oral reading 'miscues' is widely quoted, Frank Smith[2] and Gibson and Levin[3] offer a more balanced view of the contribution of individual researchers.

Goodman used the term 'miscue' to refer to errors made in oral reading. He was not happy with the implied value judgement associated with the term 'error' since his central contention was that most mistakes in oral reading demonstrate that the reader is in fact grappling with the meaning of the text and is not simply 'careless' or 'lazy'. For example, in a story written in the first person a reader might well substitute *He yelled* when reading the words *I yelled* in a story. This substitution would only marginally affect the meaning, and might simply be related to the child's greater familiarity with the third person narrative. Similarly, Goodman cites a child's saying *Might as well study what it means* instead of *Might as well study word meanings first*. The reader's version was not self-corrected, since he was quite happy with the sense. In fact, the reader has transformed the grammatical structure of the last three words of the sentence and

---

[1] K. S. Goodman, 'Reading: a psycholinguistic guessing game', in *Journal of the Reading Specialist*, USA, May, 1967.

[2] F. Smith, *Understanding Reading*, New York, Holt, Rinehart and Winston, 1971.

[3] E. J. Gibson and H. Levin, *The Psychology of Reading*, M.I.T. Press, Cambridge, Mass., USA, 1975.

changed the vocabulary, but he has retained the basic meaning. Goodman also noticed[1] that errors involving intelligent substitution were far more common than those related to letter reversals, which produced a nonsensical reading. He found, for example, that the substitution of *was* in the sentence *The chicken saw the cat* was rare, even though the misreading retains a verb and uses each letter of the original. More common were errors of the type *The windows were full of pets and kittens* for *The windows were full of puppies and kittens*. In this example the miscue *pets* can only be introduced by a reader who has read and understood the final part of the sentence. Further research on beginning readers has shown that provided they are offered texts which approximate to natural language, even five- and six-year-olds can use the same approach to good effect. In fact Goodman has cited examples of children who cannot cope with the pre-readers in a scheme which have sentences of the form *Ride in Sue* or *Ride in here*, but can read with confidence the more advanced stories in which there is more complex grammar and vocabulary. The difference is that the more advanced stories also have an increased load of meaning, and within this richer framework of grammatical structure, vocabulary and meaning the reader can use graphic information much more effectively. In short, it is easier to read sense than nonsense.

Reading, then, is not to be seen as a precise letter-by-letter or word-by-word scanning process. Clearly, without graphic input there would be no reading, but a model which stresses only the decoding of graphic input will fail to correspond with the experimental evidence available. The reading process is more complex, more dynamic and more flexible than this. In the past it has been normal to regard writing as an active language skill and reading as essentially passive, like listening. In fact, reading can be much more of an active process than listening. When a listener misinterprets or fails to hear part of a lecture or broadcast, it is usually impossible for him to recall the exact form of an utterance or its context after more than a few seconds, and he has to choose between reflecting on what was missed and missing more discourse, and ignoring the omission and keeping up with succeeding sentences. A reader, on the other hand, has much more control over how he chooses to process the text an author has written, and this fact is admirably crystallized in the phrase used in the Report which describes effective reading as 'the active interrogation of a text' (8.10).

What is a good reader?

The answer to this question is closely related to the concept of an active interrogation of a text, and can be linked directly to our description of the reading process. Once a child has begun to move

[1] K. S. Goodman, 'Analysis of oral reading miscues: applied psycholinguistics', in *Reading Research Quarterly*, Volume I, 1969, pp. 9–30.

away from the first reading scheme, in which there is naturally a heavy emphasis on graphic information, the meaning of a passage comes more and more from an accumulation of partial information obtained from graphic cues on the basis of which tentative decisions are confirmed or rejected. When they are rejected, for example because a phrase seems anomalous, the text is scanned again in order to find an alternative meaning which is syntactically and semantically acceptable. The good reader is therefore one who (a) has a fairly extensive working knowledge of possible language structures, and (b) is alert to anomalous meanings when they occur. It is important to note that the first requirement does not imply that all children should be taught rules of grammar from the age of five; the emphasis is on the availability of structures, not on an awareness of the rules which govern them. In fact, up to the age of nine or ten, much of what children encounter in books is no more complex linguistically than their own speech, and therefore this criterion is fulfilled.

The emphasis in the definition of a good reader therefore rests on an awareness of whether or not what is being read makes sense. This point might seem banal, and yet it is one which deserves emphasis. What is suggested is precisely that a bad reader is one who is unaware of whether or not he is understanding a text. Every reader sometimes has the experience, perhaps when fatigued, of suddenly realizing that two or three pages of a book have been read without a single fact or incident impinging on the consciousness; in one wit's words, the text has gone 'in one eyeball and out the other'. This is the most glaring example of ineffective reading, and yet there is good reason to suspect that describes much reading in schools, especially if the vocabulary and grammatical structures are so unfamiliar to the reader that the guessing-game process breaks down. The reader then is in a more hopeless position than the six-year-old child who cannot cope with a pre-reader because the language structures are unfamiliar. At least in that case the meanings of the individual words are known to the reader. With an 'O' level course book in physics, biology, or geology, for example, one would also anticipate that many of the crucial words would only be partly understood, thus introducing extra difficulty. It would of course be nonsense to suggest that a textbook should only be used when its content has already been assimilated; the reason for introducing this example is rather to throw light on some of the special difficulties associated with some textbooks as opposed to other kinds of school books.

Another important determinant of effective reading relates to a concept which will be developed and expanded later in this chapter, and this is the notion of flexibility. A crucial research finding is that poorer readers are also those whose rate of reading is least flexible.[1] In other words, those who read every passage at exactly the same pace,

[1] E. Rankin, *The Measurement of Reading Flexibility*, International Reading Association, Newark, Delaware, 1974.

regardless of whether it is complex and dense, or a relative simple story, are also the lowest scorers on tests of reading comprehension. Another aspect of this phenomenon was noted by the Schools Council *Effective Use of Reading* project team in a videotaped session in which a group of twelve-year-olds discussed the content and implications of a series of passages which together linked up to produce a story. It was noticeable that one reader was always the first to declare that he had read the instalment and was ready to discuss its implications. In fact his answers showed him to be one of the poorest readers in the group. Normally, one perhaps tends to associate fast reading with effective reading, but in this instance it was clear that while the boy's *scanning* of a passage was swift, the quality of reflection on what was read was low, which in turn meant that his understanding of incidents, and their cause and effect, was much more shallow than that of other members of the group. The good readers, however, slowed down their reading when they encountered what they took to be a section which needed closer attention, or perhaps it would be more accurate to say that they allowed more time for reflection between bursts of reading, in order to tease out meanings.

This process of re-reading and reflecting on points in the text which present difficulties or anomalies is absolutely crucial, and yet it needs to be stressed that until very recently the notion of going back and re-reading chunks of text was frowned upon in some circles and by some teachers. Experiments with tachistoscopes[1] had demonstrated that many poor readers did not read a line of print in the same way as fluent readers. Instead of having about five or six fixations per line their eyes dotted about forward and backwards searching for cues, and not surprisingly they failed to build up meanings in the way better readers could. Gradually regressive eye-movements came to be regarded as harmful, and in some reading clinics students were trained on a tachistoscope in such a way that they came to avoid regressions during reading. The term 'regressive' often has unfortunate value implications, and it has become necessary to reassert the importance of re-reading as a concomitant of effective reading. One would really want to go further and suggest that a total absence of regressive eye-movements would almost certainly imply a low level of reflection on the text being read.

Reading in school—beyond the reading scheme

During the early 1970s three major research projects were funded to consider specifically the use of reading in British Schools and the ways in which teachers encouraged the reading development of those beyond the infant stage. In Scotland, James Maxwell's wide-ranging project has given attention to the whole school age-range, and in

[1] A tachistoscope is a device that can present information to the eye for a controlled period of time.

England two Schools Council projects, 'Extending Beginning Reading'[1] and 'The Effective Use of Reading'[2] have focused on 7–9 and 10–14-year-olds respectively.

Extensive observation in the classrooms of a number of schools has revealed that reading seems to play a much smaller part in learning than one might have expected. In top junior, first-year secondary and fourth-year classes only about 10 to 12 per cent of overall lesson time in what many teachers regard as the core subjects of English, mathematics, science and social studies involves children in actually reading. In fact, the team discovered that at top junior level the salient language activity was writing, while in both secondary age-groups the language activity which accounted for most classroom time was listening to the teacher. As an example of what commonly happened one can cite an English lesson in which an eleven-year-old child spent 35 minutes working steadily on a reading comprehension exercise; the girl was fully involved with the task, and completed it successfully, finally re-writing her answers in an exercise book from an initial version in rough. The total time she spent in reading and re-reading the passage was only $1\frac{3}{4}$ minutes. She did in fact spend most of the lesson writing down and re-writing her answers. *The reading comprehension exercise, as tackled in many classrooms, is much more a writing exercise than one concerned with developing reading skills or comprehension.*

Many teachers at first-year secondary level feel that since books are so expensive they can only be purchased for groups which are approaching public examinations. Others have phased out textbooks altogether in certain subjects because they do not suit the course the teacher has planned. Many teachers also feel that since expecting a child to learn from a book is a chancy business, it is more profitable to put their faith in the spoken word and teacher exposition. When the Effective Use of Reading project began, its aims included obtaining information about what teachers expected children to gain from that reading, what in fact the children gained, and accounting for any mismatch. What was half-expected was that the team would discover that teachers tended to have unrealistically high expectations about what children were gaining from their reading. This was by no means what was found. In the event, it seems that teachers do not expect children to learn much from reading, and since, despite their high cost, books only play a relatively minor supporting role in many classrooms it is not surprising that the teacher's low expectations are confirmed.

The question which must be squarely faced is 'Is the book dead?'

---

[1] T. Dolan, 'The incidence and context of reading in primary and secondary schools', in D. Moyle (ed.), *Reading: What of the Future?*, UKRA conference proceedings, Ward Lock, 1974.

[2] E. A. Lunzer and W. K. Gardner (eds.), *The Effective Use of Reading*, Heinemann Educational Books (forthcoming).

The answer from the project team is emphatically negative. Their concern is rather to suggest how printed sources can be used much more effectively in classrooms, and can be given more prominence in learning, not less. One crucial reason for this response relates to a paradox which has been noted in many secondary schools. The same teachers who have tended to phase out the printed word in the lower age groups are also conscious that in many fourth-, fifth- and sixth-form courses the ability to accommodate new learning through the printed word is vital in coping with their subject. Many science courses, for example, now include options involving projects which demand wide critical reading. Some 'A' level courses have 'unseen' examination questions in which experimental data, results and tables are offered for criticism and explanation, and the answer is essentially a high-level reading comprehension exercise for the student. How adequately can a diet of workcards and blackboard notes prepare a child for the very heavy demands of textbooks in the later years of secondary schooling? Even though a teacher accepts that writing is itself a vital part of the learning process, and that discussion and exploratory talk should play a significant part in the curriculum of the first two years, this must not be taken to imply that the development of reading should be neglected.

Developing reading across the curriculum

In order to simplify some of the organizational issues related to implementing a policy for developing reading, it seems worthwhile to group the issues under two main headings: those which must be decided upon at the administrative level within a school, and those on which a headteacher or head of curriculum studies might wish to initiate discussion, but which would relate more to decisions at departmental or classroom level.

Areas for decision-making at administrative level

1. *Obtaining and using data on reading performance.* If a headteacher wishes to know the reading ability of each child in a first-year intake of two or three hundred children there are a number of ways he can tackle the problem. Currently, giving each child a screening test (discussed in Chapter 7) is a solution which many heads are considering very seriously. The advantages of the school's administering a test in the first term of secondary schooling are many: firstly, the data from feeder primary schools may be difficult to interpret, either because certain tests used are unfamiliar to the new school, or because even when the same test has been used in different primary schools results indicate that it was administered or marked in a different way; secondly, a child might have improved or regressed in reading since he or she was last tested, and the test results could well be six or nine

months out of date; thirdly, a screening test can provide valuable information about which children need fairly immediate help with reading, and in a mixed ability setting the cooperative nature of working could mask problems for crucial months.

The decision to screen a whole year is not one which can be taken lightly. Tests cost money, and although many are pirated or completed in pencil and reused, they are demanding in terms of organization and classroom time, and take many man-hours to mark. A useful booklet giving details of the most widely used reading tests in this country is available through the United Kingdom Reading Association.[1] There is considerable literature on reading tests, and the main issues are summarized in Chapter 7. A point which needs emphasis, however, is that all tests are inaccurate, and only give an estimate of true competence. At the same time the object of a screening exercise is to spot children who need help, and it is not therefore necessary to contemplate using a test with a diagnostic battery of subtests. A word-recognition test, for instance, tells you nothing directly about how well a child can read sentences. It is designed on the principle that, generally speaking, good readers will tend to obtain high scores and poor readers will tend to obtain low scores. It is then up to the test user to home in on the warning light of a low score and to establish the specific nature of a child's problems.

This leads us to another important aspect of testing: test data itself is worthless unless applied. There is little point in going to a great deal of trouble collecting data if it is not used effectively in terms of classroom action. Many primary teachers despair because their secondary colleagues take little or no account of information which has been painstakingly collected and put on to record cards for the benefit of the new teacher. This is often because the administrators in the school fail to make the information available to class teachers, but it may also relate to a desire on the part of the new teacher to avoid prejudging a child's ability. Heads and their deputies have a clear responsibility to make sure that test data from any source is put to the best possible use, and this means for example, sharing it with other departments besides English. In the classroom observation study, a researcher from the Effective Use of Reading project found more than one case of first-year pupils who had convinced a teacher in one subject that they could not read (and therefore received simpler tasks) but who read perfectly adequately for a teacher in a different subject. The problem here was one of communication between teachers.

If all teachers understood the problems associated with reading in their subject, and were sensitive to the problems of each reader, there would clearly be no need for reading tests. But while this is not the case, and where a head feels the information would be put to good use,

[1] J. Turner, *The Assessment of Reading Skills*, UKRA bibliography No. 2, UKRA, 1972.

a case can be made out for some sort of screening, though it need not necessarily be formal. A cloze test constructed and administered on a classroom basis by each English teacher gives quite an effective pointer to those children with reading problems, and it offers a less threatening situation than the 11+ atmosphere created by many norm-referenced tests.

A cloze passage is simply one in which every nth word of a normal text is omitted, and the reader is asked to choose a suitable replacement. The following is an example:

> Once upon a time, in a .... small county
> town, at a considerable .... from London,
> there lived a little .... called Nathaniel
> Pipkin, who was the .... clerk of the
> little town.

At first sight a cloze test might seem to be little different from a multiple-choice comprehension test, but in fact it has many more uses. The reading project team have used cloze tests as the basis for silent reading and group discussion activities, and in helping to measure textbook difficulty. In the present case, a cloze test can be valuable in giving the teacher some diagnostic information about how well or how poorly a child is reading. For instance, in the passage above one regularly finds that a poor reader will put *boy* in the third gap, while better readers will offer *man*. The teacher can use cloze test responses as a window into the child's mind, and returning to Goodman's model, can examine how effectively the reader is using the cues supplied for this guessing game. The word *man* can only be guessed by working backwards from the information that the person was a clerk, and therefore *boy* would not be likely. Apart from any difficulty associated with the word *clerk*, it is also the case that poorer readers tend to use what are called 'backward acting' cues less effectively than good readers. The potential value of cloze tests in the classroom is all the greater because they enable a teacher to learn something about the reading process in the reader who tackles the passage, and this is certainly not a claim one would make for multiple-choice comprehension tests.

2. *Provision for poorer readers.* Broadly speaking, there are three alternatives available as a basis for giving selective help to those who are poor at reading or who have special problems: remedial classes, selective withdrawal from lessons, and provision within the normal class grouping (the broader issue of pupil grouping is discussed in Chapter 7).

The advantages and disadvantages of having remedial classes are well known: resources in terms of both appropriate materials and specialized teacher expertise can be centralized, the feeling of constantly failing can to some extent be overcome, and learning tasks can be matched more easily to the whole group than in a mixed-ability situation. The main disadvantage is that the remedial class functions more as a long-term isolation ward than an out-patients' department, and those in such classes rarely emerge to share in the greater school learning community, or possibly emerge to join it after a three-year course of treatment totally unprepared by their workbooks and regimented lessons for the experience of a Mode 3 CSE course.

Selective withdrawal functions more as an out-patients' clinic, and given on a rotated timetable allows poorer readers to receive help while missing no more work in normal lessons than the child who goes to flute lessons twice a week or who plays football for the district team. This system has the disadvantage that the rest of the class know where their neighbour is going, but this need not be a stigma. In some schools it is recognized that this kind of help may be needed by bright children as well as slower ones. If it is decided to establish some kind of reading centre there is no reason why it should not be an attractive place with special displays and furniture, equipped with, at the very least, tape-recorder playback facilities, such that it would come to be regarded as a place it is at least interesting and at best fun to visit.

While one would imagine remedial teaching would for many children consist of one-to-one tuition in phonics or word-attack skills, it is important to mention that technical innovations such as the synchrofax and taped stories (possibly school-produced) can be used by secondary children without constant supervision. Reading while listening is currently recognized as an invaluable aid for some poorer readers, who have hitherto been held up as much by poor articulation as anything else, and the technique has brought about significant gains in reading ability.[1] Another much-discussed innovation is the use of fluent readers, usually parents or sixth-formers, as helpers of poorer readers. This help would normally simply involve listening to a reader and correcting errors, and very little is known about its potential benefits or dangers. The experience of workers in the adult literacy field, however, makes it clear that giving this kind of assistance is a delicate business, and unless the learner is highly motivated and the helper sensitive and sympathetic the result could be harmful, and destroy confidence rather than build it up. The implications of this are that despite the compelling needs of older non-readers, a successful bond is more likely to be established with a first- or second-year child, and even then one would only allow volunteers who seemed well suited to the task to give tuition. One shrinks in horror at the attitude of some schools in which this exercise is regarded as a sort of social work, begun on the basis that even if it does not work out the sixth-former will have learned something.

[1] M. H. Neville and A. K. Pugh, 'Context in reading and listening: a comparison of children's errors in cloze tests', *British Journal of Educational Psychology*, **44**, 1974, pp. 224–232.

Making provision within normal class groupings for poor readers is in many ways the hardest problem of all to tackle, since it places on each individual teacher the responsibility for offering appropriate remedial help. The most cogent argument in favour of this strategy is that since each subject has its own special language demands, and often its own special language, it is appropriate that the problem should be tackled at departmental level. The excellent monograph *The Learning of Reading*, produced by teachers at Clissold Park School, demonstrates that teachers can inform themselves about reading development and go on to share the responsibility for achieving it in every child, rather than leaving it to the remedial department. In fact, whether remedial classes or selective withdrawal are used, it is the theme of this book that the responsibility for developing reading must be accepted at the departmental and classroom level and by every department and class teacher.

3. *The use of library and resources areas*. Before considering issues at the departmental level, some comment must be made on staffing and using library/resource areas. Norman Beswick's comprehensive books[1] deal with this complex subject very fully. The intention here is merely to raise some issues specifically related to reading and the accessing of printed sources.

The Effective Use of Reading team have studied the use of resources in topic and project work, and have made time-lapse ciné films of the use in a school library of card indexes, reference books, and special collections of materials. What they found has confirmed what many librarians suspected, which is that the crucial resource is not the indexing system but the librarian. When no librarian is present, researching a subject very rarely extends beyond the consultation of encyclopaedias, even with fourth- and fifth-year groups. In many school libraries a great deal of time is devoted to updating and cataloguing books on the Dewey system, and yet it may be consulted no more than two or three times a day. The plain fact is that from the child's point of view the system is difficult to understand, time-consuming to use, and can often lead to frustration. Since the child's need is usually immediate, any book not actually available on the shelves is of no interest to him.

Librarians have tackled this problem in a number of inventive ways. In some schools a booklet produced by the county library service is hung at strategic points; it contains an alphabetically ordered list of topics together with their Dewey number. Over the geographical section a librarian can mount a map of the world, with major countries labelled and numbered. This kind of innovation can ensure fuller use of library resources and help children to find the books they seek more readily.

[1] N. Beswick, *School Resource Centres*, School Council Working Paper 43, Evans/Methuen Educational, 1972; and *Organizing Resources*, Heinemann Educational Books, 1975.

Special collections on local topics, and 'project trolleys' containing perhaps thirty or forty books culled from the shelves or borrowed from the county library stock can also assist children with a specific task. The greater problems, however, are those associated with educating children to use the books they have chosen in a purposeful manner. The library is a complex system, and can be a valuable aid to learning in every subject, and yet in many schools children receive no more than one lesson a year on how to use it. This is comparable to a mathematician's giving one lesson a year on logarithms. Children need to be taught how to use the indexing system, dictionaries, encyclopaedias and special collections, but this is only the first step. The crucial skill of a good library user is not that of finding a book, but rather that of being able to reject a book which is unsuitable. Too often, a child sees the topic under consideration mentioned in an index and immediately assumes that the book he holds will be appropriate for his purpose. It may be that his topic is an account of the ecological benefits of the bicycle, but for him any reference to bicycles will do, even a list of Olympic Games results from 1964. As teachers we often assume that children know how to use books to obtain information, and since most teachers are reasonably fluent readers it is sometimes difficult for them to imagine the child's problems.

A video recording made by Tony Pugh of the Open University demonstrates the difficulties even a fluent reader can have in using a book effectively. His film shows a sixth-former who had been given a standard university psychology textbook and a fairly straightforward task on the lines of 'What contribution did Miller make to work on human memory?'. The girl read the question, took up the book, consulted the list of chapter headings, and began reading at page 1. Twenty minutes later she was on page thirty, and when the tape ran out she was still reading steadily, not having reached the point where Miller's name was first mentioned. Pugh's interest was in how students used books when making notes, and he had not expected to encounter a situation in which the reader did not even reach the section on which the notes would be based!

As teachers we need to be aware that for many children the only readily available strategy is to begin reading a book at the first word and to carry on to the last. By contrast the reader may care at this point to consider the route by which he or she has arrived at this line on this page; it is unlikely that it has followed word by word the path from the editor's introduction. If a different route has been taken this will be because the reader has a specific purpose in mind and is using a strategy suited to it. What Pugh's subject failed to do was to use an appropriate strategy. If children are to use books effectively, in the library or in the classroom, they must be taught two things. The first is that there are different ways of reading and using a book; the second is that they should consider what approach best suits their particular task. No doubt Pugh's sixth former could use an index perfectly well; what she failed to do was to realize that she was in a situation which required her to use that skill.

Areas for decision-making at departmental and classroom level

1. *Defining the problems at departmental level.* One clear outcome of the Report has been the need to redefine the maxim 'Every teacher is a teacher of English'. This used to be interpreted in terms of all teachers taking a share of the responsibility for improving the grammar, spelling, and punctuation of those they taught. The new interpretation rests more on the necessity of every teacher realizing that most learning takes place through the medium of language, and that each subject has its own special language demands. In some subjects such as biology and geology, there are special difficulties associated with vocabulary. In most science subjects children have to come to terms with the passive voice and highly objective writing. In history one might suggest the need to obtain information from a variety of sources and to assess bias in writing as special areas of difficulty. The implication from the Bullock Report is that teachers must ask themselves what special language problems are associated with reading in their subject, and how these should be approached.

If a head teacher or head of curriculum studies wishes to establish how well-prepared a department is to undertake an analysis of the part reading plays in its courses, he could ask the following question: 'Are books used in your subject in the same way they are used in English lessons, or do you think there are some differences?' If, despite the transparently leading nature of the question the answer given is 'No', he may assume the ground is somewhat stony. If the answer is 'Yes', there is a basis for action, since the next and most difficult task is to try to articulate the differences.

As a framework for discussion a department could be encouraged to take two year groups, perhaps first and fourth initially, and attempt to clarify what kind of written sources are used in lessons over the year's course, and the part they play in the curriculum. For example the department could note the use of worksheets, textbooks, reference books, the blackboard, posters, etc., and then examine how each was used, whether to generate activities, give instructions, provide model answers to be copied down, to convey facts, to support the teacher's factual presentation, for diagrams, or as a basis for note-taking. The group could then begin to consider whether the use of resources could be improved, and whether it emerged that specific skills were necessary for a child to cope successfully with the course.

As the next step it would be valuable for this analysis to be extended over each year group up to sixth-form level, and the teachers would be able to ask themselves to what extent the language demands of their courses were sequential, and adequately prepared for by work in preceding years. At the same time, if other departments were attempting a similar exercise it would be advantageous for cross-fertilization of ideas to take place, and for other teachers to gain some insight into their colleagues' conclusions and special problems. One would ask, for example, whether making notes in one subject does in fact involve different skills from making notes in another, how primary sources are used, and at what age most children can cope with the task successfully.

2. *The need for flexibility in reading.* It has already been emphasized that in reading the concept of flexibility is an important one, and that a child who reads every text at the same speed and in the same way is likely to be an ineffective reader. Research evidence to support this is found in the work of Laurie Thomas and Sheila Augstein of Brunel University, who designed a machine which produced a visual record of the way in which different readers read a passage for a specific purpose. They were able to show that certain approaches to a task were much more profitable than others.[1] They used their reading recorder with college students and examined which types of approach to reading an article resulted in high scores on multiple-choice comprehension tests, and which approaches led to their producing a coherent summary of a passage. They discovered that a 'smooth read' straight through the passage, followed by a sentence-by-sentence read resulted in accurate multiple-choice answers, but was not a good preparation for writing a summary. A summary based on this type of reading tended to consist of an arbitrary selection of facts, and lacked any appreciation of the overall argument and implications of the article. By contrast, they found that a successful summary writer could also score highly on multiple-choice questions, and tended to remember the facts of the passage for a longer period. The following is an example of the reading strategy of a good summary writer:

1. Smooth read straight through the article.
2. Sentence-by-sentence read of whole article.
3. Paragraph-by-paragraph read of whole article.
4. Pause for thought.
5. Search read (through whole article; much skipping forwards and backwards).
6. Pause for thought.
7. Final smooth read.

The volunteers who worked with the reading recorder gained from the insights they obtained into their own reading habits, and as well as improving their summary writing most went on to achieve higher grades under the continuous assessment scheme of their college course.

[1] L. Thomas and E. S. Augstein, 'An experimental approach to the study of reading as a learning skill', in *Research in Education*, **8**, 1972.

Since so many people have encountered references to speed reading courses, it is appropriate to make some comment about advisability of attempting to teach children to read faster. Much of the literature on speed reading has been based on armchair psychology and sold more on railway stations than in university bookshops. Two myths which have sprung up need to be firmly uprooted: the first is that one can greatly increase reading speed without decreasing comprehension; the second is that one can take in the gist of a page by attempting to fixate an imaginary line running down the middle of that page.

The first myth has been given some credence partly because many speed-reading courses only test recall of factual details such as dates and proper names. If a student learns to scan a text quickly it soon becomes possible to register such details in half the time it would take to read the whole passage, and therefore he will feel he has read it twice as quickly. In fact, what has happened is that he has really only half-read the passage, and if faced with the task of summarizing it would no doubt do it ineffectively for exactly the same reasons as Thomas and Augstein's student who read only for factual points.

The second myth has been viewed with some amusement by those with some knowledge of visual perception. When the eyes fixate a text the area clearly in focus is an ellipse not much larger than a two pence piece; certain distinctive letter-features can be perceived up to about one-and-a-half inches from the point of fixation, and the partial information from one fixation is confirmed by partial information from the next. In normal reading five or six fixations per line are necessary to ensure that a line is read completely, so one can imagine how little information would be gained by attempting to read straight down the middle of a page. The reader of this chapter may care to see how much can be understood of the following page if to begin with he or she covers all but a two-inch wide strip of print down the middle of the page. The chances are that only the occasional phrase which has been left intact will carry much meaning, and this will not be organized within any overall framework of argument. If someone were able to train themselves to achieve the considerable feat of reading down the middle of the page one would expect them to gain less from their reading rather than more.

In fairness to the authors of the less disreputable courses on speed reading one should point out that some courses do encourage flexibility of reading rate according to the task in hand, which is much more important than pure speed. Of course there are children in remedial groups whose reading is held up because they fixate every word on a line, and find it difficult to grasp the overall meaning of a sentence because its meanings remain fragmented. It may well be beneficial to encourage increased reading speed and fewer fixations per line in such a case, but this by no means implies that this emphasis should be continued once a person is reading fluently.

3. *Encouraging flexibility in reading.* It would be foolhardy to assume that all children will spontaneously develop a set of strategies for different reading tasks, although many do unconsciously in employing the 'principle of least effort'. For example, as every English teacher knows, many children approach a comprehension exercise by looking at the questions first, and if these do not demand an overall appreciation of the passage the text as a whole will remain unread. Nevertheless it is worthwhile noting three of the most widely quoted alternative strategies to a straightforward 'smooth read' of a text, not least because some experts firmly believe they should be specifically taught to children. The strategies are scanning, skimming, and SQ3R.

Scanning is the term used for the rapid searching for a specific piece of information in a text, such as a date or a name. Skimming involves a closer inspection of a text, in order to obtain a general impression of its content or argument. This would perhaps involve concentrating on a few key words or phrases, but would not go into details. For example, a reader might turn to the correspondence pages of a journal to establish whether the editors have printed his letter; this would involve scanning. He might then quickly skim all the letters in order to decide whether any of the issues raised interested him enough to merit a full reading. There is some doubt about whether readers can be taught to scan more effectively, but skimming is much more clearly a strategy which can be taught, and it is reasonable to suggest that both strategies are valuable at some stage in practically every subject. Skimming is particularly important in situations where a reader is using a number of books in order to complete some topic or reference work. It can help to avert the situation in which a child is half-way through copying out or making notes on a passage before he realizes that it is not after all dealing with the issue he wanted to raise.

SQ3R is a more complex approach to reading a passage for information than simply scanning or skimming. The mnemonic was first used by Francis P. Robinson[1] to describe a system introduced to help college students read more effectively. The characters stand for Survey, Question, Read, Recite, Review, and they can be glossed as follows: Survey—skim the passage to gain an idea of the main points (and to ensure it contains the information sought); Question—formulate questions to guide your thinking during the intensive reading (these would depend on your initial purpose); Read—read the passage intensively, pausing for thought and re-reading as necessary; Recite—say aloud the answers to your questions, the salient facts, a summary of the overall argument, or whatever (alternatively these could be recalled without speech, or written down); Review—go over what you have learned (this stage could

[1] F. P. Robinson, *Effective Study* (new edition 1961), Harper and Row, New York, 1946.

also include evaluation of the content, thinking of connections with previous learning, considering the possibility of bias, etc., as appropriate).

Some authors (see for example Niles[1]) have suggested that this technique is too difficult for school pupils to learn, but this argument can be countered by those who have simplified some of the stages where necessary and introduced SQ3R from the upper years of junior school onwards.

4. *Hierarchical models of comprehension and their relevance to classroom planning.* Much of what has been written above relates to improving what a reader gains from his or her reading, or in other words developing reading comprehension. The authors have suggested that children should be taught how to use books more effectively and to be aware of the possibility of using their reading in different ways. Good reading has been described as being related to the quality of the reader's reflection on what is read, and the strategies associated with SQ3R and the Thomas and Augstein work are valuable in that they provide a framework in which this active interrogation of a text is more likely to occur.

There remains the question of whether teachers should be seeking to enhance specific subskills of comprehension. Table I shows three examples of comprehension hierarchies, based on the work of Davis,[2] Barratt, and Dolan and Waite.[3] In what is a celebrated article Davis suggested on the basis of a complex statistical analysis of test results that reading comprehension consists of a number of separately isolable subskills. Since 1944, any number of comprehension taxonomies have been suggested by experts in the reading field, and that of Barratt is included because it is well known in this country through the Open University's Reading Development course.[4]

The great attraction of such a taxonomy is that it offers the teacher a ready-made strategy for improving children's reading. If the teacher can use a diagnostic test to establish the areas in which a child is weak on comprehension, for example in drawing inferences, it is then simply a matter of giving special attention to that subskill in order to improve overall reading performance.

It was partly with the intention of developing such a diagnostic test that Dolan and Waite carried out a major study on reading compre-

---

[1] O. S. Niles, 'Comprehension skills', in A. Melnick and J. Merritt (eds), *The Reading Curriculum*, University of London Press, 1972, pp. 228–234.

[2] F. B. Davis, 'Fundamental factors of comprehension in reading', in *Psychometrika*, **9**, 1944, pp. 185–197.

[3] T. Dolan and M. Waite, 'Does comprehension consist of a set of skills which can be separately examined?', in A. Cashdan (ed.), *The Content of Reading*, UKRA conference proceedings, Ward Lock, 1975.

[4] See A. Melnik and J. Merritt (eds), *Reading Today and Tomorrow*, ULP, 1972.

hension, using a list of putative subskills which has much in common
with those of Davis and Barratt.

TABLE I. *Three examples of comprehension skill hierarchies*

Davis (1944)	Barratt (undated)	Dolan & Waite (1974)
Word knowledge		Word meaning Word meaning in context
	Literal comprehension	Literal comprehension

Reasoning	Reorganization
	Inference
		Inference from single
		    strings
		Inference from multiple
		    strings

Following organization		

Recognizing literary
    devices
		Understanding
		    metaphor

Focusing attention on
    explicit statements
		Perception of salient
		    points

	Evaluation Appreciation	Evaluation

Unfortunately, they discovered that despite careful controls it did
not appear to be possible to isolate specific comprehension subskills;
readers were broadly speaking good, average or poor at comprehension, and did not show any consistent weakness in any one area of
comprehension. Furthermore, it soon became clear that the work of
Davis had been the subject of the most heated debate, during the
course of which the distinguished inventor of the statistical method
Davis had used had denied the validity of his results, and pronounced
that they showed clearly that reading comprehension was made up
of one general ability.

This section, therefore, may be a slightly disappointing one for
some readers, but one should not infer from it that teachers should
give up attempting to improve children's comprehension. The
debate between the experts is partly a theoretical one concerning
what can be accurately measured. If teachers go on attempting to
enhance what they feel are specific subskills it is likely that they will
tend to improve overall competence, and the orientation of their
teaching towards specific goals may also be an asset, simply because
of the structure it provides.

Other methods of attempting to develop comprehension have been investigated by the Effective Use of Reading team. In particular, they have taken and extended some of the ideas for group reading and discussion in Christopher Walker's book *Reading Development and Extension*.[1] The work is to form the basis of a separate publication, and will elaborate a number of Silent Reading—Group Discussion (SRGD) techniques. These involve structuring reading situations in which a small number of readers (at least two, not more than ten or twelve) have to analyse the words, organization and meaning of a passage. This is done orally, although the passage has been read silently, and an initial evaluation of the techniques has proved very promising. As an example of one of the approaches used one could take Group Cloze. For this activity groups of two or three readers consider a cloze passage which has been prepared in a similar way to that on page 89. The object of the activity is for the small group to discuss which word seems to be the most appropriate for each gap, and any guess must be supported by references to the surrounding text. When two small groups have agreed on their versions, they join up and discuss points of difference, again referring to the text to support their points.

In general the team have found that while children enjoy doing this kind of exercise it is improving their reading, and also results in fairly good recall of the passage and a high level of overall evaluation of what has been read. It seems likely that SRGD techniques will become more widely used in this country.

5. *Worksheets, textbooks and vocabulary control.* In the school as a whole, printed materials tend to be used for two main purposes: for generating activities and for learning. To some extent this distinction is an artificial one, but it allows a number of points to be made which relate to one type of text rather than another.

Activity generating materials may well not be textbooks at all, but rather workcards or worksheets. The crucial need here is for teachers to monitor pupil performance continually and to rewrite or edit where necessary. In the hurly-burly of the classroom a series of questions from children about a certain workcard may simply be regarded as related to the difficulty of the task itself when in reality the fault may lie in the workcard. What is needed is accurate record-keeping on the teacher's part to help to spot poorly written or poorly organized workcards. The research of the Effective Use of Reading team into levels of prose difficulty showed that teacher-produced worksheets for one first-year mixed-ability group were comparable in difficulty with the standard 'O' level textbook in the same subject. Writing simple prose is far from easy, and it poses extra problems for a subject specialist, since he may feel unhappy about oversimplifying a complex subject, and will introduce qualifications and exceptions which will baffle the child who has yet to grasp the central point.

[1] C. Walker, *Reading Development and Extension*, Ward Lock Educational, 1974.

A further important point is that instructions need to be in simpler prose than anything else a child reads. There are two reasons for this. Firstly, if a child only partly understands an explanation or a definition, that partial understanding may nevertheless be an important interim stage in learning; if however he only partly understands an instruction he is quite likely to fail altogether to engage in the learning experience which the teacher had in mind. Secondly, one must bear in mind the fact that readers find it more difficult to understand prose which they find uninteresting, and there is very little of generic interest to most children in the instructions to set about a task, even if the task itself is a stimulating one.

A teacher must be aware however that it is much easier for a child to say 'Sir, I don't see what we've got to do' than for him or her to read a worksheet carefully, so it is important not to allow the children too much freedom to by-pass reading altogether, which a harassed teacher might be tempted to do. He could persuade the child to discuss the worksheet with a friend and then to say what they thought the task seemed to be. If the teacher gives the impression that children are not expected to work from the worksheet the group will soon conform to that expectation.

When books are used as a stimulus for learning, rather than for generating activity, the crucial factor to be borne in mind is that of vocabulary. Research into the readability of texts has shown repeatedly that vocabulary is more important than syntactic complexity in determining text difficulty, and this does not surprise many teachers. It is part of every department's planning commitment to decide what concepts are to be introduced each term, and what content should be covered. One might suggest that this kind of analysis could be extended to include specialist vocabulary. In some schools the teachers have been enterprising enough to provide a glossary for children containing words which have caused difficulties. Difficulties are not only associated with words which the teacher expects to cause problems; sometimes a simple word is incomprehensible simply because of the way it is used. Consider for example words such as *salt*, *relief*, or *solution*. These are used quite differently from one subject to another, and while they may be used consistently within a subject, the teacher needs to take account of the child's day consisting of perhaps six or seven different subjects, each with its own vocabulary and prose style.

6. *Motivation and readability*. A classic study on motivation in reading was carried out by Shnayer,[1] who investigated to what extent interest in a passage affected the scores children were able to achieve on comprehension tests. Shnayer first gave a standard reading comprehension test to hundreds of pupils, on the basis of which he assigned

[1] S. W. Shnayer, 'Relationships between reading interest and reading comprehension', in J. Allen Figurel (ed.), *Reading and Realism*, 1968 proceedings, Volume 13, Part 1, Newark, Delaware: I.R.A., 1969, pp. 608–702.

them to one of seven notional ability groups. Next he gave them a number of comprehension tests on other fairly difficult passages, this time asking the children to state how interesting or how boring they found the test passage. Shnayer reported two important findings: firstly, with the exception of the bottom group (which clearly had fundamental problems with reading) there were no significant differences between groups in test scores on passages which were rated as of high interest—in other words, some children's reading ability seemed to improve when they were interested in what they read; secondly, Shnayer found that his good readers found more passages interesting—the poor readers only occasionally found a difficult passage interesting.

The importance of motivation in reading is seen as the more problematical when one considers that a school textbook has been defined (by John Holt) as a book which no one would read unless they had to. In a pilot study for the Schools Council project, Harrison[1] found science and social studies texts were assessed as more difficult than sources from other subjects by both teachers and readability formulae. The special problem with science texts is that apart from often being the hardest of all to read and comprehend, they tend to be used as a support for homework and may hardly be dealt with in class at all.

The terms *supported* and *unsupported* may be used to describe the conditions under which a book is used. At the supported level, the teacher is present and either actively explains what is in the text or is at least readily available to deal with any problems. At the unsupported level, however, the child is isolated from adult support either working in a resource area for example, or doing homework. Now it is not uncommon for a reading expert to suggest that the texts for reading at the unsupported level should be about two years simpler in terms of 'reading age' than those a child encounters at the supported level, and there are various measures of prose difficulty which would help the teacher to select a suitable text. What seems to be the case, however, is that the most difficult texts in the whole curriculum are used more often at the unsupported than at the supported level.

Those interested in measures of readability may consult a monograph by J. Gilliland[2] which introduces the subject quite fully. A guide for teachers which will present data on a cross-validation study of twelve formulae, together with the results of a survey of prose difficulty levels in different subjects is being prepared by the first author of this chapter, and should be available in 1977.

For the teacher not so interested in detailed analysis, but who would wish to gain some information about how well a group can cope with a textbook, one can suggest giving the class a cloze test

[1] C. Harrison, *Readability and School*, Schools Council project discussion document, University of Nottingham School of Education, 1974.
[2] J. Gilliland, *Readability*, University of London Press, London, 1972.

based on a passage from the book. The procedure might also be considered as a revision exercise after some work has been covered. In either case the results will give the teacher some insight into how well individuals as well as the whole group have coped with the text.

7. *Additional issues for the English department to consider.* This section is brief because many of the special problems of developing reading within the English department of a school have been covered in some detail by the Bullock report. In addition, two Schools Council projects, Children's Reading Habits and Children as Readers, have examined the reading of literature in depth, and Kenyon Calthrop's excellent book *Reading Together*[1] offers many more useful ideas for tackling fiction in English lessons than there would be room for here. Most English teachers would accept the importance of fostering a habit of reading, being seen reading themselves, discussing books, encouraging library usage, developing classroom libraries, and maintaining a school bookshop.

One point which needs to be made concerns the value of accurate record-keeping in developing and encouraging reading. The Effective Use of Reading project team felt it was no accident that of all the schools they visited, the one which seemed to be making most progress in developing reading at all levels was the one which had the most comprehensive records. Each child had a book-review notebook, in which details of teacher-initiated and private reading were kept, and apart from screening test scores the Head of English had in her mark book the names of each novel read by every child, and thus could see at a glance which children were not making progress in reading, or found it difficult to find a book they would read by choice. The children were invited to share the sense of achievement they felt when they had read a book, and were encouraged by the teacher's genuine interest in what they read. This teacher was of the opinion that there are in fact very few reluctant readers; there are however many who are reluctant to read what we as teachers want them to read.

The final issue to be dealt with is one which is currently hotly debated—the use of reading 'laboratories'. The Canadian firm of SRA is the best-known one in the field, but English rivals are available, published by Ward Lock, Longman (Reading Routes), and Drake Educational (Language Centre). The Bullock Report criticized this type of approach to reading on two main counts. The content of the laboratories was felt to be arbitrary, with the emphasis on factual content at the expense of any literary merit. Also the laboratories purport to improve reading ability, and there was only evidence of a very limited sort available to suggest that they do so.

The first criticism still stands, and those who wish to attempt to improve reading within the context of specific subject areas will not use a 'laboratory' approach. The second criticism, that the evidence

[1] Heinemann Educational Books, 1974.

of improved reading ability was flimsy, has been challenged by the work of a primary head, Roy Fawcett. His Ph.D. study examined the gains in reading ability over a year of 1200 top junior, first-year secondary and fourth-year secondary pupils, half of whom began the academic year with a one term burst of SRA and half of whom acted as controls and simply took their normal English lessons. He found that in each age group the boys and girls who took the SRA course outperformed the control groups on two separate comprehension tests. Six months after the experiment was over, he gave a late post-test, and discovered that far from reverting to their previous form, the SRA groups maintained, and in some cases increased their superiority over the controls. Not surprisingly, these results have proved unpalatable to many educationalists, particularly English teachers. The Effective Use of Reading team, with whom Roy Fawcett worked, are concerned to stress that his results in no way suggest a blanket endorsement of SRA. The experiment was conducted simply because the materials are already in many schools and it was felt more information was needed about what they might achieve. E. A. Lunzer, the project co-ordinator, has stated that the results show clearly that it is beneficial to devote a specific effort to improving reading, but that there could well be equally effective methods which would allow teachers the freedom to introduce their own material, rather than being restricted to bundles of facts of somewhat doubtful educational value. His own feeling is that the SRGD techniques referred to above hold this kind of promise. What SRA does is what any reading improvement programme must do, and this is to encourage careful reflection on what is read, and to encourage flexibility in reading.

Conclusion

The main argument of this section is that reading cannot be allowed to develop wholly spontaneously, any more than learning can develop wholly spontaneously. The task of the teacher is to provide the conditions within which learning can take place, and if that learning is to be through reading it is likely to be much more effective if the teacher understands each child's strengths and weaknesses, and has designed reading assignments in such a way as to use the strengths and remedy the weaknesses. The need, therefore, is for an accurate monitoring of each child's reading, using all the information available in the school, and supplementing it during the school year. The teacher needs to have a clear idea of the reading demands within his or her own subject, otherwise it is impossible to gauge the level of a child's success or failure. Finally, having isolated the nature of the specific demands the teacher must assist the child in meeting them. This final injunction may seem banal, and yet it represents a challenge which we are only beginning to meet in any organized manner.

Subject reading strategies
Introduction

How does one assist the child in meeting the reading demands? The previous section has made it clear that we suffer from inadequate understanding of the reading process, we give pupils too few reading opportunities, we provide unsuitable material, and we do not prepare pupils to read for meaning. The majority of teaching of reading beyond the basic skills is with narrative material; the majority of reading for learning is, however, with non-narrative material.

We talk about 'the ability to read', but a moment's thought reminds us that there are very different *kinds* of reading—and pupils are not necessarily equally competent in all kinds. One person takes in most non-fiction readily, but finds prose fiction difficult to read. More commonly there are many readers who find fiction easy, but struggle with various kinds of non-fiction. There are differences between the texts in these two kinds of writing at every level; it is not merely the addition of a difficult technical vocabulary that marks off informative prose. Computer analysis[1] has shown that the frequency of even the most common words varies from genre to genre. *I, he, you, me* appear far more frequently in general fiction, whereas *than, by, which* appear far more frequently in learned and scientific writings.[2] There is also a very marked difference in sentence structures and lengths; all categories of imaginative prose have shorter mean sentence-lengths than those of informative prose. According to an American computer analysis the average sentence length for 'fiction: general' was 11 words compared with 21 words for 'learned and scientific writings'.[3]

Reading in literature, science, the humanities, and mathematics obviously shares many overlapping skills, but there are other skills which are more particular to one or the other areas of reading. It is partly a matter of vocabulary, but also of specialized ways of treating ideas, and different patterns of writing.[4] The differences are worth considering and I would suggest that different subject Departments in a school select key passages from important texts, whose reading demands can then be analysed and compared. The American reading specialist Nila Banton Smith carried out such an analysis on a large number of school texts used in science, social studies, mathematics, and literature,[5] then classified the reading response patterns

[1] H. Kucera and W. N. Francis, *Computational Analysis of Present-Day American English*, Brown University Press, 1967, p. 276.

[2] *op. cit.*, pp. 275–293.

[3] *op. cit.*, p. 376.

[4] A. Sterl Artley, 'Influence of the Field Studied on the Reading Attitude and Skills Needed', in *Improving Reading in Content Fields*, W. S. Gray (ed.), University of Chicago Press, 1947.

[5] Nila Banton Smith, 'Patterns of Writing in Different Subject Areas', *Journal of Reading*, USA, 8 October 1964.

typically required for each. For instance, we must take into account the very high importance in reading social studies texts of the need to analyse the content for cause–effect relations, comparisons, and sequence of events. There are also special problems of bringing together different viewpoints, facts mixed with opinions, quotations and exposition, narrative and comment. A special difficulty, which is almost never met in the main 'reading subject', English, is the taking in of illustration and caption so that they are read with the text. The subtle comprehension skills required for reading literature are intensively taught. From the earliest emphasis on narrative in younger classes through to analysis of character and atmosphere, the teacher is demonstrating how the reader can concentrate on certain signals and infer from these. Is there anything like this training and emphasis on either the printing conventions or the comprehension skills of non-literary writing? I am convinced that there is not. It is no wonder that pupils find reading outside English so difficult, and that they are so inept at getting the sense from the text. We simply do not teach what the Report calls 'different kinds of reading strategy'. Two of the Committee's recommendations are vital here:

68 The majority of pupils need a great deal of positive help to develop the various comprehension skills to a high level.

69 An important aspect of reading behaviour is the ability to use different kinds of reading strategy according to the reader's purpose and the nature of the material. Pupils should acquire the skills which will free them from dependence on single-speed reading.

Most of the reading done within the curriculum for learning is expository; most of the higher reading tuition is in literature. It is this mis-match between need and offer which is at the heart of the difficulties in reading to learn in the secondary school.

The strategies required need to be available to all subject teachers. Their basis is simply in the idea that we must learn to interrogate print to get the meaning out of it. Straight left-to-right, no skipping, no going back, misses the main point of print. One of the special things about it, as compared with talk, TV, or tapes, is the reader's own control over his experience. The print on the page will stay there and not change, therefore the reader can go back, or look forward; he can pause to think, make notes, or compare; he can jump and join sentences from different places. Thus reading should not be a passive occupation, pupils should be encouraged to react to a text and check back, guess what is coming, and see if the guess is confirmed by what is then read. They can think of the writer as being present and themselves as an interviewer: 'What evidence have you for that statement?' 'Will you be giving more detail about that idea?' and so on.

I am now going to suggest specific ways in which a subject teacher can encourage this interrogation by taking the pupil back into the text and showing him the way through it. Whilst I am sure that some specific teaching is required from time to time as part of a careful basic programme to make sure the pupil has a growingly elaborate foundation for his work, I suggest that the main occasions for the teaching of reading are in context and as far as possible when the teacher has helped the pupil into a sequence of work in which the need to read, to get meaning from print, is felt by the pupil. This contextual teaching requires careful preparation from the teacher, for he must call on his teaching knowledge unexpectedly, whilst in the midst of some subject matter. The teaching of reading as part of the teaching of subject learning requires a ready reservoir of teaching knowledge to be drawn on as required by the needs of the pupil and his text. I have therefore tried to divide up the kinds of help that can be given, even though in practice it may be necessary sometimes to re-synthesize them.

The sense of words

Later sections consider the teacher's task in introducing vocabulary, in building up phonic word-attack skills, and in help with spelling. All these teaching activities combine to help a pupil with the reading of words which give him difficulty. However, part of the teacher's task is to help pupils develop ways of deducing the meaning of unfamiliar words in a text. When a pupil asks the meaning of a word, there are two normal teaching responses: the first is to say 'Look it up in a dictionary' and the second is to give the meaning ourselves. I maintain that it would often be better teaching to help the pupil find ways of deducing the meaning for himself. This can be done by specifically teaching word detective work at various times. The word can also be referred to in other subject lessons, to reinforce or elaborate its meaning in context, establishing meaning by context clues. It is worth sorting out the range of kinds of context clues: syntactic and semantic:

1. *Syntactic context cues: functions of words.* The pupil stuck over a word should be encouraged first to see what function it must have. This does *not* require the teaching of the parts of speech, but simply a common-sense comment. Consider possible problems in the following:

> In the crowded hovels of the poor, lacking privacy, sanitation and a water supply, few diseases could have been more horrible, but most people were unwilling to be removed to hospital and would only go as a last resort.[1]

The reader not knowing 'hovel' would see first that it must be a thing; whereas the pupil who did not know 'ultimately' in the following example would know it could not be a thing:

> 'The food question ultimately decided the issue of this war', Lloyd George wrote after the armistice.

[1] This and other examples in this section can be found in Norman Longmate, *Alive and Well*, in *Topics in History*, Penguin, 1970.

In this more difficult case, the reader would conclude that the word had something to do with 'decided'. Other factors besides word order help pupils to guess at the function of a word. Inflections obviously help. Some inflections in the two passages are very reliable: e.g., *d, ed, ing, s, ly*. Markers (capital letters and structure words) also indicate what kind of word is being dealt with. A noun, for instance, is indicated by *the, a, an*, a cardinal number, or a possessive.

2. *Semantic context cues:* Our way of writing employs a number of devices for giving the meaning of a word or phrase the writer feels might cause difficulty to his reader. A second-year maths class were working with pin-boards, creating shapes by placing rubber bands round various combinations of the pins. The pupils were working from a maths textbook. A number of times a pupil would raise a hand. The teacher would go over:

> 'Please, Sir, what's "ver . . . ti"?'
> '"Vertice". You remember. We learnt that last year. It's a corner, like this.'

Sir rapidly points to one on the pinboard. A look of satisfied understanding spreads across the pupil's face. Sir retires, pleased at his teaching skill. But has he been so skilful? Certainly he's explained *what the pupil needed to follow the instructions*, but:

(a) It is doubtful whether the pupil is likely to remember the word, as his eye was not taken back to it.

(b) He has directed the pupil to a meaning outside the book, without encouraging him or her to search for that meaning in its context.

(c) He has lost an opportunity to give the pupil some strategies for guessing the meaning of the word: e.g., indicating the stem 'vert' which occurs in many other words, and could serve as a memory prompter.

(d) He has in effect agreed with the pupil that reading is difficult.

In fact the text in the book read:

> The position of a shape on a pinboard can be given by stating the co-ordinates of the *vertices* (or corners).

The writer of the textbook used the device of giving the meaning of new or difficult words in brackets. The teacher should have asked the pupil to take him to the word, and then to read on, and skip back. He would thus have solved the instructional problem just as quickly *and* taught a general point for the future. Apart from brackets, other semantic cues are 'following sentences'.

> Suppose your counter was at L and you threw a blue 2, taking you to N. What number must you now throw if you want to 'undo' this: that is, go back to L, where you started?

This example shows that the word to be explained ('undo') need not look difficult but still might need clarifying. Other ways of defining word meanings are by example or synonyms. In all these cases the reader has to read ahead, suspending a sense decision on the troublesome word for a while. At other times words will be defined by description, comparison, or contrast. The most important skill is to work the meaning out by the overall sense, the position of the word. The teacher should not simply give the meaning of the word, thus short-circuiting the reading process. He should help the pupil deduce it from the context clues.

If the reader were stuck at 'absorption' in the following passage, the teacher should be able to help him through the passage.

> A burning sensation in the stomach suggests that it is having difficulty in digesting food. If you have eaten unwisely, the food resists being prepared for further absorption. If you are worried, the powerful juices which break down the food into starches, proteins, and sugars, do not flow readily.

The pupil would have little difficulty pronouncing 'absorption'; he might not be much helped, but the sound might remind him of 'absorb'. Certainly the '-tion' would come out clearly. That would help him look at its parts. He might realize that '-tion' can indicate an action. If he had learnt prefixes carefully he could recognize that the prefix 'a-', can mean 'into'. Therefore 'an action into'. He is still stuck, and will need to look at the word's position. The puzzling word follows 'further'—therefore it must mean more of something already named. In this sentence the food is resisting further *something*. In the final sentence the stomach is having difficulty *digesting* the food. Then unwise eating stops further *digestion*, presumably. And this is confirmed by the final sentence. If one is worried (clearly another difficulty like eating unwisely) the juices do not flow to 'break down' the food—yet another phrase for digestion. Thus the position suggests that 'absorption' is something that happens to food as part of the digestive process.

The same process can be used to work out far more difficult words. Here is a piece from Siegfried Sassoon's memories of the First World War: *Memoirs of an Infantry Officer*. He has been describing the weary return home by moonlight:

> After this rumble of wheels came the infantry, shambling, limping, strag- gling and out of step. If anyone spoke it was only a muttered word, and the mounted officers rode as if asleep. The men had carried their emergency water in petrol-cans, against which bayonets made a hollow clink; except for the shuffling of feet, this was the only sound. Thus, with an almost spectral appearance, the lurching brown figures flitted past with slung rifles and heads bent forward under basin-helmets. Moonlight and dawn began to mingle, and I could see the barley swaying indolently against the sky. A train groaned along the riverside, sending up a cloud of whitish fiery smoke against the gloom of the trees.

Supposing a pupil doesn't know 'indolently', near the end, or has only a half-formed idea about it. There is the suffix: '-ly' always ends a word that describes an action (an adverb), such as 'smoothly' or 'happily'. This therefore describes which action? Coming between 'swaying' and 'against the sky', the word must tell us how it is swaying. Then we must guess. How can barley sway? Presumably slowly or quickly. The whole mood of this piece is slow and very quiet, and there is no mention of wind. It would be reasonable, therefore, to deduce that 'indolently' means 'slowly'. This is not far from the dictionary meaning of 'lazy' for 'indolent'. So it is possible to get very nearly the right meaning—certainly enough of it to follow the passage.

Unknown words certainly hamper reading, but the skilful reader develops ways of deducing all he needs to know. The teacher's job is to help the pupil do this.

Signal words

The key to reading argument is, as I have stressed, seeing relationships. The key to relationships between ideas is a rapid and unconscious understanding of connectives, which the Americans rather nicely call 'signal' words. It is curious that virtually no teaching time is given to these words. Pupils who have devoted classroom hours to discussing the atmospheric associations of various adjectives, may never once have discussed 'accordingly' or 'nevertheless'. As the bulk of the pupils' reading will have been in fiction, which has a very low use of such words, the pupils will have had neither experience nor tuition when they come to tackle such connectives in their subject reading. And yet, as one writer shrewdly pointed out, there is less difficulty in reading if the reader comes across an unfamiliar noun, such as 'elephant' or 'helmsman', than if he comes across a connective, such as 'since' or 'although', without fully grasping its function. A sentence in an historical text in which 'despite' is not understood is rendered meaningless. Even an apparently easy small word can be difficult, and yet vitally important to the sense. How often do any of us teach the sense of the word 'if'? Yet consider these three uses from a school textbook:

(a) If the range was close, the guns fired grape-shot or cannister.[1]
(b) If the Americans were going to fight against a great power like Britain, the Congress had to set about raising an army.[2]
(c) If British soldiers had suffered much, the Loyalists had suffered more.[3]

None of them are simple conditional uses ('If it rains, I'll stay indoors'). (a) has the meaning of when. The sense in (b) is really very different. By this stage in the book it is in fact clear that the Americans were going to fight. The point of the 'if' clause is the nature of 'a great power'. 'If', here, really means 'as' or 'Because of the fact that'.

---

[1] R. E. Evans, *The War of American Independence, Cambridge Introduction to the History of Mankind*, CUP, 1976, p. 17.
[2] *ibid.*, p. 12.
[3] *ibid.*, p. 41.

Paraphrased, the construction could be rendered: 'As Britain, against whom the Americans were to fight, was a great power (with all that that means in terms of a professional army), Congress had to . . .'. In other words, this sentence is simply not a straight conditional. 'If' is used in the sense which the Shorter Oxford English Dictionary gives as 'given or granted that', a sense with which our pupils are less familiar. Example (c) is similar, except that the conditional is even weaker. The reader knows by the time he has reached this sentence that the British soldiers had indeed suffered much. The sentence means something like: 'Certainly the British had suffered much, but in fact the Loyalists had suffered more.'

It is clearly insufficient to expect word recognition to be adequate for connectives. Equally, pupils have inadequate experience from fiction, and must be helped to see the *function* of these words. I find the following analysis a helpful one. It classifies connectives by the kind of signal they give the reader about the sense relationship.[1] Obviously these are not precise or exclusive categories, but a consideration helps the reader understand the structure of ideas and to respond to the writer's intentions:

1. *Go Signals.* These indicate a continuing idea, an equivalent example, and the same line of thought:
and
first, second, third
next
furthermore
likewise
in addition
similarly
moreover
at the same time
also

2. *Caution Signals.* These warn the reader that the writer considers the point following requires concentration; it is likely to be a conclusion or summary:
thus
therefore
consequently
accordingly
in retrospect
hence
in conclusion
in brief
as a result

[1] Adapted from H. Alan Robinson, *Teaching Reading and Study Strategies,* Allyn and Bacon, 1975.

3. *Stop Signals*. These are stronger than the former, and clearly indicate that a statement of special significance is to follow:
without question
significantly
without doubt
hereafter
unquestionably
absolutely

4. *Turn Signals*. The reader is warned that he is approaching an opposing idea, or a change in the direction of the discussion. They are all varieties of 'but', and I consider are worth special emphasis:
yet
on the contrary
nevertheless
notwithstanding
on the other hand
otherwise
in spite of
although
despite
conversely
however
I find these are frequently not recognized for their real meaning. In the following sentence, for instance, very many of the pupils arrived at precisely the opposite meaning to that intended:

> Although Hinduism is the main religion of India, most of the Indians in Britain are in fact Sikhs.

5. *Relationship Signals*. These are the most important. They articulate the structure of ideas, and above all they clarify the argument. The most important are:

cause and effect	because
	since
	so that
	accordingly
condition	if
	unless
	though
illustration	for instance
	for example
apparent contradiction	despite the fact that
	although

I do not suggest that the teaching of the analytic groupings is itself a great deal of help. However, I believe that they should be taught specifically to provide an underlying understanding. This is best done both by taking the words out of a passage, and by working to a passage from the words. One device is to find a long form for the compressed meaning of the word, e.g. 'although' in example 4 means: 'We have just learned one thing which will make the next thing I am going to say surprising to you.'

This specific teaching is useless, however, without being allied to contextual teaching whenever print is used in the content subjects.

Paragraph sense

Our emphasis on reading texts through without re-reading, our withdrawal from the teaching of reading after the initial stages, and our avoidance of non-narrative material leaves the pupil to cope unaided with more complex argumentative writing—the stuff of school textbooks and virtually all information sources! In such writing, paragraph structure offers a problem. Narrative is basically linear, but argument rarely is. The central problem of reading non-narrative paragraphs seems to me to be summed up by this comment by a linguist:

> Problems of clarifying meaning are constantly with us, too pressing to be evaded. If we find it hard to understand well, the fault is not altogether that of the writer or speaker. Even at its most lucid, discourse is inescapably *linear*, doling out scraps of meaning in a fragile thread. But significant thought is seldom linear: cross references and overlapping relationships must be left for the good reader to tease out by himself. Much, also, must be 'read between the lines'.[1]

Thus the problem for the reader is re-organizing the linear thread of discourse into the three-dimensional structure of thought. It is assumptive teaching to presume that this is understood, even unconsciously, by the pupil. It is over-hopeful to presume that the thirst for knowledge, even in a well-motivated project, will itself lead pupils to develop the necessary skills. These cannot be truly isolated; they cannot be fully taught. However, considerable help can be given by analysis of sense structures as specific teaching and by adequate preparation before reading assignments. The subject specialist should have studied the structure of the paragraphs of the material he is asking the pupils to read. His prime task is to help them see the main idea of each paragraph and the ways other sentences support it.

Most paragraphs have a main idea, and the experienced reader readily picks this out, usually without thinking about it very consciously. When a reader has found the main idea, the supporting ideas seem to fall into place in one's understanding quite naturally. The key sentence may give an answer to the general question of the paragraph; it may define a term which is essential to the argument; or it may sum up the point of a series of examples or details. Obviously

[1] M. Black, *The Labyrinth of Language*, Pall Mall Press, 1970, Penguin, 1972, p. 21.

the main idea sentence may come at any point in the paragraph. Sometimes it is not placed obviously. Here for instance are two paragraphs, from an essay by an art critic, Eric Newton, called *Looking at Pictures*:

> Perhaps one of the most valuable and unexpected results of what is roughly known as 'modern' art is that it has given us all a shock and compelled us to ask a question. We may admire Picasso's pictures or we may detest them (almost everyone seems to pick on Picasso as the most extreme example of modernism, so one may as well quote him as a type rather than as an individual); but all of us, with the exception of the arrogant philistine—to whom this article is not addressed—agree that he needs explaining. And the explanation we all hope for is in the answer to a question.
>
> Let me put the question in its simplest form—the form in which the intelligent but uninstructed layman, anxious to learn rather than to scoff, would phrase it. 'I like pictures to represent something I can recognise: I like them to be more or less realistic—if that's the right word. I also like them to be beautiful, though I'm not such a fool as to think that the beauty of a picture is the same thing as the beauty of the object or objects it represents. My difficulty is that modern art seems to me to fail too often in both respects: for me, it lacks both realism and beauty. Yet responsible critics praise it. I assume, therefore, that there must be some quality they find in it that I don't. Please tell me what that quality is. I'm willing to believe that I've missed something but I want to know what that "something" is.'

The first paragraph has the main idea at the very start: '. . . one of the most valuable . . . results of . . . modern art is that it has . . . compelled us to ask a question.' The rest of the paragraph defends and explains that point. The paragraph ends with a link, and in the next paragraph we think we are going to get an immediate statement of that question, and probably at the start of the paragraph again. In fact, the question is not stated until the penultimate sentence: 'Please tell me what that quality is.'

Inexperienced, nervous, or superficial readers frequently miss the main idea, and pick as the most important something that catches their eye because it is well known, or startling.

For instance, in this section of an article by Gillian Tyndale in *The Guardian*, titled 'Gillian Tyndale talking about easy marriage',[1] I found many sixth-formers thought that the writer was writing mainly against difficult mortgages. Housing was an easy subject to understand, and it leapt to the eye. The main idea had become subordinated in the pupils' minds to what was only an example.

> Why, when divorce is protracted, often expensive, and occasionally (even today) unobtainable, when to get a job you need an employment card and to have a baby in hospital you have to book months in advance, when a passport requires two reputable referees, to obtain a mortgage on a house is a complex manoeuvre, and to go to university requires a sustained effort of form-filling and form-studying apart from the examinations themselves
>   —why, in this intricate, inevitably docketed existence that is civilised

[1] Reprinted in *Relations Between the Sexes*, The Humanities Curriculum Project, Heinemann Educational, 1970.

life, do we treat one of the most important steps most people ever take with an airiness bordering on levity?'

There is also often confusion between the main idea and a topic. In some textbooks, for instance, as in some magazine articles, a word or phrase is printed about a paragraph or group of paragraphs, telling us what this paragraph is going to be about. However, it is often not the main idea, because it does not convey the gist of the content. For instance, an article might have 'The Balanced Diet and Calories' as a topic heading. The main idea of the first paragraph could prove to be an explanation of what a calorie is, and the second could define a balanced diet. Thus the top heading would be a guide towards the main idea, without being it: it would be the topic of the paragraph.

Although a writer does not usually plan a paragraph in any particular way, it is possible to see that each paragraph of factual and argumentative writing especially tends to have one of a fairly limited number of patterns. The pupil's ability to grasp the logical structure of the ideas is helped if he is shown what these patterns are. It is also a considerable help for such procedures as note-taking, summarizing, abstracting, and, of course, the comprehension questions of examinations. The underlying patterns show the relationships between the main paragraph ideas, their supporting points, and the examples or details that illustrate those points.

1. *Lists.* After a general statement the writer can give a number of examples, which are of broadly equal importance and could be rearranged in any order. You could draw a diagram of such a paragraph like this:

main idea

supporting examples

In these cases not only is the precise order of the listed examples not important, but also the number of listed ideas does not matter: an editor could take a couple out or put another in without spoiling the logic of the paragraph. It is important for pupils to realize that in note-taking or summarizing they must find a general description for all the examples, and not pick out the one or two which especially appeal or are rather better known.

2. *Chronological order.* In historical writing the ideas and details are obviously arranged sometimes in the order in which they happened. You could show the simple time chain in a diagram like this:

□→□→□→□→□→□

3. *Comparison and contrast.* It is sometimes harder to follow the thread of a writer's ideas if he uses neither 1 nor 2, but is showing the truth of an idea which has a comparison built into it, such as: 'In many ways ours is the most successful civilization that has existed'. Such a paragraph is likely to have many comparative words like *more, less, never, so, rather than, so many,* etc. Pupils sometimes lose the thread of the writer's point of view in such examples.

4. *Cause and effect.* Often a writer is building his argument round the relationships between cause and effect. He may be giving a list of effects and deducing their cause, or describing a cause and then listing its effects. Frequently the thread of the argument is complicated by alternative causes being compared.

5. *Expansion.* Perhaps the most common pattern is one of the loosest, in which a main idea is supported and expanded. Sometimes the writer builds up to the main idea, and at other times he states the main idea first, and goes into great detail to expand it. It is important to watch out particularly for the function of 'signpost' phrases like 'Nevertheless . . .', 'However . . .', 'On the other hand. . .'. Sometimes these phrases mark the turning point in the argument.

Obviously such a catalogue of organizational patterns is artificial. However, if a reader is to grasp the argument of a piece of writing, it is important that he senses the logical structure of the passage. This usually means seeing how secondary ideas support or explain the main idea, and how examples or details back up the secondary ideas. An important skill is to be able to sift the supporting detail from the main ideas and within the supporting detail to see that which is essential and that which is unimportant. Of course, nobody draws diagrams when they read, but a diagrammatic analysis may help pupils see how our unconscious mind should see the *relationship* of facts to each other and of the facts to the ideas. It is well worth getting the feel of this supporting structure, for much mis-reading results from not sensing this relationship.

Consider these two paragraphs from a widely used second-year humanities textbook. They are on the basic effects of climate on man's life. Each has a logical structure which the reader must sense if he is to follow the argument:

> Man does not like cold climates. Polar and sub-polar regions have the lowest human population densities of all. In these areas people are very likely to catch respiratory diseases. Also the shortness of the growing season cuts down the amount of food which can be produced, and it may be that the long periods of darkness and lack of sunlight have other physical and psychological ill-effects on man, about which we do not yet know much.

High temperatures, when combined with high humidity, allow plants to grow very rapidly so that more than one crop can be harvested per year. The warmth also cuts down the need for food and shelter, so that high densities of people are possible in tropical and subtropical countries. However, in these warmer climates, insects, fungi and bacteria can reproduce in large numbers so that there is an increased chance of the spread of disease in man, crops and domestic animals. In colder regions the winter serves as an annual check on reproduction, but there is no such seasonal control in the tropics.

The first paragraph makes a statement: *Man does not like cold climates.* Then it gives evidence to prove this: *Polar and sub-polar regions have the lowest human population densities.* It then gives three reasons for this: *increase in respiratory diseases; reduced amount of food produced; possible psychological effects.* And for two of those reasons it gives causes: *shortness of growing season; long periods of darkness and lack of sunlight.*

The reader must sense that there are four levels of logic here, which can be shown diagrammatically, the lowest explaining the one above it (except for the increase in respiratory diseases, which the writer leaves you to infer is caused by the cold):

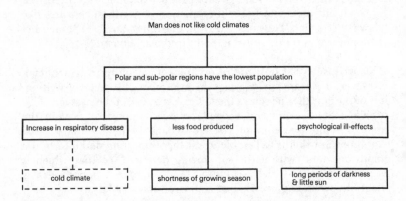

The three reasons explain the basic fact, and that justifies the main idea. In this kind of pattern you can cut off the diagram at any low level and still have the basic sense quite firmly. If you wanted to shorten intelligibly, however, you would really have to remove *all of one level.* Similarly, when summarizing, it would be wrong to include, say, the reduced food and leave out the psychological ill-effects, each of these being of the same level of significance.

The second paragraph is far more complicated. Although it is mainly about warm areas, it is not a simple catalogue of advantages, but contrasts the good with the bad, an example of pattern 3. The writer explores four results of 'high temperatures . . . combined with high humidity', and contrasts the good with the bad. Further in the last sentence he is contrasting one of the results with the colder regions.

This argument can also be represented in a diagram. The dotted lines lead to a point which is not *stated*, but which the reader is expected to *infer*. The *x* indicates a contrast point.

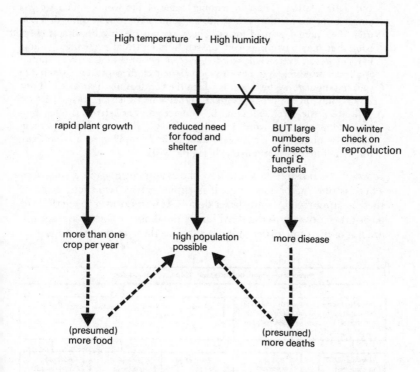

It is noticeable how many key signpost words there are in this paragraph. This is in itself an indication of the greater complexity of the argument. Simple listings, as in the previous paragraph, require fewer signpost words. We find: *when* (with the sense 'if'); *so that*; *so that*; *However*; *so that*; *but*. In each case, *so* signals an effect. *However* warns the reader that a contrast is to be expected, and that the paragraph is swinging round to look at the bad effects of the heat.

It is interesting that the last sentence looks at first as if it is changing the subject back to colder climates, the polar and sub-polar of paragraph one. But it is not. 'In colder regions . . .' presents a contrasting condition not experienced in warmer climates, and the final sentence is actually giving a reason for the fact in the sentence *before* it.

Here is a passage from a more advanced book. It is likely to deter the reader because of the rapid introduction of difficult words, but, as in many mathematical or scientific arguments, the *point* is actually very simple, virtually common sense. Many readers get lost, however. One picked out the point about mis-spellings and claimed the author was saying that it is a bad thing that careless people let mis-spellings get into books:

> What is commonly called perception is a mixture of perception, illusion, and hallucination. Thus, in reading, some of the words which we feel ourselves to see are not seen at all, and others are seen as quite different from their actual printed forms. There are mis-spellings in almost every book, but they pass unnoticed, unseen by the mental eye while reading. Parts of words, even whole words, are often not present as sensory stimuli at all, the mind making them up out of whole cloth. So also in listening to spoken language we hear words which the ear does not hear at all. If one says rapidly, in the proper context, 'What time tis it?' or 'Please pass me de butter,' the error will often be undetected. The letter *t* is often pronounced as *d* in such words as *ability, certainty, falsity,* but only experts in phonetics notice the fact. Again and again in rapid speech, words are totally omitted without anyone being the wiser.

It would be possible to show how the argument goes in a diagram. There is one major idea, and it is explained by two facts. Each of these is supported by some lesser details. It is important to see that the parts taken down into the third line in the diagram for the paragraph are not of the same order of importance as those in the second line.

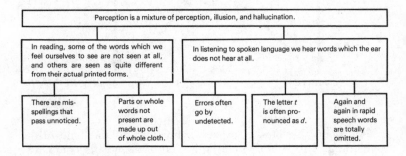

Probably the most important reading skill after the initial stages is the ability to re-create the argument the writer converted into the linear sequence of a paragraph. The pupil can be helped to see possible paragraph structures, sometimes as an isolated exercise (when the paragraphs can be chosen specially for their structural clarity), but more often in context (when the specific teaching can be drawn upon by pupil and teacher alike). Usually the method will be simply to highlight by question or pointing the structural articulation of the paragraph. Sometimes, however, visual techniques, such as the flow-chart diagrams I have demonstrated, listings, underlinings, etc. may be used to make the sense structure clearer. Each of us must give the necessary help in our own subject and with our special material.

Overall structure

We have a long, vigorous, and on the whole very successful tradition of helping pupils see the structure of narrative, drama, and poetry. We almost never do the same for the factual. Yet a chapter from most textbooks *has* a structure, and the pupil needs to be able to follow it if he is to grasp the argument. Consider, for example, a typical piece of biology reading, a chapter from the widely used Nuffield CSE Biology textbook;[1] called 'Smoking and Health', it is a 4-page essay with diagrams. It is also appropriate to consider such an example as it is very similar to articles that adults are likely to meet in a range of papers and magazines. If the reader is really to understand the writer's meaning, he must involve himself in the structure of the argument. I have found that fifth-year pupils reading this essay lose the steps in the progression, partly being pulled away by the illustrations and partly giving too much attention to details. I suspect that the pupils whose reading of this passage I observed had never had argumentative structure explained to them. They could not see the wood for the trees. Attention to paragraph structure would have helped pupils grasp the overall structure of continuous pieces of writing, whole chapters, papers, essays or articles. Clearly as much help as is given to using a test tube should be given to *using* the overall argument of such a chapter.

The first task is to help pupils realize what is meant by *argument*, which is the pattern of the ideas. Arguments can be built up diagrammatically in flow-diagram form, using very few words, in an expansion of the method used to interpret a paragraph.

To understand overall structure it is also worth teaching that paragraphs usually *have a purpose*; they do a job in building up the sequence of an argument. Each paragraph is then a step of one sort or another. Thus paragraphs *do something* for the argument, they don't just 'go on'. Even the youngest pupils in the secondary school can have this idea made explicit, but by fourteen there can be some classifying of paragraph functions:

1. *Explanatory*. These are the most common paragraphs outside narrative; they outline facts by informing or explaining.
2. *Definitional*. Many chapters have one or more paragraphs devoted to clarifying the meaning of a word, phrase, clause, or concept. This may be necessary, for instance, before a sequence of explanatory paragraphs is embarked upon. The reader needs to study these especially closely, and mentally keep his finger on such a paragraph for back reference. Frequently such a definitional paragraph needs to be read *before* the explanations, but then again *after* them, for only then will the full force of the definition be clear. It is worth asking oneself *what* is being defined and *what* it means.
3. *Introductory*. These are often broad, focusing the nature of the

[1] *The Maintenance of Life*, Penguin/Longman.

argument that is to follow. Sometimes they are signalled by obvious phrases: 'This chapter is about . . .', 'Now we shall see . . .', 'It is important to outline. . . .' However, not all are so baldly signalled, and, indeed, many introductory paragraphs deliberately start dramatically but obliquely, a combination which throws most pupil readers. Here are two introductory paragraphs from different chapters (4 and 2) of a book on the pyramids for younger secondary pupils.[1]

> How did the ancient Egyptians move the stone from the quarries to the pyramid being built? As we know, the larger pyramids used up millions of tons of stone, most of which was in two-and-a-half-ton blocks. This was no easy task, yet the Egyptians managed to find a way.
> The pyramids still stand today and some of them look much as they must have done when they were built thousands of years ago. Most of the damage suffered by the pyramids has been at the hands of men who were looking for treasure, or more often for stone to use in modern buildings. The dry climate of Egypt has helped to preserve the pyramids, and their very shape has made them less likely to fall into ruin. These are good reasons why the pyramids can still be seen today, but perhaps the most important reason is that they were planned to last 'forever'.[1]

Both paragraphs are introductory but they work in different ways. Whereas the first announces the subject of the chapter in its opening question, the second deliberately postpones it to the final 'but . . .'. It is worth pointing out these techniques in general terms. If the pupils are expected to read the chapters, it is worth, as part of the readiness preparation, establishing the announcement function of the paragraphs and sorting out 'which words tell you what the chapter is going to be about?', and 'why are the other facts put in?'

4. *Summarizing and concluding*. Pupils tend to switch off towards the end of a piece of reading as their stamina wilts. In fact the summarizing and concluding paragraphs are vital for review and check. (Indeed, they are often worth looking ahead for as part of a previewing technique.) It is important to note that not all conclusions are summaries—often the conclusion gives the writer's retrospective judgement or future speculation. Review signal words should be thought of: 'Thus . . .', 'We can therefore see . . .', 'It is therefore clear . . .', 'The evidence can be seen . . .'.

6. *Transitional*. I consider the transitional function especially important but easily missed by the pupil:

> Although Hinduism is the main religion of India, most of the Indians in Britain are in fact Sikhs. The word 'Sikh' means 'disciple', and Sikhs follow the teaching of Guru Nanak, who lived in India from A.D. 1469 to 1539. The title 'Guru' means 'Teacher', and although Nanak was brought up as a Hindu he later combined what he thought was the best in Hinduism with what he thought was the best in Islam. He taught that 'There is no Hindu, there is no Muslim, but only one human being, the Sikh'.[2]

[1] J. Weeks, *The Pyramids*, Cambridge University Press, 1971.
[2] Roger Street, *Focus on Faiths*, Nelson, 1974, p. 11.

The 'turning word', 'Although', needs pointing out. This is *not* going to be about Hinduism. Like most transitional paragraphs, this one refers backwards first. It is worth discussing the structural function of transitional paragraphs, and finding actual examples. They are important for the structure of the piece, and for the pupil's understanding of the argument.

7. *Narrative.* In expository writing, narrative paragraphs are often used to illustrate points being made, although they can also be used simply as introductions or to add atmosphere. The reader needs to be used to the idea that the story is there for a purpose, and to ask himself what that purpose is. The narrative thus requires a closer and rather different kind of detailed scrutiny to that given to prose fiction.

It needs adding that a diet totally of worksheet and gobbet will ill-prepare pupils for continuous reading of argument. It has been shown that of the reading done in class very little is continuous. Indeed, about half of all reading in class is in bursts of less than a quarter of a minute in any one minute. The table shows how little continuous reading there is. Obviously we are not training our pupils to understand structure in continuous reading!

Patterns of continuity in reading for each age and subject group, given as a percentage of the overall reading time recorded for reading in the group

	Type 1	Type 2	Type 3	Type 4
ENGLISH				
Top Juniors	46	29	11	13
First year Secondary	53	27	10	10
Fourth year Secondary	34	25	14	27
MATHEMATICS				
Top Juniors	41	47	11	0
First year Secondary	70	22	8	0
Fourth year Secondary	72	24	4	0
SCIENCE				
Top Juniors	69	26	5	0
First year Secondary	75	21	3	1
Fourth year Secondary	57	36	4	3
SOCIAL STUDIES				
Top Juniors	60	28	8	3
First year Secondary	60	28	8	3
Fourth year Secondary	44	42	9	5

Type 1 = Total reading during time-sampled minute was 1–15 seconds.
Type 2 = Total reading during time-sampled minute was 16–30 seconds.
Type 3 = Total reading during time-sampled minute was 31–45 seconds.
Type 4 = Total reading during time-sampled minute was 46–60 seconds.
Thus Type 1 represents only intermittent reading, and Type 4 continuous reading.
Source: Schools Council Project, *The Effective Use of Reading*, Second Interim Report, 1975, Table 4.

It is interesting to take a piece of argument from one of the most popular papers. How would school leavers cope with it? How should teachers help? As an example, we have reproduced an editorial from the *Daily Mirror*. Similar pieces of writing can be taken from the popular daily papers almost any day. It has three difficulties for pupils:

(a) range of reference and background knowledge required;
(b) breadth of vocabulary;
(c) complexity of argument.

The courage of Jack Jones

JACK JONES is a man of the Left.

There's no mistaking that. He is against Britain remaining in the Common Market. He favours more state participation in industry.

He is leader of Britain's biggest union — the Transport and General Workers — and a dedicated supporter of the Labour Party.

But Jack Jones is a constructive radical. Not a ritual extremist.

Builder

Where many Left wingers are self-confessed wreckers and apparently proud of it, Jack Jones is a builder of bridges.

● He has striven to hold all sides of the Labour movement together.

● He has striven to heal the self-inflicted wounds in Britain's industrial relations by successfully advocating worker participation.

● Above all, he has striven to uphold the social contract as a means of creating a more equal society.

More often than any other TUC leader he has spelled out the importance of unions sticking to their side of the contract.

His appeal at the Scottish TUC annual congress was the most powerful yet.

Where is the chorus of TUC voices that should be supporting him?

For the most part, they are as silent as the grave they are digging for the social contract.

Blunt

Today it is sometimes hard to remember that the social contract is the official policy of the **whole** TUC.

Some of those who voted in favour of the contract last year are now undermining it at every opportunity.

The good sense of Jack Jones has gone hand in hand with the blunt warnings of Denis Healey.

If more trade union leaders had taken their advice in the last twelve months, today's Budget could have been a lot less severe.

The far Left might even have got the reflationary Budget it wants but obviously now cannot have.

Such an example, reproduced in facsimile, could be used either *in context* (e.g. current affairs, social studies, history, newspapers, the media) or *specifically*, as an example to illustrate written argument.

In either case the teacher's approach would be broadly the same, though the emphasis would be somewhat different.

The teacher's approach, I should suggest, would be to tackle the difficulties in the order in which I have just listed them. First, through discussion, establish the background facts: 'Left', 'TWU', 'worker participation', 'social contract', 'Denis Healey'—whichever of the facts need filling in. Secondly, the teacher would pick out, or have the pupils pick out, the difficult words, and explain them: 'participation', 'ritual', 'striven', 'advocating', 'congress'.

Then, the real point: here are some fairly simple sentences, placed, however, not in a simple series, like a string of beads, but arranged by the author to advance some opinions. Each opinion is justified by one or more reasons, and sometimes the reasons are supported further by examples. Interestingly, there is also a relationship or progression between the main opinions—the third opinion, which is in the form of a question ('Where is the chorus of TUC voices that should be supporting him?') being the central one. Interestingly it is cast as a question to give it more force, but it *means*: 'We consider the TUC should be speaking up for him.'

Pupils can annotate the originals to analyse the argument, or can produce their own list, as shown. By one means or another the teacher can show the structure of the argument. This benefits the current lesson objective, and the wider aim of teaching reading.

Opinion 1: Jack Jones is a man of the Left.
Evidence: 1 Against Common Market
           2 For more state participation in industry
           3 Leader of biggest union
           4 Dedicated support of Labour Party.
Opinion 2: He is constructive.
Evidence: 1 Builds bridges
           Examples: (i) works to hold all sides of Labour together
                    (ii) tried to heal industry by recommending worker participation
                    (iii) tried to uphold social contract.
           2 Spells out importance of unions keeping contract.
           Example: (i) recent appeal to Scottish TUC.
Opinion 3: TUC are not supporting him.
Evidence: 1 They keep quiet over contract
           2 Some even undermining it.
Opinion 4: (conclusion) If they had, Budget would have been less severe and nearer to what the Left want.

Pupils' work on overall structure should be done in three ways:
1. specifically by theoretical study on limited occasions, of the idea, with illustrations;
2. as part of the study of an argumentative piece of writing for its own sake, but chosen to allow a study of structure;

3. by readiness techniques, help during reading, and subsequent review by all subject teachers who use print.

Graphic conventions

A publisher uses a number of graphic conventions to help convey meaning. Leaving aside those best thought of as punctuation, these range from type fonts to the use of illustrations.

1. *Typographical aids.* I do not wish to exaggerate reading difficulties, but it is important to realize that the teacher of English takes trouble to explain the typographical conventions of prose fiction (for instance, the layout of story dialogue), of verse (for instance, the problem of line endings), and of drama (for instance, the italicized stage directions in speeches, which are not to be read aloud). Any experienced teacher knows that most pupils do not just pick up the ability to read these typographical conventions. The teacher returns to them year after year—often spurred on by the failure of the pupil to use the tuition in his own *writing*. The result is a fairly methodical approach to the teaching of the typographical conventions of the presentation of literature forms, even with the least able. Nothing similar is done for conventions used outside literature. I suggest that there should be specialized teaching of the possible use of bold type, italics, sans serif (e.g. to differentiate captions from text), etc., and the subject teacher can and should then draw on this knowledge in guiding the pupil through texts.

2. *Illustrations.* Consider the complexity of layout of many of the most carefully and ingeniously designed modern information books. It is generally felt that illustrations help the poor reader. Actually this seems to me an arguable and unproven point. For flipping through, an illustrated book may be more attractive visually, but it is not necessarily easier to read its text; indeed, it may even be harder. This is because the continuous text is broken by a variety of visual devices, chosen and reproduced to be eye-catching, and laid out by a graphic designer to make a pleasing *visual pattern* of the double-page spread, and a variety of such patterns from spread to spread.

Modern technology—particularly offset litho—has opened up new design possibilities. Of these the most important is the simple one of making it possible to print half-tone illustrations on ordinary paper. Previously a coated, glossy paper was required. This led to a choice either of line drawings, or of grouping the half-tone on 'plates' gathered in one or more sections of the book. The new freedom, encouraged by other visual trends in our culture, has led to a 'graphics explosion' in information books, including school books. Picture researchers use their ingenuity to extend the range of kinds of illustration available—a diversity which, whilst considerably enriching the evidence available also makes it harder for the pupil to grasp the total effect.

The pupil needs help in the art of synthesizing graphics and text. The continuity of reading is severely fractured by captions, drawings, and photographs. The ability to step forward and backtrack is made more difficult. The mental organization of caption, illustration, and main text is extremely difficult.

Pupils need help in coping with this kind of book. Such help involves discussing what elements a book has; how they are arranged; how to differentiate captions; the possible orders of reading; and how to integrate the elements. Time must be taken to explain to the pupils the various ways in which graphics are used:

(a) Immediate reference within the text, with the sentences directly referring to and or broken by the graphics.

(b) Reference from the text to a nearby graphics, probably with its own caption.

(c) Added graphic, to be studied separately and synthesized by the student.

Within the curriculum specific attention should be given to study of visual sources: graphs, maps, photographs. When books are used, the interaction of graphics and text should be prepared for and discussed. To reintegrate the static breaks of the illustrations with the impetus of the text is difficult. This is a reading skill—paradoxically, one which modern attempts to make books easier for the 'less academic' have often made more acute.

Preparing for reading assignments

The subject teacher who has planned that his pupils should read as part of a sequence of work should normally, I would suggest, devote class or group time to pre-reading preparation. This is especially necessary for subjects such as science and mathematics in which not a great deal of reading is normally done in class.

The first aim is to generate interest in the passage. Too often we say: 'read pages 22 to 34', leaving the author the entire task of raising the interest. Excerpts, non-print material, key questions, anecdote—there are a variety of possible approaches.

It is considerably easier for the pupil if reading purposes are defined. The ideal reader does this for himself, but when all the pupils are to read, the teacher and group can do it together. Too often the reading is purposeless, or too unfocused ('find out all you can about . . .'), or the purpose is discovered only retrospectively in the following lesson when the questions are asked too late. Rather, a question (or variety of questions) should be posed, and the reason for reading the passage made clear.

It is frequently necessary for the pupils to be led into the text. I see six possible techniques that will need to be used on occasion.

1. *Background facts.* The text may presume and depend upon knowledge that the pupils have not got. Whilst avoiding giving a

subordinate rival lesson, it is worth planting this information. I have seen pupils unable to make sense of a passage, which is well within their competence, merely because of some unfamiliar references in it.

2. *Previewing*. Attention to headings, sub-headings, and typographical devices ('Why is that sentence in bold type?') will help the pupil see where the reading is going.

3. *'Stopper words'*. This American phrase nicely describes those words which 'stop' reading. Again, a brief pre-reading session should not be converted into a laborious vocabulary session, but key vocabulary should be picked out. In my observation it is not mainly the true technical vocabulary of the subject being studied which confuses, but use of a less common non-technical word. This passage, for instance, is from a 'Geography for the Young School Leaver' pack:

> Some of the most exciting new parks and open spaces in heavily built-up urban areas have been created from derelict industrial areas. The city of Stoke-on-Trent, for example, is creating a chain of parklands out of colliery slag heaps, pottery claypits and disused railway lines.

The style is very simple, but 'derelict' is likely to stop some readers. Admittedly the word is virtually defined by illustration in the following sentence, but I suggest that most pupils should be given some help—either by pre-definition, or by reminding them that whatever 'colliery slag-heaps, pottery claypits, and disused railway lines' have in common must be what is meant by 'derelict'.

4. *Structure words*. In many cases the structure signal words that I talked about on page 109 are worth highlighting in advance.

5. *The structure*. On other occasions the structure of the argument is worth outlining in advance: e.g. 'The first three paragraphs are about this point of view. Compare them with the next five, which put the other point of view.

6. *Graphics*. If a graphic representation is a crucial part of the argument, it may be worth reminding pupils of how it works and its relationship to the text. Graphs often give difficulty, as do certain numerical tables. It is sometimes helpful simply to point out in advance: 'When you get to the last paragraph, the graph opposite needs studying. It tells you the same thing as the words in the paragraph'.

The aim of this preparation, therefore, is to give the necessary background, purpose, and way in. It helps to guide the pupil reader by showing him where the reading is going and how it is getting there. It is, after all, no more than a teacher would do in preparation for any other study activity, such as experiment, visit, or simulation. If helped in this kind of way a pupil not only gains more from *this* reading: he gains more reading experience to help other reading.

Reading aloud

Reading aloud is not favoured by teachers, a generation of whom are still reacting against plodding through a novel from pupil to pupil week after week. Mixed-ability groups have now made the use of the technique less easy, and where it is used, it has become associated solely with English lessons.

I would suggest that the technique has value in helping pupils grasp the intonation patterns that even in unvocalized silent reading are necessary to make sense.

The value of reading aloud is illustrated in the following example from mathematics. Merely *looked* at, the passage seems nonsensical: it has to be vocalized to be understood, with intonation patterns clarifying the sense groups. It is also a good example of the extreme importance of understanding the place of the comma in clarifying sense groups: a pupil who has not considered the comma would be less likely to understand this, and a pupil who has been helped to understand this in his maths lesson would be helped to gain a feel for the comma:

> If we start at 0 each time, the shift plus 1 takes us to the point plus 1, the shift plus 2 to the point plus 2, the shift plus 3 to the point plus 3, and so on. In the same way, each time starting at 0, the shift minus 1 takes us to the point minus 1, the shift minus 2 to the point minus 2, and so on.

(It seems to me that quotation marks round the phrases 'plus 1', 'plus 2', etc. would have made the sense clearer.) The point is that there is nothing *mathematically* difficult about the idea in this passage which refers to shifts on a number line:

There is, what's more, nothing difficult in the words, or the syntax. There are merely two factors that create difficulty:

(a) The need to understand the sense of 'takes us', a phrase which is omitted from the clauses following its first appearance.

(b) The repetitions marked by commas.

If the teacher, or a good pupil reader, reads it aloud, not only is the sense immediately clear, but help has been given to the pupil to similarly reconstruct sense by his intonation patterns for other examples. Obviously the pupil should be encouraged to vocalize such a passage.

Subject teachers will need to choose carefully when they ask pupils to read aloud. It is at its best for highlighting key passages, or supporting pupils' opinions. Obviously less able readers should not be abruptly exposed to the whole class, but small groups on prepared occasions can get round these difficulties.

Conclusion

It is too readily assumed that all that is said about the teaching of reading in the content area applies only to the less able, or maybe at most to the average and below average. This is not so. Fluent reading by competent pupils can mask the fact that they read the text merely as a string of statements, and that they do not read the reasoning process. These are the pupils of whom one American declared: 'There are many students who read too well for their own good in most schools'.

I have suggested teachable clues to help grasp meaning. Mere teaching of these clues as an analysed series of skills does not itself improve reading, but equally leaving the pupil to develop ways of working out sense entirely on his own is to leave him with insufficient help. We must keep providing opportunities, and support those opportunities with pointed help.

The question of time will naturally be raised. If one is not careful the idea of teaching reading is seen as an added task laid on top of a subject teacher's present load. But the teaching of reading outside English is not *something* to teach, but a *way* of carrying out part of the teaching, one which not only helps the pupil gain the ideas, knowledge, or skill currently being explored, but also increases his ability to learn other aspects on other occasions, independently and at will. It will be rare that a lesson sequence or the work of an individual or group of pupils will be stopped for specific reading tuition, but whenever print matter is used as a source, the teacher can integrate his reading help with the lesson. Thus time is saved—for the time of the pupil devoted to the text will be more valuably spent, the knowledge will be more thoroughly grasped, and the pupil will have been helped for the future.

A subject-teacher's reading policy

A school might consider these points for its whole-school policy:
1. Make sure that print is a necessary source.
2. Judge the suitability of each item.
3. Provide a variety of kinds and sources, including continuous passages of some length to teach structure and short passages for intensive study.
4. Structure the moments of reading, to provide both group guided reading and individual varied reading.
5. Devise functions to focus the purpose of the particular reading occasion.
6. Prepare for most reading occasions by introduction and pointer.
7. Allow adequate uninterrupted time for reading.
8. Help individuals through the text where necessary (not by offering alternative explanations).

The use of talk

'I can't even speak English proper because you never talked about anything important.'[1]

The pupil's limited range of language may be a serious barrier, preventing his access to learning. This is, as we have seen, especially true of reading problems. Conversely, however, the school's limited uses of language may restrict the pupil from deploying his language in learning situations. A language policy is concerned with helping him get *at* the understanding and knowledge on offer, and it must also help him get *into* the understanding and knowledge, since without comprehension, access itself is of little value. The way into ideas, the way of making ideas truly one's own, is to be able to think them through, and the best way to do this for most people is to talk them through. Thus talking is not merely a way of conveying existing ideas to others; it is also a way by which we explore ideas, clarify them, and make them our own. Talking things over allows the sorting of ideas, and gives rapid and extensive practice towards the handling of ideas. It is also, as Nancy Martin's contribution to this chapter makes clear, a valuable step towards writing.

John Dixon has asked: 'How did classroom dialogue, a central method—*the* central mode?—of teaching and learning come to be so neglected? Why is there still so little published discussion among teachers and research workers on dialogue between pupils as a mode of learning? Why is linguistic theory, so original in other respects, still so weak on the most elementary form of discourse?'[2] And he might have asked why a method so long recommended has been so little used. After all, the Report's predecessor, the Newbolt Committee, fifty years earlier had spoken of 'the conversational method'. What that committee had to say is now agreed to by all linguists: 'So-called knowledge is not knowledge if the thinking powers are not applied to it, and . . . the only way to get a child to think about it . . . is to get him to talk about it.'[3] This is what the Bullock Committee had in mind when it stressed the value of talk as an educative activity in itself. From infant conversation to university seminar, the student needs the opportunity to talk about his learning, indeed to learn through his talking.

The failure can be seen only too clearly when the pupil gets older. It is, I think, well put by a speaker from an Agricultural College talking about the Suffolk boys who come on from school:

They make statements—big, flat statements. They never explore ideas. Nobody has taught them how to use words to convey theories, so now that

---

[1] Beatie Bryant in *Roots* by Arnold Wesker (Penguin edition, p. 55).

[2] John Dixon, 'Talk and Collaborative Learning', in H. Rosen (ed.), *Some Appraisals of the Bullock Report*, University of London Institute of Education, 1975, p. 28.

[3] *The Teaching of English in England*, HMSO, 1921, para. 74.

all the old village story-telling has died out their talk is very poor dull stuff. Although sometimes you'll get a flood of the old richness when somebody has to relate a bit of gossip. There is terrific animation. Eyes light up. The man isn't really gossiping in the trivial sense of the word, he is story-telling.[1]

The teacher's task is to help the pupil extend from the possibility of story-telling (and to nourish that tradition too) into the 'conveying of theories', and not merely into the dead-end of 'big, flat statements'.

The first problem of such aims is the need to establish an atmosphere in which talk is possible and to build up relationships in which talk is wanted. We know from commonsense and linguistic research that genuine talk is not possible in certain atmospheres, nor is it possible on one side of certain relationships. We have all experienced occasions when we or others have been made virtually speechless by an intimidating atmosphere—whether in interview, or because of a particular individual. Labov, the American linguist, has demonstrated[1] how fluent black children can be reduced to mono-syllables in teacher-dominated situations. We know that from our own memories or reading. This exchange, although from a novel, records the kind of relationship which makes a pupil literally speechless. Saville is unable to answer the teacher's questions, not because of any deficiency on his part, but because of the nature of the verbal exchange:

He examined the register once again. 'Father's occupation.' He wrote something down on a piece of paper. 'Now "colliery worker" means that he works at a coal-mine. Is that correct?'
'Yes', he said.
'Yes, *what*?'
'Yes, sir', he said.
'Now there are any number of people who might legitimately say they work at a *coal*-mine. The *manager* of a *coal*-mine might say he works at a *coal*-mine.'
He waited for an answer.
'Yes', he said, then added, 'Sir.'
'I take it, of course, he's no such thing.'
Colin waited, unsure of what to add.
'He's not the manager, Saville?'
'No.' He shook his head.
'No, what?'
'No, sir', he said.
'He's not the deputy-manager, either, I imagine.'
'No', he said.
'Does he work on top or, as they have it, underneath?'
'Underneath.'
'Does he superintend the men down there, or does he actually hew the coal itself?'

[1] Ronald Blyth, *Akenfield*, Allen Lane, 1969, p. 169.

'He hews the coal', he said.
'E'ews the coal.'
'Yes, sir.'
The class had laughed.
'In other words, Saville, he's a miner?'
'Yes, sir.'
'Then why couldn't he put that on the form?'
He bowed his head and wrote in the register for several seconds.
'Well, Saville double l, have you got an answer?'
'No, sir.' He shook his head.[1]

Saville (who was grilled earlier about his father's mis-spelling of his surname) is made to look a fool, indeed to be a fool, by the teacher's use of language as a weapon to maintain his superiority. There can be few of us who, however we feel schools have changed since that kind of exchange, do not recognize the linguistic pattern as one which we use from time to time, thus driving a pupil into inarticulateness. However, we try more often, and frequently succeed, in creating an atmosphere and setting up an exchange in which we can build on the pupil's natural way of putting things.

Secondly, and related to that, pupil talk is most likely to flourish when there is a genuine interest in what is being communicated. Although speech education still has a place in schools, for some pupils and on some occasions, its tradition can be very unhelpful indeed. There will be times when concentration on clarity, modulation, expression, and projection is relevant and meaningful for the pupil. Indeed, the art of public or semi-public use of the voice is one which will always be worth working on, whether for use in reading aloud to children round the fire, at the rugby club dinner, or in quasi-professional roles. However, that is virtually a separate concern, and its methods have little to offer the encouragement of communicative talk in a school. Indeed the vestigial remains of elocution and performing can cramp talk for the many by emphasizing the manner rather than the content.

The teacher's response must be to the totality of the statement, not to the triviality of part of the expression. An important statement can accommodate a vague confusion of phrase, just as a printed statement can carry a blurred word, and still be fully explicit. The teacher has to choose whether to respond to the overall sense, which he has probably taken quite clearly, or to pull out the weak phrase for examination. If he does the latter, he will lose the former. In general, a school policy will want to place emphasis on a genuine interest in and response to the pupil's ideas and intention.

But this is to describe pupil talk as if it were merely talk to and with the teacher. Certainly the teacher as sympathetic adult will be important, as will any other adult audience that can be arranged, such as visitors, other professionals, parents, local people being

[1] David Storey, *Saville*, Jonathan Cape, 1976.

interviewed, and so on. However, the greatest speech opportunities, and potentially the most valuable, are those between pupils. On these occasions the pupils can think on their feet. They can explore ideas in a way which can sharpen, intensify, and even speed up the process of thinking. During and through the speech the pupils can create new perceptions, new ideas, and new knowledge.

The humanities are too often seen as the main talking subjects. Possibly, though this is no more than a personal hunch, there is too much reliance on the exchange of views in subjects like social studies. More certainly there is a gross underestimation of the value of pupil discussion in other areas of the curriculum. Music, for instance, is rarely mentioned in this context, yet the exchange of opinions and reactions in small groups is a real possibility. Group music-making offers an even more promising opportunity, in which small improvised compositions are planned and rehearsed. These demand cooperative talk, as the suitability of musical material is offered, doubted, considered, and decided. (Do we get louder or softer at the end? Should we repeat that note pattern? When should we bring in the metalophone?) Similarly, in three-dimensional crafts, design problems lead to small-group talk, bringing memories and experience of life to bear on the challenge of materials and techniques. Similar group planning, analysis, and thinking through can be a part of science, mathematics—indeed most subject activities.

A school considering the place of talk in learning is likely to want to study classroom approaches in some detail, for increasing the value of pupil talk is probably the hardest actual pedagogical problem within a language policy. Crudely translated into: 'They've got to do a lot more talking', the ideas of the Report could be at best a waste of time, and at worst could produce disruptive chaos. Some schools might not yet feel ready to go far in this direction. But a school planning to do so might well consider in seminar and staff meeting how pupil talk is encouraged, the kind of occasions, and the kind of teaching required. The following headings could be looked at:

Contexts

Talk flourishes best when it grows in a context. The kind of purposeful developmental talk that Douglas Barnes has described in his two books[1] usually comes in a carefully arranged situation, with some form of suitable learning material to use in discussion, and with a suitable setting. What kind of contexts can a teacher set up to encourage such talk? The staff of a school can compare contexts that seem to have worked and ones that do not. They can work towards developing their own guidelines that will help others create promising talk contexts.

[1] *Language, Learner, and the School* and *From Communication to Curriculum.*

Disciplinary patterns

The traditional school injunction of 'silence' has the practical virtue of clarity. No doubt there will always be occasions on which it will be the most appropriate disciplinary injunction. When it is discarded, however, and talk is expected and encouraged, with what is silence to be replaced? There can be a genuine disciplinary problem to which too few educationalists give any thought. Talking situations can get out of hand, and the noise level with a full class in an ordinary room rises so high that the aim of productive talking for learning is broken by the sheer hubbub and the teacher's eventual need to shout above the noise. The injunction of 'reasonable noise' is too vague, and offers no guidance to the participants. Teachers therefore need to develop in a school alternative acceptable disciplinary guides, working out alternative injunctions such as 'No talking outside your group' or 'Each chairman will decide who is going to talk'.

Time constraints

Are there any generalizations about time and talk that would be helpful to a school? Obviously the question 'How long is a good discussion?' is a fatuous one. Yet a staff can help itself develop good classroom talk if it does give attention to the effects of increasing or decreasing time for talk: too little and the session barely gets going; too long a session for the material and the talk flounders.

Discussion techniques

Most valuable talk will be virtually unstructured. Nevertheless there is advice which can helpfully be given to pupils about talking together. We do, after all, give them advice on most learning techniques, and it would be strange if this were omitted. Some consciousness of the problems and methods of group discussion can be of great help. This worksheet below is from the Abraham Moss Centre in Manchester, a school which takes pupil discussion very seriously and has developed ways of discussing discussion.

When you are taking part in a discussion remember the following points. They are *very* important.

1. Remember you are taking part in a discussion
(a) to learn
(b) to help other people to learn.

2. Always have a paper and pencil handy during discussions.

3. Ask for anything you do not understand to be explained.

4. If two people have misunderstood each other, help them out.

5. If someone has said something which you think is important, remind the group about it.

6. Always let other people 'have their say', even if you are bursting to say something.

7. Be prepared to change your mind if you have been proved wrong.

8. Do not shout people down just because you don't agree with them.

9. Do not show off in a discussion.

10. You must take part in a discussion even if you feel shy.

11. Listen carefully to what everyone else in the group says.

12. Always have one member of the group writing down the most important points discussed and any decisions that the group has made.

End product

Talk is frequently, though by no means always, sharpened by a function—that is if the talk is leading towards some form of end product: establishing a hypothesis, choosing a design, planning a strategy, drafting a report, making a decision. It will often help if the teacher focuses the talk by choosing such an end product in advance. A school staff can consider what kinds of end products have proved the most profitable.

Perhaps the hardest problem in talk is that of the place of the teacher in situations somewhere in that rich but uncharted area between teacher-dominated 'discussion' (which certainly has a place) and pupil-to-pupil discussion without a teacher. If the pupils are always to be dependent on the teacher for the sense of direction in talk, how will they learn to cope without him? Yet his ability to alter course, to focus, to weave in the relevant reference is valuable not only for the discussion of the moment, but also for the pupils' growing awareness of the opportunities and methods of purposeful talk. It is possible for teachers to develop strategies for participating without dominating, but these techniques are at their hardest in subjects with few periods and much explaining—such as science. They are at their easiest in the more personal parts of the humanities, and for this reason those teachers whose experience has been wholly in literature, for instance, often have great difficulty in even under- standing the difficulties of a teacher trying to find participatory ways in pupil discussion in other areas. The core of the problem seems to be the knowledge which needs to be deployed in much of this discus- sion, and the teacher's fear that the conversation will confirm wrong ideas if he does not oversee, intervene, and correct. Preparation seems doubly valuable in these situations, and it is vital to ensure that the background information to the talk has been learnt earlier. Sometimes information cards can be a useful source of facts, basic ideas, and key vocabulary, available to all the participants.

In the next section we shall see the uses of such exploratory talk, between teacher and pupils and between pupils and pupils, in the context of a science practical lesson. Following that we shall look at the uses of writing, seen initially as a form of recorded inner talk. A final point about talk, however, needs making. It is not a question of how to find time for talk, as if this were to be an *added* activity competing with the main learning and therefore requiring spare time. The opposite is true: the speed of real learning in most subjects is likely to be *increased* by talk—so that the task is therefore not to find time, but to choose the best time.

Talking and learning in science, an example

Irene Robertson

As a starting point we could look at a common-sense distinction that most of us work with: the distinction between a science ('biology' or 'physics' etc.) and the language of science or scientific language (I use language here to denote all signing systems, e.g. algebraic, pictorial, that a scientist may use). We can consider that science *is* the language in which it is reported, taught, received. This could apply equally to a doctoral thesis, an 'O'-level textbook, the talk that goes on when a teacher gives a lesson on electricity, or the talk that goes on among pupils as they conduct their experiments in school labs.

We can view the teacher then as teacher of his subject-cum-language. In learning that subject-cum-language, the teacher has come to see the world in particular ways. He has organized it scientifically. I may see a jug as an everyday object to hold water; in a pottery class I may see it in terms of the structure of its clay and the movements of its making; in a science lab I may see it in terms of a concern with the physics of liquid.

The science teacher can share particular ways of seeing with his pupils. I use *share* here, because I want to get away from a simple notion of the direct transmission of knowledge from teacher to pupil. For if we agree that coming-to-know-in-language is the issue, then we must recognize that this is a process within each individual. All of us, teachers and pupils, are responsible for our own enquiry (here scientific enquiry) and we can truly know only what we have come to experience and express for ourselves. Nobody else can do it for us. As teachers, we probably recognize this most clearly when we distrust work that a pupil has simply copied from a book. We feel that he has not understood or made it on his own. We should be suspicious for the same reasons when we find ourselves filling blackboards and getting the pupils to copy our own formulations.

How to share these ways of seeing with our pupils? We probably feel, perhaps unfairly, that when pupils initially come to us they are ignorant of science's ways of seeing the world. After all, that is what they come to us to be educated in; that is why we are teachers. We should equally remember that those pupils are already competent in working with language. We all live by explaining the world and ourselves in it. Our pupils' explanations may in detail be different from ours, just as yours may be different from mine. The detail is not the issue; the possibility of enquiry is.

If we can respect the pupil as his own enquirer, and remember that becoming educated in science is doing your own scientific enquiry, then we should bear this in mind when we make provision for him in schools, in lessons. When we as adults do our own enquiry we can turn to books, and are probably willing to admit that this may be a particularly difficult or uncomfortable thing to do; we turn and talk to others; we talk with ourselves. We are then in a whole network of dialogues with ourselves and books, ourselves and others—and it is the interplay of these dialogues that are our learning and coming to know. For instance, whatever we may gain from this paper, whatever we may count as knowledge for us, will be what emerges in the talk we engage in with the paper and with others sharing it. In turning to this account of lessons, we could consider how enquiry was enabled; where it fell down; and we could listen to what these boys say of what doing physics was all about.

In the physics lessons which I shall describe, boys were learning about speed and internal combustion engines. Speed was already a common-sense notion which the boys had experienced and talked about on countless occasions previous to the lessons in which they measured speed in terms of the formula distance/time. The boys weren't being handed new knowledge; rather they were coming to focus differently.

There are, of course, ways of knowing to which we need never give utterance; an example of this can be found in the account which follows when pupils at work do not need to express the fact that they know how to start a two-stroke motor, since their knowledge is displayed in their activities. But in schools we are largely concerned with public, communicable ways of knowing and understanding; we talk with pupils, we read what they have written—listening and looking for their understanding.

These activities of shaping and sharing understanding are what I was listening for in the lab which is the setting for this account. I try to place them in the context of the lessons as a sequence; the organization of space and time; the teacher's concern with his purposes; the pupils' views of what they are doing when they practise science. Other issues could have been brought into focus, and may well be by those who read the paper. The account is in no way intended as a blueprint for a set of practices to guarantee good lessons, but rather is offered as an occasion for us to continue our own enquiry into our endeavours as teachers.

Working in the lab

What is described here is a sequence of lessons in physics experienced by a group of mixed-ability fourth-year boys at Sir William Collins School. The lessons dealt with speed, the measurement of speed, two-stroke and four-stroke engines, the kinetic theory of gases. The teacher of the class, Tony Hoskyns, usually plans a piece of work to last for about five weeks. The class has two one-hour physics lessons per week. This points to what I see as a major concern of the way this teacher works. As the boys are preparing for examinations, the teacher makes an initial decision about lesson topics with this in mind, but also draws upon his sense of the boys' interests. The boys have enough time to work on a project in a way that enables them to feel a responsibility for their own learning. To put it another way— for five weeks the boys know that they will be working in a particular area; the twice-weekly lesson is not a surprise given to the boys by the teacher—the rabbit out of the hat.

In the lessons on the measurement of speed, Tony Hoskyns had suggested to the class that they made trolleys. For this he provided wood, wheels, tools and a design for a trolley which he and another teacher had produced. In the eventual making of the trolleys the boys used the design simply as a guide, and adapted it considerably. How the materials were used depended on the discussions and decisions made by the boys themselves.

Initially the problem presented to the boys was—If we wish to measure speed, what kind of movement do we want our trolleys to make? Answer—straight movement. For two weeks boys worked together in groups of two or three, constructing trolleys, and afterwards fitting them with small diesel two-stroke motors (thus anticipating the topics to be looked at in the later stages of this lesson sequence). They were asked to measure the speed of their trolleys—first when pushed by hand and secondly when driven by motor.

During these lessons very little of what we usually take to be formal teaching or formal learning was taking place. To the layman the physics room probably looked more like a workshop than a science laboratory. Boys were grouped round the benches working on their constructions, or making an enormous row and smell in trying to start-up their two-stroke motors.

Overtly the boys were paying little attention to the problems of physics as such. Problems arose and were worked on in terms of getting the motors to start and keep going; making the trolleys strong enough to take the weight of a motor; adjusting weights to get the balance to make the trolleys run straight.

It was at this stage that I experienced my first dilemma as a researcher for the Oracy Project, committed to a notion that children, like adults, need the opportunity to talk out, to enquire. Many of the activities I've described took place without very much talk, or at least without the kind of talk that researchers usually offer as evidence of learning.

Yet when asked (in very much the way of their teacher who was visiting groups and asking), one group of boys told me readily that their motor would start once it had heated up; that once hot, it would keep going; that cutting down the supply of fuel would slow down the motor; and that the up-and-down movement of the piston turned the propeller.

How did the boys know all this when they had been given no formal teaching, but had simply been asked to make a trolley, measure its speed, and get their motors to work? One answer, I feel, lies in the teacher's trust of the boys' own common-sense. They were left to read the maker's instructions that came with their diesel motors; to spend time pushing the propellers to create the heat to get the motors going; to play with varying the fuel supply. At this stage, as indeed at any stage in their work, the boys could also consult their textbooks. At the beginning of the year, each boy is given a copy of the book *CSE Physics* by Nelkon, which he is asked to keep always at home, and which he is invited to use as and when he wishes. It becomes another resource, rather than a programme of learning.

Using resources in the course of problem-solving is, I think, well illustrated from the actual measuring of speed. Tony Hoskyns simply handed out clocks (second-timers) and a metre measure.

One group measured out a length of five metres on the floor and marked it in chalk. One boy propelled the trolley down this; a second boy operated the stop clock. Their problem was to get the trolley to go straight and it was one they did not solve until they saw a second group at work. The other group, on their own initiative, threaded through the trolley a piece of fine string, tied to a stool at one end and held taut by a boy at the other end. When they pushed their trolley it went along the straight line of the string, making the measuring of speed easy.

The blackboard note for the lessons on speed indicated: *speed* = *mt/sec*. The teacher assumed that the boys already knew about speed, and could make explicit this knowledge in measuring the speed of their trolleys, converting feet per second or miles per hour (their already familiar notion) into metres per second. The formula for speed was on the board then, but was not taught as such.

The boys would push their trolleys over the measured distance. A typical exchange between a boy and the teacher was:

B Just over a second for five metres (pause) five metres, 1.1 second.
T So what's the speed?
B Five metres in 1.1 seconds.

This I see as the teacher simply checking and affirming the boy's understanding of speed.

The second part of this sequence of lessons concerned heat, engines, and the kinetic theory of gases.

Pinned on the notice board was a paper, a guide for work for the boys, which read:

> *Unit:*
> *Heat. Engines.*
> *The Two-stroke Motor.*
>
> Diagram with parts
> How does it work?
> Advantages over four-stroke
> Disadvantages
> Kinetic theory of gases
> Petrol/diesel

Throughout the lessons concerned with this topic, an overhead projector was set up, showing a mobile transparency of a two-stroke engine (mobile so that the action of compression and combustion could be shown). This was then available for the boys to come and look at and work with as they needed to, either alone, or with a friend, or with the help of the teacher. The transparency showed in diagram form the essential parts and piston movements of the engine.

In the following exchange the teacher was working with a boy (B1) and was joined by a second boy (B2).

T Now if you look up on the board! How does it work?
   Just give me a minute on how it works.
   (The teacher then leaves the boy time to think.)
   (The boy calls over his friend, B2.)
B2 Four-stroke. I know it.
B1 It's a two-stroke.
B2 Two-stroke, it's just the same.
B1 How does it work then?
B2 Right. First of all the piston comes down, opens the inlet valve. In comes the fuel. They're both shut. The piston comes back up, compresses it. As the piston comes down the outlet valve opens and pushes it all out of the exhaust.
T That's the four-stroke, though.
B2 Aah—but they're the same principle.
T Yes, what actually happens? How does it work?
B2 On the two-stroke you haven't got a spark plug. A two-stroke ignites itself under pressure and you get a spark off the thing.
T Now just a second (turns to B1) can you give me a minute on how it works?
B1 (The boy uses the transparency as he talks.) Well, you see, it lets the air in and lets the fuel in and this comes up like this and ignites it.

T   Why does it heat up?
B1   Because of the pressure?
T   Because of the pressure inside here? (indicating)
B1   Yes
T   Fine.

What interests me in this exchange is the question of the rightness or wrongness of B2's knowledge—the question of his understanding. In looking at the model of the two-stroke engine he in fact talks about the four-stroke engine (only the four-stroke has valves, not the two-stroke).

What the boy insists upon is the principle behind the two kinds of engine. It seems to me that the teacher, by not saying to the boy 'you are wrong' accedes to this. The wrongness of the boy's explanation is in the detail. He does know well what an explanation of an engine requires: an account of piston movement and fuel ignition. Instead of having his explanation discredited, he is able instead to listen to B1, who does indicate clearly the two strokes of the two-stroke engine and the way in which fuel ignites. B1 in turn is not sure of this second point. The teacher, I feel, senses this, and so indicates the pressure chamber to remind the boy. It's an important bit of teaching smoothly incorporated into the boy's own explanation.

B1, along with many of the boys in the group, is also unsure about the petrol/diesel distinction, as the following exchange shows. The teacher and B1 are talking about the disadvantages of two-stroke engines. They are looking together at a duplicated sheet of information about engines, a further resource available in the physics rooms.

T   There's a tendency to overheat. Why do you think this is?
B1   It ain't sparking. It's heating up from the pressure inside there (indicating the pressure chamber).
T   This could have a spark-plug here just as easily.
B1   I know but that ain't made for a spark-plug is it?
T   Well this would be a two-stroke petrol engine, if it had a spark-plug up here, instead of a diesel. So we're comparing a two-stroke with a four-stroke. Why do you think it would overheat compared with a four-stroke? You do of course get this pressure cycle every two-strokes instead of every four strokes. So you're getting heating. . . .
B1   Twice as fast.
T   Right.

The boy then is not clear of the petrol/diesel distinction. But he has learnt that on the model in front of him there is no spark-plug and so the firing of the fuel and air is caused by pressure. His suggestion that this is what causes the engine to overheat is a plausible one, and in fact not entirely wrong. It needs only a bit of prompting by the teacher to point to the cause of the overheating: the *frequency* of the pressure cycle, and he can finish the explanation for himself.

The boys of course shared enquiry with each other as well as with the teacher. Here two boys are at work on a diagram of the parts of an engine:

B3   Bill, what's that called?
B4   Piston crank.
B3   Piston Rod.
B4   Piston Rod.
B3   What's that one?
B4   That's connected on to the crank shaft (pause) that is, yes that's the
     crank shaft. That's what's meant to be connected on to there really,
     because that's what pushes it. That's just there to measure it see—
     that's just a diagram. The piston rod is connected on to the crank
     shaft which makes the piston go up and down. See.

B3 is the one who starts the conversation by asking for clarification,
but I think we can argue that B4, in starting to answer B3, making
his own thinking clearer; is coming to name the parts properly; is
seeing that a diagram has to be read as such and isn't the real thing;
and is giving a very clear explanation of the connection between
crank and piston. The boy doesn't know what he knows, until he
says it. And this remains, perhaps, the single most powerful argument
for all kinds of classroom talk.

Writing in these lessons is linked to the talking that goes on, not
least because Tony Hoskyns is constantly talking through work that
the boys have written. In the task assigned, a boy would come to the
teacher when he had completed a stage in his writing. The teacher
then would read aloud to himself and to the boy, that particular
piece of work: 'At compression the molecules of air and fuel crash
into the sides of the cylinder and bounce back at the same speed.
This means that the molecules are elastic; when they bounce back,
they collide with other molecules, thus producing heat from the
collision.' Then followed the teacher's remark: 'Beautiful.' And later
from the same piece of writing:

T   'When the air and fuel is let in, the exhaust opens and some mixture
     goes out, so there isn't as much mixture being compressed as there
     would be in a four stroke'. Yes that's good, that's well put. (teacher
     remark)
     'This would mean that it wouldn't go as fast as a four-stroke engine.'
     Why wouldn't it go as fast as a four-stroke engine? (teacher question)
B5   Because there's not so much pressure inside.
T   Beautiful. Thank you very much indeed.

Here it seems writing takes its place not as a burden for teacher and
pupil, but as another occasion to share understanding. The boy here
could go away and add his point about pressure, arrived at in that
exchange. The writing, too, is treated not as teacher's way of testing
pupil knowledge, with all the misery for teacher and taught that that
involves, but as another resource among the many in the room that
two people can meet over. Each boy has an open-top clip-file in a
filing cabinet where completed work is banked, available for reference.

A group of the boys talked of the importance of writing for them as a way of checking their own understanding. In coming to write, they felt that they had to work out their ideas more clearly. Sometimes, they would go to the teacher with a problem, but sometimes, too, they could get a sense of what they didn't understand from trying to write.

Some of the boys, too, had a sense of the public nature of writing, and of science as a public discipline. As one boy said: 'If you didn't know what a thing is called—you wrote down that blue thing with the red knob on, they (whoever was referring to your work) wouldn't know. And you've got to know what you're talking about'.

Many of the boys did express a concern to get through exams, to get a job in which their physics would be useful—and a useful physics is one that is communicable with others. The teacher shares this point of view with the boys. Written work is brought along as a communication for people to share.

Still interested in seeing the work from the boys' point of view, I asked a group of them what they reckoned an experiment was. One boy said: 'An experiment to us is reality to the teacher because with us at first we're just trying it out. We don't know what's going to happen but the teacher knows what's going to happen and how it's going to happen. We've got to find how, what, when.'

If the teacher already knew, and if the boys knew that he knew, I wondered if they would not simply prefer to be told. 'No, we want to find out for ourselves,' one boy said. Another added: 'You've gone wrong somewhere, go and check it. He'll never tell you exactly.'

One boy talked of building a circuit: 'Building helps you understand. If you're just given it on a piece of paper you wouldn't know because you wouldn't know what went into building it.' Another boy explained: 'If you've done the experiment yourself and you know in your head that if the piston goes up, and it says well what happens when it goes up, well you think, well when it went up, it sparked and made it come back down, so it must compress when it goes up, and you'd work it out that way.'

What I want to argue from this is that the boys feel that being told something does not necessarily enable learning; that the knowledge in a teacher's head cannot simply be transmitted to the pupils' heads; that to understand, one has to be responsible for one's own enquiry; that science is about tackling problems.

From the boy's point of view, where does talk feature in all this? I asked: 'Does it help if you talk?'

'If everybody talks about what they're doing and how they're figuring it out, everybody takes an interest in everybody else.' And: 'Discuss between you, you get more and more to do it properly first time. There's an incentive to do it properly first time.'

Writing [1] Nancy Martin
Why write?

Every day in schools children write—in exercise books, in rough work books, on file paper, on worksheets. They write reports of experiments, essays about climate or causes or persons, stories, recipes, poems, occasionally journals; they write exercises and answers to questions on what they have just been told or read; they copy a great deal off the blackboard or from books. Why do they? What is all this writing for and what does it achieve?

When the Project team (Writing Across the Curriculum) asked pupils and students about their recent experience of writing in school we found, not surprisingly, that the teacher figures prominently in their recollections. He structures situations, he makes demands, he influences both implicitly and explicitly by his responses to what is offered. The teacher has his own ideas about what his subject is and what learning is and these inform his practice. He may be more or less aware of the criteria on which he bases his teaching but in either case his pupils soon know what pleases him. But what pleases the teacher, what he considers to be the appropriate language of his subject and the appropriate way of using it, may not be helpful— indeed may actually impede—the understanding of his pupils.

> Our history teacher used to make us put down—she gave us a load of facts to make into an essay. Well, I couldn't do that. When I was confronted with a whole list of facts I just couldn't do it and I failed my history exam and she told me I'd fail 'cos I couldn't do it. (Technical College Student)

> I knew what he was on about but I only knew what he was on about in my words. I didn't know his words. (Technical College Student)

> In my exams I had to change the way I learnt, you know. In all my exercise books I put it down the way I understood, but I had to remember what I'd written there and then translate it into what I think *they* will understand, you know. (Technical College Student)

The teacher as the only audience for the pupils' writing is a point which will be discussed later. Meanwhile, it is clear that if the teacher sees writing mainly as a means of recording and testing this will inevitably influence the expectations and attitudes of his pupils.

> . . . our lessons consisted entirely of bending pieces of glass over bunsen burners and copying down endless notes of dictation. Our involvement in the learning procedure can be measured by the accuracy of my notes. Every time he dictated punctuation I wrote down in long-hand, taking 'cover' instead of 'comma' so that a sentence might read: 'Common salt cover to be found in many kitchens cover is chemically made of sodium cover represented Na cover and chlorine cover represented Ch full stop.'

---

[1] This section refers to work undertaken by the Schools Council Writing Across the Curriculum project, and includes quotations from the book based on the project, *Language Policies in Schools*, Ward Lock Educational 1977. For a full list of the books based on the project, see page 303.

Dictation was similarly rife in other subjects. (College of Education Student)

In RS right up to the fifth year we were not allowed to make our own notes on the Apostles, everything was copied from the blackboard. This was a weekly exercise in neat writing and nothing else; we never discussed the work, nor was there any homework set. What I do not understand is why everybody passed the O level. Maybe there is some loose connection. (College of Education Student)

A major concern of some teachers was technical accuracy which took precedence—or so it seemed to the pupils—over content. Handwriting, spelling and punctuation were frequently referred to:

Girl 1: Well, mostly they just mark spellings and they're so involved in getting all the spelling right that they forget the story and there's so many papers to mark they can't go over it twice.

Girl 2: And they just make sure you've got the punctuation right and everything. (Third-year pupils)

The power of the teacher was dramatically illustrated by the recollections of some of the students who could remember clearly how a single remark by a particular teacher influenced their feelings about writing for months—even years—afterwards. Sometimes the effect seemed beneficial, sometimes not, but either way it seems that teachers may often underestimate the effect that their opinions can have on their pupils.

My first notion of the change in emphasis between junior and grammar school came when I had to write an essay on Neolithic man for my first piece of history homework. I started 'My name is Wanda and I am the son of the head man in our village.' The history master read it out to the rest of the class in a sarcastic voice—everybody laughed and I felt deeply humiliated. I got 3/20 for covering the page with writing. I hated history after that until the third year. (College of Education Student)

We also asked many teachers what they set writing for and what they thought it achieved. We received very varied answers which I think are representative both of the different ways teachers see the functions of the writing they set, and also of the varying purposes for which writing is used both in our society and in schools. Some idea of this span is illustrated in the following examples.

A science teacher said he used written work to provide a record of work done which could be learned. He thought the act of writing itself helped pupils to learn what had been presented to them. He said it had not occurred to him that writing might aid independent thinking and the making of connections by pupils. He reckoned this was done more appropriately in talk. A history teacher said: 'you can't arrive at judgements about evidence—which I take to be the aim of history teaching—without envisaging of all sorts. So I set a lot of writing about hypothetic situations and events and ask the pupils to place themselves in these. But they must have something to work on. So I do a lot of input teaching before they do this kind of writing. I am pleased with the results—as a history teacher.' Another history teacher said that independent writing (not notes) helped memory, clarified unfamiliar information and ideas and allowed the writer to discover what he thought and felt about the information.

Teachers of most subjects said they were concerned for their pupils to pass their examinations and they therefore set their pupils a good many written exercises involving written answers to comprehension questions and copying accurate information from the blackboard. Other teachers said, 'you have to survive. It's no good discussing what would be best. That won't help you on Monday morning when it's how to survive that matters. So I make them copy, or write answers.'

An English teacher said: 'they write to explore—themselves, their experiences—growing up—their reading—literature—and what they learn from their own writing of stories and poems. I ask them to write to help them learn—about themselves and about the world.'

A history teacher said about his first-year tutor-group 'What they think English is depends on what junior school they came from. Some of them thought it just consisted of handwriting and punctuation and spelling. "Are we going to do spellings everyday, Sir? Are we going to have a test everyday?" The other response was, well, it was creative writing. Already by 11, they've got it drummed into them what a subject involves. And it's very difficult to break them out of it.'

It is all there, in these documentations, if one has time and patience to unravel it. Teachers set written work to test, this is universally recognized and practised. After this the intentions vary, not so much by subject as by individual pedagogical philosophies. Writing is to record, to aid memory, to induce specific imaginings, to clarify information, to discover what one's knowledge and opinions are, to learn specific information, to explore the self and the world, to learn what the different subjects are by the kinds of writing the teachers demand—and as a means of class control.

Within these varied uses for writing one can detect different functions. There is an inner role which is concerned with learning and thinking, and an outer role which is to do with external features, the skills of presentation, paragraphing, punctuation, spelling, titles, spaces, underlining, etc. These skills carry powerful social prestige but would seem to have little to do with the inner role of using language for thinking. History may account in part for these differing aspects. When the majority of children had only elementary education the focus was on basic literacy—to read and to write with some measure of educated spelling and punctuation. With the coming of universal secondary education the focus began to change. Many more children began to move into further and higher education where good hand-writing and spelling were not enough. The student needed in addition to master the kinds of writing shaped by the thinking problems which he encountered. The Bullock Report is concerned with both these complementary aspects of writing. How is it that they are so often seen as polar opposites? The reason may perhaps be found in increased numbers of pupils who, since 1944, stay on till 16 to take public examinations. In a more affluent and socially mobile society most school students want the ticket of attainment offered by examinations, and the types of examinations that have been most widely developed in this country have put a premium on the giving back of information presented to the students by the teacher in accordance with a prescribed syllabus; furthermore, the fact that the students are examined by written answers has put a premium on writing of a certain kind, impersonal and classificatory. Thus, the shaping of writing by the thinking problems of the student has not been much in sight before the sixth form because the public examinations at 16 have not generally been concerned to test the pupils' capacity to think. There are, of course, some exceptions. Some of the CSE examinations have attempted to break away from this pattern of academic tennis (returning the ball of information served by the teacher), and most notably some science teachers and mathematics teachers have been aware of the long-term danger, and have developed programmes of work leading to specific examinations which have set out to test the student's capacity to use his knowledge in new situations, i.e. to think for himself. It is perhaps not insignificant that the Project team (Writing Across the Curriculum) has found more interest from science teachers in the ideas we were briefed to present and more cooperation in attempting to widen the range of writing available to school pupils than from any other subject group apart from those teaching English.

Writing, and Contemporary ideas about language

On the whole people tend to regard language as they regard breathing —something you take for granted until you notice something wrong with it. Thus language becomes something to be put right, cured, corrected; its active role in learning is not understood. Written work suffers particularly in this context. It is a visible product, there to be corrected, and while talk is, today, often seen as a useful part of the process of learning, writing is seldom seen as having this function. The written language of school pupils cannot be dealt with at anything but a superficial level without taking account of language more generally, when one is in a position to single out the features and problems peculiar to writing. At the risk of giving altogether too simplistic an account I want to try to identify those ideas about language which need to be understood if writing is to make a more effective contribution to learning.

First, there is the fact that language is learnt by use—by encountering it and using it in a variety of situations. It is therefore, important to note the difference between the use and the study of language. Essays, science reports, notes, stories, written accounts of all sorts are examples of use—in these, language is the means not the end. Study of word meanings, parts of speech, clause analysis, literary devices and style, analysis of texts and other matters of this kind undertaken by English teachers, are aspects of the study of language. Language is here the end as well as the means. There is no research that I know of at school level which shows that the *study* of language has any effect on how pupils *use* language, and much that shows it does not, and since these researches are fairly widely known many English teachers have given priority to experience of *using* language, whether it be in the form of purposive use or practice exercises.

Second, because language is closely linked with thought, the utterances which each individual constructs are outward expressions of his thinking and are therefore a crucial part of his learning. To assimilate new information and incorporate it into our existing knowledge we have to restructure it for ourselves in our own formulations. We have seen how children have expressed to the Project Officers their difficulties in learning in the words of their teachers. This is particularly true of younger children, and it is interesting to note that some of the special science programmes referred to above, advise that younger children write up the reports of their science work according to their own lights and not in a predetermined form. Thus, while notes copied or dictated may be the most effective way of getting children to learn specific material, or of maintaining control of the class, they rob children of opportunities to use the language as an aid to their own thinking. If teachers understand this dilemma they can solve it in terms of their own priorities.

Third, conversation is the most immediate and effective way for most people to penetrate and assimilate new knowledge. The feedback from others checks and expands one's own understanding. Consider the following example.

Keith Harvey is a probationary physics teacher. One of the Project team tape-recorded a group of children working together during one of his lessons. The pupils had previously done some worksheets on ways of measuring time. For this lesson they had been asked to bring a candle or jars and tins (which could be fixed together to make sand or water timers). Some of the pupils had had difficulty in deciding how to measure the amount that their candles had burned in a given time but it was clear that different candles had produced different results. This is a short extract from the end of the transcript.

Julie   Sir, Mr H. You wouldn't be able to make a reliable candle clock.
Teacher   Why?

Julie	'Cos both our candles burnt down different times. It depends on the candle.
Girl	Unless you buy the same candle.
Julie	Because her candle burnt slower than our candle.
Teacher	There's all sorts of things (indecipherable).
Julie	And the wind.
Teacher	And the wind, yeh.
Girl	Like the candles you put in candelabra last longer than these ones.
Teacher	Well, they're different thicknesses, aren't they?
Boy	No they're not, they're posher.
Teacher	What, they're made out of something else?
Girl	And then twisted. That's what I mean.
Voices	Yeh, those twisted ones. Burning slower
Girl	Yeh, because when we had a power cut two weeks ago we had a candle like that and one of them fancy ones in a candelabra. And the candelabra lasted longer than that one.
Julie	So it depends on the candle.
Boy	Those twisted ones do burn slower.
Teacher	I can't see why.
Boy	'Cos it has to go round the bend (Laughter).
Girl	It's a different wax, I suppose.

During the lesson there was a great deal of talk about the details of measuring and the variables that influenced their results. Now, with the teacher, these pupils are here reflecting on the implications of what they have been doing—and are bringing experiences from outside the lesson to bear too.

Keith Harvey commenting on the transcript said: 'I like practicals. I think you can get a lot more—not what you expect—but you get a lot more from the children. It seems to be a good way to teach children to think for themselves. I think the learning itself is far more diverse than simply having an objective. The objective here is connected with the idea of time and yet I'm sure they learned far more about candles—and general principles of exactly what they're doing. They're out on a limb—they haven't been told what to do.'

Fourth, in the absence of this kind of talk, expressive writing is a good substitute. Practical work and field studies by their very nature allow for exploratory talk as part of the operation, which might make exploratory written work redundant. But as this kind of talk is more difficult to organize in classrooms, personal, near-to-speech reflective writing will fulfil some of the functions of exploratory talk, and in addition provide opportunities for sustained reporting and reflection which talk does not. Here is another illustration concerning Sue Watts, a chemistry teacher. She asked her first year mixed-ability class to keep a diary of their work. These diaries are in addition to the record of experiments which the children keep. I quote from two of them.

Carol

Today we played another sort of guessing game on one of the benches we had three trays half full of water one was hot one was cold and the middle one was warm. first of all we put our hands into the cold and hot trays then after a minute we put our hands into the middle tray and they felt very different my right hand felt cold and my left hand felt warm but this was wrong because both of them should have felt the same because the water was all the same temperature. After we had done this we were given a thermometer and we found out the temperature of my fingers and my temperature is 35 °C.

Ann

In the science laboratory we have been looking at many different things, I was particularly interested in mercury and why it is so heavy. I once learned that you get mercury in a thermometre and that if you drop the thermometre and it smashes all the mercury will spread over the floor and turn into silver balls. You mustn't touch it because it is poisenous. My mother once dropped a thermometre when she was a child and that is how I know.

These diaries give the children the chance to reflect on what they are doing. Thus Carol thinks that it is 'wrong' that her two hands felt different in the same bowl of water. She is initiating a question about the relativeness of subjective judgements and her teacher will respond to this when she reads the diary. Ann selects the things she is 'particularly interested in' and brings together school knowledge and knowledge from other sources. Neither of these children could have initiated this reflective awareness of the work they have been doing in their formal reports. Both kinds of writing are important and have different functions within the subject area—in this case, science. The diary entries are like talk in some ways, though there is not the instant feedback that comes from discussion. On the other hand they give an opportunity for coherent and extended reflection which talk does not.

Many teachers have said to us—and pupils too—about this kind of writing, 'But that's English'. This is both sense and nonsense. It is sense in that everyone interprets the present in the light of expectations built up from past experience. In as far as school experience has taught both teachers and children that different kinds of writing are, in school, associated with different subjects, they are right, but in the world, language alters according to the situations of which it is a part, i.e. what it is intended to do, and who it is for—so the diaries being primarily for the writer with the teacher as a subsidiary interested reader, are different in purpose and audience from the formal reports. Neither is functionally peculiar to science or to English.

A school-wide view of writing activities

One of the features of the subject organization of secondary schools is that teachers of one subject have only the haziest ideas of what goes on in other subjects. A valuable result of the Committee's recommendation with regard to language policies is that teachers have begun to look at the overall picture of language activities in their schools. A recent sample offered by a school to the Project team for discussion was a surprise to the staff. It consisted of all the writing done in one week by three school pupils of varying abilities from three different classes. Each pupil was found to have done: (1) a piece of independent, extended writing for English, set after class discussion but free to be treated in any way; (2) notes or extended pieces copied from the blackboard; (3) answers to comprehension questions on the blackboard or on worksheets. (2) and (3) covered history, geography, European studies, religious education, and science. So a bird's eye view of written language activities offered to these three classes in one week showed a very narrow range, with five-sixths of the writing (coming from five subjects) giving the pupil little or no chance to use his own language, or to write extended prose as distinct from short answers. *No teacher pursuing his own teaching conscientiously was aware of the heavy weighting in one direction which the total picture revealed.*

Given that teachers are beginning to ask how much and what kinds of language there should be, it is clear that they need some tool of analysis. Teachers need to look at the part played by language in their lessons and communicate this to each other, then the first steps towards a language policy will have been taken. To develop a useful policy further, teachers of all subjects must then be prepared to incorporate in their thinking the sort of knowledge about language and its import for learning which has been indicated in this book. What are the implications for writing?

The writing research models of discourse

The writing research team, funded by the Schools Council to investigate the development of writing abilities at the secondary level was faced with essentially the same problem as teachers examining language use across the curriculum; they asked themselves the same questions—what kinds of language should pupils have opportunities to use? Are some kinds more important than others to the pupils' learning? Are some kinds more difficult to acquire? What are the circumstances most favourable to acquisition?

A first step in attempting to answer such questions was to survey a wide sample of school writing (2,000 scripts). To do this and to describe them we developed a model of mature written discourse. We assumed that the socializing effect of school would cause school writings to approximate—more or less—to adult models, though we did not discount the possibility that we might find some writing which existed only in schools. This model allowed us to place each piece of student writing at some point on one of two scales; not scales of quality, but scales of (1) function and (2) a sense of audience—what the writing was for and who it was for. Though other dimensions might be examined, these we felt, were of primary importance in affecting what and how the writer wrote. Models are developed for particular purposes and we were seeking a model which would allow us to classify school writings by other categories than those of subject and thereby enable us to study the comparable intellectual problems which would be, we predicted, reflected in the writing from various subjects. These would be masked, as they are in practice today, if we viewed various kinds of writing as being proper only to various subjects. We thought that intellectual growth transcended subject boundaries and we should be able to trace this more generally by looking at kinds of writing across the curriculum since verbal–mental operations such as report, explanation, argument, classification, comment, narrative, etc. are not peculiar to any one subject.

1. *The Function model.* First, then, the Function model was designed to help us look at what writing is for. This is not exactly the same as a writer's purpose because our culture has itself developed distinct language forms which are typically associated with certain situations. We know quite well, for instance, when we are in a story, or a sermon, or being persuaded to buy something—because we have internalized these kinds of language from our day-to-day encounters with them. When children come to write in similar situations they draw on their pool of language experience which helps them to know what kind of language to use in certain types of situation. For instance, no-one teaches children in an infant class to begin their stories 'Once upon a time', or 'Once there was a little pig . . .' but most of them do this because this beginning is so obviously a 'marker' of stories which they have listened to or read.

The boundaries are by no means hard and fast but it has been found possible and useful to distinguish three broad categories of function to which recognizably distinct kinds of writing belong. What distinguishes them is that writer and reader mutually recognize the conventions that distinguish one 'job' from another. It is true that there are often linguistic differences but these are the markers of the different functions whose essential difference lies in the sort of things the writer takes for granted about his reader's responses. To take a simple example, if we read 'Once upon a time there was a flying horse' we know the writer is taking it for granted that we recognize a story and shall not quarrel about whether horses can fly.

Our model distinguishes three main 'recognized and allowed for' functions of writing, EXPRESSIVE, TRANSACTIONAL, and POETIC.

THE EXPRESSIVE FUNCTION

The central term of the model is taken from Edward Sapir,[1] who pointed out that ordinary face-to-face speech is directly expressive

[1] E. Sapir, *Culture, Language and Personality*, University of California Press, 1961.

and carries out its referential function in close and complex relationship with that expressive function. Since much writing by young children is very like written-down speech we described the expressive function as that *in which it is taken for granted* that the writer himself is of interest to the reader; he feels free to jump from facts to speculations to personal anecdote to emotional outburst to reflective comment as he wishes, feeling that none of it will be used against him. It is all part of being a person *vis-à-vis* another person. It is the means by which the new is tentatively explored, thoughts may be half-uttered, attitudes half-expressed, the rest being left to be picked up by a listener or reader who is willing to take what is expressed in whatever form it comes, and the unexpressed on trust.

The Writing Research Team said: 'The more we worked on this idea of the expressive function, the more important we felt it to be. Not only is it the mode in which we approach and relate to each other in speech, but it is also the mode in which, generally speaking, we frame tentative first drafts of new ideas. By analogy with these roles in speech it seemed likely to us that expressive writing might play a key role in a child's learning. It must surely be the most accessible form in which to write, since conversation will have provided the writer with a familiar model. Furthermore, a writer who envisages his reader as someone with whom he is on *intimate* terms must surely have very favourable conditions for using the process of writing as a means of exploration and discovery.'

We quote in illustration three examples taken from metal-work, middle school science and social studies which contain many of the features of expressive writing. The first is an excerpt from a long account of a project in metal-work by a boy of twelve.

The becoming of a gnat killer
the name Gnat Killer came to me after the project for maths I had been doing, you see I was going to do a project to see how many people spelt Gnat rong they ither spell it Kat, Gnate, Knate, Knatte, and even Knatt. well when I started to do my project, I thought well I will call it the Gnat then Killer came into my mind because I am mad on Horror. So I called it the Gnat Killer, it may sound violent but it isn't well at least I don't think, it is only another name been created to the world for the perpose of a project, I dont know if my turnin two the dictionary, it will read

> Gnat Killer
> name for
> a dagger used
> by Ricky Baker
> in 1972 8th dec:
> (not spelt nat killer)
> in italics:

that is only my idear thoe not that it will work.

In the second case, the children watched an egg hatching in the science lab. They were asked to write about it in any way they liked.

We quote two examples to show the variation in perceptions and focus.

The Chick Hatching (In the science lab.)
The egg was begginning to crack, the chick inside was using all the strength it had to get out from being trapped inside the shell. I thought to myself, if just I could get a knife and crack the shell gently, then I could see what the chick look like. I kept seeing bits of the chicks wing as it was slowly cracking. The chick was gradually pushing it's way out, but could not go no further, because the other eggs were in the way, so our science teacher (Mr bowman) gently lifted the lid of the incubator and the egg that was cracking was moved away from the other eggs, Now the chick was not having such a struggle. you could see it pushing up against the top of the shell, and then going down for a rest. I said to Mr bowman will the chick be hatched by the time the bell goes, and mr bowman took it as a joke, put his head down to the incubator and said will you be hatched by the time the bell goes." don't worry the chick did not reply.
The chick was just about hatched now, all it had to do was struggle out of the top of the shell, it was just about out, as it got out all the class shouted, "it's out!
It was just standing up properly, with all it's feather's sticking up on end, it looked around in wonder, when the bell went and mr bowman but the lid back on the incubator.

'*The Egg . . .*'
The egg begins to hatch, the crowd of children cluster around the humid inqubator. The egg cracks about 3cms, the egg tooth on the chick's beak can be spotted, the chick pants as he catches his first breath of fresh air then he goes back to work the egg opens about another centermeter then the chick lays back gasping for air it rests for about a minite then on it goes to crack the egg it pants and gasps catchies abreath then back to work in about ten minutes the egg is hatched the chick's feathers are wet and flat and the chick lays panting in about two minits time he is stood up then the feathers begin to dry off and fluff up then it becomes steaddy and soon enough it will be walking around.

The third is an excerpt from a fourth-year boy's account of his work in social studies. Of his project on 'The British political system' he writes:

This was the first big project I did and now when I look at it I marvel at how pathetic it is . . . I have placed emphasis on the wrong things and made all the mistakes I was warned about . . . so it ended up in my eyes as a great failure. But I have learnt more from that project than any other piece of work I have ever done at school so it was only a failure in terms of what it was, not what was learnt from it. I learnt not only how to improve my work from this project but believe it or not I also learnt a great deal more than I already know about the British political system although most of it is not in the project.

These writings have many of the features that characterize speech— the utterances stay close to the speakers, reflecting the ebb and flow of thought and feeling, and like speech this expressive language is always on the move. It moves according to the demands of what it is for—all are towards the transactional in that they are giving information—what the reader wants to hear, and how the writer's language resources allow him to meet these demands—his own and other people's. All three would seem to have the self as audience and also their teacher whom they believed when he told them to write as they wanted. In addition Ricky Baker and the fourth-year boy had some vague sense of a wider audience in that they knew their writing was for someone at London University to read.

THE TRANSACTIONAL FUNCTION
The transactional function is that *in which it is taken for granted* that the writer means what he says and can be challenged for his writing's truthfulness to public knowledge, and its logicality; that it is sufficiently explicit and organized to stand on its own and does not derive its validity from coming from a particular person. So it is the typical language in which scientific and intellectual inquiry are *presented* to others (not necessarily the kind of language in which these activities are carried out); the typical language of technology, trade, planning, reporting, instructing, informing, explaining, advising, arguing and theorizing—and, of course, the language most used in school writing. It can be more or less expressive too, but the more familiar the writer is with the information, or the arguments or whatever, the easier it is to respond to the demand of explicitness and the less is the need for expressive features.

Ian was in the same metal-work class as Ricky. His project was a brass dish and he wrote a long piece about brass and how you work it and how he made his dish; but, although there are expressive features in his writing, his purpose is firmly transactional. He feels himself to be knowledgeable about brass and sets out to *inform* his readers. The differences between his piece and Ricky's (quoted above) illustrate the differences between writing that is focused on a transaction and writing following the free flow of the writer's thoughts and feelings.

About Brass
Brass is an yellow alloy of copper and zinc in varying proportions with quantities of lead tin and iron brass is very malleable, fusible ductile and readilly cast and machined, Muntz or yellow metal is a variety of brass containing 60% copper, As it resists corrosion well, it is largely used for shop propellors, bows and fittings, corrosion means rusting away.
Some examples of what brass can make:
1. electrical fixtures
2. unexpensive jewelry
3. metal decorations
4. table lighter
5. trombone
6. screws

7. marine hardware
A percentage table

copper	60%
brass	37%
white alloy	3%
	100%

In the famous Praha football stadium, nearly everything in side the walls are made out of copper including the goalpost, the team that play here are Sparta Prague. Mallable means easy to work with, and very dicible.

THE POETIC FUNCTION

This function is that *in which it is taken for granted* that 'true or false?' is not a relevant question at the literal level. What is presented may or may not in fact be a representation of actual reality but the writer takes it for granted that his reader will *experience* what is presented rather in the way he experiences his own memories, and not *use* it like a guidebook or map in his dealings with the world—that is to say, the language is not being used instrumentally as a means of achieving something, but as an end in itself. When Huck Finn said all Tom Sawyer's great stories were lies he was mistaking the function of the stories (the poetic function) and operating the 'rules' of the other 'game'—the transactional. So a reader *does* different things with the transactional and poetic writings: he uses transactional writing, or any bit of it, for any purpose, but who can say what we 'do' with a story or a poem that we read, or a play we watch? Perhaps we just share it with the writer; and not having to 'do' anything with it leaves us free to attend to its formal features—which are not explicit —the pattern of events in a narrative, the configuration of an idea and, above all, the pattern of feelings evoked: in attending in this non-instrumental way we experience feelings and values as part of what we are sharing. The term 'poetic' is used here in a narrower and more specific sense than in its general usage. We use it here in the sense of the Greek from which it was derived to mean 'created'. Its examples in school use are the stories, poems and plays which children write.

In the context of these function categories it is perhaps worth drawing attention to the ways in which knowledge—and, by implication, learning—in secondary and higher education is organized; systematically by subject disciplines and presented in the explicit, often specialized and generally formal language of those who know to those who are beginning to know. In contra-distinction the kind of knowledge (and way of learning) that goes on outside school is random, unsystematic and may or may not be linked by the learner to school knowledge. The bridge between systematic and unsystematic knowledge would seem to be the learner's own language, his own formulations which are the means by which he incorporates the

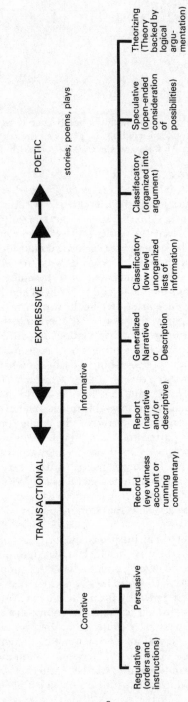

TRANSACTIONAL EXPRESSIVE POETIC

stories, poems, plays

Conative
- Regulative (orders and instructions)
- Persuasive

Informative
- Record (eye witness account or running commentary)
- Report (narrative and/or descriptive)
- Generalized Narrative or Description
- Classificatory (low level unorganized lists of information)
- Classifacatory (organized into argument)
- Speculative (open-ended consideration of possibilities)
- Theorizing (Theory backed by logical argumentation)

new into his existing corpus of knowledge. Most people do this by talk, but in school the expressive and poetic functions of writing give children opportunities to recognize and evaluate new knowledge and new experiences and thereby gain self-knowledge.

Our transactional category clearly needed to be broken down in terms of the kind of transaction undertaken, since the great majority of school writings are in this category. If teachers want to gain some idea of the range of writing opportunities that their pupils are getting *across the curriculum* the diagram we used is one way of enabling them to do this.

To quote from *The Development of Writing Abilities*,[1] 'This, then, is the broad picture, and taking the view currently being put forward that linguistic competence embraces rules of two very different kinds, grammatical rules and "rules of use", we suggest that the expressive function may mark out an area in which rules of use are at their least demanding, an area of comparative freedom in this respect. Thus, it may be that, as a writer moves from the expressive into the transactional, he increasingly takes over responsibility for rules of use that, in sum total, constitute one kind of order, one mode of organisation by which we encode experience—the cognitive order described by psychologists and codified into laws of logic by the philosophers. And it may be that, as a writer moves from the expressive to the poetic, he takes on responsibility for rules of use that represent, in sum, a different kind of organisation: one that we can recognise in a work of art, while at the same time we know little about the general principles that govern it.

'All this has obvious bearings upon our developmental hypothesis. From the area of least demand as far as rules of use are concerned, the learner-writer progresses by increasingly recognising and attempting to meet the demands of both transactional and poetic tasks, and by increasingly internalising forms and strategies appropriate to these tasks from what he reads and incorporating them into the pool of his resources: thus in the course of time he may acquire mastery of both varieties of rules of use.

'There exists always, of course, an alternative hypothesis: if you limp about long enough in somebody else's language, you may eventually learn to walk in it.'

2. *A sense of audience: the child and his reader.* The notion of audience, like that of function, has powerful implications for school writing in spite of the fact that almost all of it is produced for one sort of reader —the teacher. What makes for differences between the pieces of writing is not, objectively, who the reader is, but how the writer *sees* his reader; and children see their teachers in very different ways. Not only may different children's views of the same teacher vary, but a child may see his teacher as a different sort of reader on different

[1] Britton *et al.*, *The Development of Writing Abilities (11–18)*, Macmillan's Research Series, 1975.

occasions. Furthermore, the process of writing is more complicated even than this suggests. The monitoring self is always a part of a writer's sense of audience, as well as those others—the class, friends, examiners sometimes, parents perhaps, and a shadowy 'public'— who lurk behind his shoulder. In speech the actual or potential feedback from the listener continuously modifies what is said because the audience is physically present and sooner or later will speak too and thereby modify what you say next. In writing there is no such feedback, but somewhere, out of the direct focus of attention, a sense of an audience remains, ready to take shape when summoned, or stepping forward uncalled. We think it likely that one reason for the great amount of inert, inept writing produced by school students is that the natural process of internalizing the sense of audience, learned through speech, has been perverted by the use of writing as a testing or reproductive procedure at the expense of all other kinds of writing. When a writer's focus is on returning as exactly as possible what he has been given, the sense of any other audience, including the monitoring, reflective, independent self, disappears, leaving incomprehension, resentment or despair, or alternatively the satisfaction of producing something to satisfy someone else's demands. We think the following conversation throws light on some of these matters.

Andrew (a third-year boy) is talking to one of the project officers who knows his school and his teachers well. They are talking about Andrew's humanities project on 'The industries and populations of towns' and are referring to an anecdote he had included about slavery:

BN   There's an anecdote about a grave . . . it was something about slaves —it was something about, er, in a cemetery near Harlow there's a gravestone which says on it 'Here lies so-and-so, the property of somebody-or-other . . .' How did you find that out?

A   Well, we just moved—'cos we don't live far from that end, we'll go to church fairly often, and, we went round to see that church 'cos we saw it from the road and I like looking at gravestones and that and I saw it sort of fitted in with that.

BN   And who are you asking the question of 'Rather unusual to put on a grave, don't you think?'

A   Well, that's to anyone who reads it.

BN   Do you think of your reader?

A   Yea

BN   Who do you think of?

A   Anyone who reads it. Mainly Sir, 'cos he reads it. And anyone else.

BN   But I mean, when you put a thing like that, or your jokes, do you think to yourself 'How will Mr S . . . react' or do you think in more general terms, how will anybody react—you know?

A   More general, I think, how would anyone.

BN   You do? So you're not just thinking of him.

A   Oh, no.

BN   Would you, I mean, it's kind of a bit odd because you say that mostly these just get stockpiled, you know, so they're not read by anyone else normally.

A   Not really, no. But we're always told to write it as though we're trying to explain to someone else of our own age—so we just get used to it.

BN   So you do it, I mean you do actually think of other people reading it even though you don't expect them ever to do it?

A   Yea, that's how we have to. They always write out 'as if to someone of your same age', and you've got to tell them about it. . . .

BN   In some of these things you give your opinions, don't you?

A   Oh yea, most of it.

BN   You like giving your opinions, do you?

A   Yea

BN   Do you very often get asked for them?

A   Mostly, yea. Especially in this subject. (Some talk about the humanities projects of the class.)

BN   It looked to be as though you were looking for the chance to give your view.

A   Well, perhaps, yea . . .

BN   This is a bit you wrote about *To Sir, With Love*, you said 'On reading this section from the book . . . I felt thoroughly annoyed to think that those businessmen wanted a man for the job but when they found that he was coloured, they rejected him and what was more annoying was that those men probably gave the position to a less intelligent white man.' That was just how you began. So already you're expressing an attitude—you're saying what you think about it.

A   Yea. I don't think we were asked to put our opinion on that but I was annoyed. When I usually do something, I always position myself as the person like now, I mean I was treating myself as the coon who got turned down.

It seems that Andrew, in his writing, takes account both of his actual audience—his teacher—and some potential wider audience. Earlier in this conversation he had said that he often puts jokes in his writing because his teacher enjoys them and he himself likes them. This seems near to a trusted adult audience, which we think the most fruitful in developing writing ability because it allows a writer to experiment with safety. Andrew also understands the convention which requires him to write *as if for* some particular audience—'they always write out "as if to someone of your own age", and you've got to tell them about it'; and he understands that this convention allows him to express his own opinions and feelings within the framework of the 'as if' situation.

We have found an increasing number of teachers who have tried to create situations involving an audience other than themselves— real or imagined—as a context for the writing they have asked their pupils to do. On the whole this tends to come from teachers concerned with the humanities. In the sciences and among older students there is perhaps an unspoken sense that this is a device for younger children or for less serious students, yet the American psychologist George Kelly in a paper called 'The language of hypothesis' describes an attitude and a corresponding use of language which would help to bridge the gap between the known and the unknown. Kelly calls this the use of the invitational mood. He says that at moments of risk we would be greatly helped if we deliberately abandoned the indicative mood and operated in the invitational mood with its language form, 'let us suppose . . .'. He says that this procedure suggests that things are open to a wide range of constructions and 'there is something in stating a new outlook in the form of a hypothesis that leaves the person himself intact and whole'. When students reflect on their work or even report what they know, they put themselves at risk in terms of their teacher audience, or any audience for that matter, and we would stress the value of the invitational mood both with regard to a hypothetical audience as well as hypothetical ideas. We quote an example here because the 'as if' situation is directly one of audience, 'Suppose that you wanted to explain what diffusion is to a younger child who has not done any science and does not know what molecules are':

Explaining diffusion (Frances, 14)
We all know that gases are invisible, in other words we can't see it there but it is present. Gases are made up of molecules, for the moment let us call molecules 'marbles'. These marbles are present in solids as well, but here they are squeezed together and are unable to move. But in a gas the marbles (which cannot be seen with the human eye, only with an electronic microscope) move about freely and do not move in one specific direction, they move at random. . . .

This, of course, was an 'exercise', but it was also a game played by the children and the teacher—a combined knowledge and language game. The pupils had to manipulate their knowledge and their language to serve an audience other than themselves and their teacher, and, as their teacher observed, you only really understand ideas like these when you can play with them—supposing this, and supposing that, in Kelly's terms.

Our next examples come from situations where the writing was directed to real audiences other than the teacher. First, the *Cleveland Evening Gazette*, where the English adviser arranged for the paper to carry a weekly feature page, 'Report from the Cleveland classrooms'. A different school would be responsible for the page each week. This feature would run for six or seven weeks, and then be picked up again later in the year if it interested the readers. One issue was contributed by pupils of a sixth-form college. The page carried reports, a story—'What a north-east town might be like when the iron and oil had run out'—opinions and a poem).

Continuously, monotonously,
the tall concrete towers

Churn out clouds of never ending smog.
As time goes by,
Slowly the whole landscape
will become engulfed by a
network of structural steel,
While beneath this mechanical mass
Life still goes on.
Life without aim,
Life without meaning,
Just one repetitive day after day.
Each morning, men of all ages,
Hurry to their industrial employment.
Karen Robson

We include below the categories of a sense of audience which the Writing Research team devised to help them in their descriptions of school writing:
child (or adolescent) to self
child (or adolescent) to trusted adult
pupil to teacher as partner in dialogue
pupil to teacher as examiner or assessor
pupil to other pupils, or peer groups
writer to his readers, or public audience.

The two models of 'Function' and 'A Sense of Audience' make it possible for us to look at the range of writing which children are doing in all their school work; and it allows us to be quite precise about the development of their ability to write appropriately for different purposes and different audiences which was how we defined progress.

'Development is to a large extent a process of specialisation and differentiation: we start by writing the way we talk to each other — expressively, and envisaging as our reader a single, real, known person; gradually we may acquire, *in addition*, the capacity to use the transactional and the poetic, and to write for an unspecified, generalised or unknown audience. Further, this differentiation ideally occurs as a result of coming to hold those adult purposes for which the mature forms of writing have been evolved, and of learning to anticipate the needs of different and remoter audiences. So the development of writing abilities is partly conditional on the more general development of the child out of egocentrism; but that general development may itself be aided by the practice of writing.

Yet, the findings of our survey showed that the range of kinds of writing that children have opportunities to use in the secondary school narrowed drastically as they moved from year one to year seven. The dominant kind of writing was classificatory for an examiner audience. James Britton (*et al.*, 1975) commenting in the Research Report says:

If, as we had predicted, the development of writing abilities showed itself as a growing range of kinds of writing shaped by thinking processes, we should have expected to find in the sample a great deal of expressive writing in the early years, in all subjects (instead of the 6% we actually found), and an increase in the later years of classificatory, speculative and theoretical writing, as well as persuasive and poetic—all these compensating for a reduction in the expressive; and at the same time, a proportion of expressive writing maintained and developing into its maturer forms and purposes.

It would appear, however, that the pressures to write at a classificatory level of the informative—and in the main for an audience of the teacher as examiner—were great enough to inhibit early expressive writing and to prevent all but minimal development into the more abstract levels of the informative; strong enough at the same time to cut down drastically in the seventh year the output of the poetic. We believe an explanation for this unexpected narrowing of the range must be sought *in the whole curriculum and its objectives* [author's italics]. The small amount of speculative writing suggests that, for whatever reason, curriculum aims did not include the fostering of writing that reflects independent thinking; rather, attention was directed towards classificatory writing which reflects information in the form in which both teacher and textbook traditionally present it.

The Writing Across the Curriculum project team—and many of the teachers they worked with—have this to say about these findings:

Writing (like talk) organises our picture of reality, and, at the same time and by the same process communicates it to someone else. It is true that for educational purposes the first is more relevant than the second: we ask children to write so that they will organise their world picture, not so that we can learn things from them. But it is a fact of life that we can't have one without the other. Language *has* two faces and we are well advised to take account of both. The moral we draw from this is that, if we want writing to be a means of thinking and of active organising, we must make sure that the writer feels he has a genuine communication to make and is not merely performing an exercise—which was how David, aged thirteen, saw it: he said, 'You write it down just to show the teacher that you've done it, but it doesn't bring out any more knowledge in you.'

'Genuine communication' for a child, in whatever context—writing for history, English, science, a letter, a diary—is very often going to mean an inseparable blend of giving an account of the topic and expressing a response to it. If this is so, we should accept the mixture; if we discourage the personal element in it, we risk making writing an unwieldy and alien instrument instead of a natural extension of the child's own mental processes. And accepting it means more than simply allowing it to happen: it means agreeing to be communicated with in that way and making ourselves a real audience to a child by giving an authentic response to the communication as a communication rather than by giving back an evaluation of how well he has accomplished the task.

What emerged from the Project, 'Writing Across the Curriculum'

The Project team reported what seemed to us the most significant things that emerged from four years' work with teachers in schools. We identified also some deep dilemmas which teachers will need to resolve for themselves in the light of both their individual priorities, and the school priorities arrived at by collective discussion and decisions.

'We observed that the examples of children's written and spoken language which seemed to reveal language operating as an agent of thinking came from individuals or small groups of teachers who were interested in our research and made use of it. They did not generally represent changes in the work of a whole class, let alone a whole school. We therefore began to suspect that the changes we found were 'exceptions' or 'isolated cases'. We think these children were probably already 'committed' to learning and therefore responded most positively to enlarged opportunities. We think the majority of the children remain generally uncommitted.

If this is right it means that special programmes for this or that will have little effect. This hypothesis suggests that every piece of writing (and the circumstances that gave rise to it) represents a network of past experience, relationships and expectations linked to a continuum of other such networks. We have attempted to identify what have emerged for us as the most significant features in these webs of learning and language. But, as might be expected, the items which we see as significant are themselves networks. This interrelatedness throws light on why efforts by individual teachers to make a change here or a change there have only resulted in what we have referred to as 'isolated cases' of progress. We think changes have to be more wide-spreading to be effective.' We summarized the chief enabling or disabling features in the circumstances from which school writings arise as follows:

1. *How a learner sees himself.* His view of himself as a school student depends a great deal on how his teachers see him. How his teachers respond to his efforts, or lack of effort, depends in turn upon how the teacher sees *himself*, and his view of his role as a teacher is closely related to his view of learning. When we look at language in these contexts we find the kinds of experience and of language reckoned appropriate to the classroom is closely related to the teacher's view of learning and his role relationships to his pupils.

2. *A writer's sense of audience.* We think it likely that one reason for the great amount of inert, inept writing produced by school students is that the natural process of internalizing the sense of audience, learned through speech, has been perverted by the use of writing as a testing or reproductive procedure *at the expense of all other functions of writing.*

3. *Assessment and criticism*. The most dramatic changes in writing that we observed came when teachers moved out of their role as examiner into the role of an adult consultant. The unresolved problem remains —at what points in children's engagement in the process of writing does advice and criticism assist rather than divert? (See the analysis of phases made by Medway and Goodson in the pamphlet *Language and Learning in the Humanities*)'

4. *The role of everyday language in learning*. The things we choose to put into words, and the words which come to hand to express these meanings reflect our unique interpretations of experience. We need to begin by accepting and encouraging children's own language whatever it may be. Particularly in the written language this view collides with some notions of 'correctness'.

5. *Conditions for moving into good transactional writing*. (a) These occur where circumstances encourage the interplay of first-hand and secondary experience. The validity of first-hand experience and/or reflection in writing about history or science for example is generally ignored. (b) There should be opportunities for pupils to encounter good and varied 'models' of transactional language—to be encountered rather than imitated. Generally such 'models' are limited to textbooks.

Changes in notions of progress in learning and language

With a group of science teachers we kept returning to creative thinking and creativity. With a comparable group of humanities teachers the central issue was co-operative learning. We see these as related, and also related to the constraints on intention and choice which arise from general school procedures. We think that these are important in getting more children to commit themselves to learning. We also think for such commitment to happen on a wider scale than our observed 'isolated cases', whole environments for learning need to be changed, and for this to happen there need to be enough teachers in a school who share a view about learning and language to create a different set of possibilities in the school.

How these observations have been reflected in our most recent work with teachers

1. We have moved towards case studies
(a) of individual children, their writing, transcripts of their talk and conversations with them about their writing, reading and other work.

(b) of particular teachers—transcripts of their lessons, and of conversations with them.

(c) of exam work in a particular school.

2. In work with teachers we have arranged more workshops run by teachers of different subjects which put us all in learning situations. Transcripts and discussions of what was going on for each of us, and subsequent extrapolation to classroom situations have all been fruitful.

3. Our focus has been shifted from spending the available time on the research findings and their implications to getting teachers to plan and subsequently report back on specific steps they can take to get discussions going in their particular schools about learning and language, and to plan joint action where channels for collaboration exist. Essentially we needed to shift the initiative from us to them.

4. Teachers who had worked with us for some time were able to take this lead in meetings. Reports and suggestions from them were generally more effective than presentations from the Project team. Research findings became less important and the outcomes of teachers reflecting on their work more important.

How teachers can cope

Let us look briefly at the sharpest of the dilemmas which these findings present for teachers. There are three that I should like to draw special attention to.

1. *Intention.* Teachers have intentions, aims, objectives etc. for their pupils; their pupils have them too. Where they coincide conditions for learning are probably at their best. In *Writing and Learning* we wrote:

'Intention is said to be the motivating force for thinking as well as action, so creativity (in a very general sense) would seem to be related to intention. This seems a long way from creative writing, dance-drama and work in the art room which is, perhaps, where many people would locate creativity in school. But it is clearly absurd to believe that creative thinking can be attached in this way to a limited number of activities. We needed to look at creativeness more generally and our 'across the curriculum' brief forced us to do this. In discussing problems of commitment to learning we kept returning to intention and the kind of environments which would permit it and sustain it. Young children are curious and persistent and eager. One could call intention robust at this stage. In the secondary school it is, for whatever reason, a delicate thing. If it exists in relation to school work at all, it is easily snuffed out, or it drifts away, or is superseded by another feeble interest, but since so much of schooling pays such limited attention to children's intentions it is not surprising that creative thinking or creativity don't flourish, or at best merely survive in those activities that are least susceptible to other people's programming—improvised drama or writing poems for instance.

It is unfortunate that paying attention to children's intentions has become equated in many people's thinking with giving children sole responsibility for what they do. Clearly before most of us can exercise any choice of what we do, we need to know what the possibilities are, so it is not a simple matter of lessons structured by the teachers versus unstructured lessons in which pupils do what they like, but a much more complex operation of a teacher building opportunities for pupils' reflection, choice and self-direction into the overall intention of his own scheme for a series of lessons. The following piece of writing by a first year girl for her science teacher seemed to us to illustrate both the way in which children need to be made aware of the possibilities in the work they are learning and also the value of opportunities in the work they have done.

> *The most interesting things I have done in science at school*
> The best piece of Science I have do so far is the experiment with water the first experiment we did with water we had different kinds of water like pond, Canal, Destiled, tap water. With the water we added a soap flake to each sample of water. And if it bubbled a lot we had to tick it on the chart. After we did that piece of work we had to find out were the water in our taps came from. The next experiment we had to do with water was called water and floating. With this we had things like a cork, Glass, block of wood, foam, copper, stone, polystyrene and we had to float them and on our chart we had to tick off what it did. The thing I liked about this work was that we were experimenting and finding things out for selfs by doing this work.

Of course the problems become more acute as children move up the secondary school where the bulk of school knowledge is transmitted through the written language in its transactional forms. Reading books and writing attract increasing attention and most students find both difficult. We think it important to say that we found that project work, where it was well done, gave by far the most opportunities for students to make their own sense out of new information, to re-structure it to fit into their own expanding world picture, and to remain at the centre of their own learning. In short, pupils need more opportunities for their own choices, self-direction and self-criticism, within a framework of guidance and criticism by their teachers.

2. *The conflict between children's own language and the pressures for them to use 'correct' English.* We suggest that this topic needs much discussion between members of school staffs. One solution might be to distinguish between things that children write which are essentially their own learning operations (using their own formulations and expressions) on the one hand, and on the other hand the things that they write which are presentations of information for other people (these being as 'correct' as possible). A teacher will function both as a reader of their work for themselves, and, for other people, real or imagined. The Report suggests we may conclude that written 'standard English'

is only desirable in transactional public writing and for all other forms of writing the most appropriate and acceptable will be individual, more or less expressive writing. What seems important is that pupils themselves should understand that the writing they do should vary according to who it is for and what it is for.

3. *Assessment*. Closely tied up with this matter of standard and non-standard English is assessment, and I have referred earlier to the problems and ambiguities inherent in the situation. Teachers must be concerned with their pupils' progress; children like to know how they are doing. Yet the risks and anxieties of being tested constantly operate against the children's taking risks in their thinking or their language. Again we suggest that teachers might vary their roles. They will get very different results in writing when there is no assessment attached, but only interested comment.

Listening

Of the four modes of language use, listening is the least researched and the least specifically taught. Ironically in secondary schooling as a whole, and despite notable exceptions, it is in fact the language 'activity' to which by far the most pupil time is devoted—past research has indicated well over half the time! However teaching methods change, listening will still remain important in a range of adult occupations from professional jobs to telephone sales clerks.

The Report considered whether listening abilities should be included in the suggested national language monitoring scheme. This was rejected for the twin reasons that we do not really have the knowledge of how to measure listening skills, and anyway the practical problems of testing on this scale are daunting. However, the Committee did feel that attention needs to be given within schools to the use of listening and the encouragement of improved listening ability: 'The difficulty of listening is commonly under-estimated' (10.19). Research reviewed by Andrew Wilkinson[1] showed that students listening to lectures comprehended half or less than half of the basic matter. The two questions are of what does listening consist, and how can the resultant skills be best fostered?

Attempts to analyse separate sub-skills, in the manner of analyses of reading, have not proved successful. However, the work of the Schools Council's Oracy project[2] does, it seems to me, make it clear

[1] Andrew Wilkinson and Leslie Stratta, *Listening and the Study of Spoken Language*, University of Birmingham Educational Review, Volume 25, No. 1, p. 3.

[2] Andrew Wilkinson, Leslie Stratta and Peter Dudley, *The Quality of Listening*, Evans/Methuen, 1974.

that, as in so many other aspects of education, by stopping and focusing on an activity teacher and pupil can note certain aspects. In listening, for instance, the pupil can be helped to consider how communication is conveyed. He can also be made aware of the activity required in the apparently passive act. The Report puts emphasis on what I should call a *conscious* contextual approach: 'In our view the ability can best be developed as part of the normal work of the classroom and in association with other learning experiences. But deliberate strategies may be required, for it cannot be assumed that the improvement will take place automatically.' (10.21) The 'association' involves the consideration of the listening demands of subject activities, and the 'deliberate strategies' involves both the planting of listening activities and, I should suggest, some specific practice and tuition. A whole-school policy might consider the following recommendations:

Examine the subject

Each subject should consider the listening expectations of the classroom activity. They should ensure:
1. Listening plays a part.
2. There is a variety of listening sources, e.g. not all teachers' exposition. This variety should be of speaker(s), speech situations (talks, reminiscence, discussion, announcement, etc.), technical presentation (live, tape, visitor, regular teacher).
3. The sources are of suitable length, frequency, and difficulty.

Involve pupils

Whenever possible pupils should be required to take some action. The immediate function of the listening should be clear. This may mean:
1. Simple note-taking from news bulletin, talk, or discussion.
2. Carrying out an activity after listening to instructions.
3. Analysis—by extracting one person's point of view, or one set of arguments from a debate.
4. Making a decision after hearing a discussion.
5. Simulations—such as making an order out from a phone call, taking the train times from a phone call.

Specific tuition

This should be given on occasions. That is, whereas the activities above are inserted primarily to provide material for the project, activity, or study, I am suggesting here the occasional use of listening material to consider the problems involved and to give practice. This could involve:

1. Listening comprehension tests, which have the advantage of helping pupils become conscious of the skills.[1]
2. An analysis of speech from the point of view of the listener.
3. Practice in skills, e.g. aural recognition.
4. Note-taking based on sound sources.

Monitoring communication for learning

Douglas Barnes

Teachers have always wanted to know how well their teaching was going, and have gained reassurance from signs of pupils' interest, and from the quality of work done, especially in tests and examinations. Thus their sense of success is based upon the products or outcomes of their teaching. What has been missing has been the means of monitoring what actually happens in the lessons—the events which have given rise to pupils' satisfaction or dissatisfaction, and have led to written work of better or worse quality. Teachers' attention has tended to be directed towards products rather than towards the processes which led to these products, because of the difficulty inherent in both participating as a teacher in a lesson, and at the same time observing what happens in it. The tape recorder, however, now allows us to be both participant and observer: we are the first generation to be able to monitor our own speech-behaviour

---

[1] *Learning Through Listening* (listening comprehension tests for 10+, 13+ and 17+), tapes, teachers' manual, pupils' answer booklets, Macmillan Education, 1976.

The tests comprise three tapes, for the 10+, 13+ and 17+ age groups respectively, plus accompanying test materials for pupils and teachers. The first two tapes play for about an hour, the third for about one hour twenty minutes (playing speed $3\frac{3}{4}$). The tapes include the following tests:

tests of content—designed to measure the ability to follow and understand a piece of informal exposition;
tests of contextual constraint—which measure the ability to infer missing parts of a conversation from what is actually heard;
tests of phonology—designed to measure the ability to understand differences in meaning brought about by different emphases;
tests of register—which measure the ability to detect changes in the appropriateness of the spoken language used;
tests of relationship—which measure the ability to detect the kinds of relationships existing between people from the language they employ.

The tests use unscripted speech for assessing listening ability, rather than readings from the written language.

and to understand its effects on others. It is now possible for teachers to extend their insight into their teaching beyond the evidence of pupils' interest and achievements to the monitoring of communication, which constitutes a central part of teaching and learning.

Looked at in this context, the Committee's recommendation that schools should discuss a 'policy for language across the curriculum' seems to strike a different note. Certainly my emphasis would not fall upon grammatical forms, or upon appropriate usage, or on spelling and punctuation; it would not be concerned with the forms of language but with the part played by talking and writing in learning. Nor would emphasis fall upon individual pupils' language skills, but rather upon how the contexts which teachers set up in lessons encourage this or that kind of talk, this or that kind of writing. But this must have been the Committee's intention too.

When teachers, working alone or with colleagues, plan a course they are about to teach, they may have at the back of their minds a picture of how it will go in practice. This picture includes the kinds of presentation, discussion, demonstration sessions they will have with the class, the range of individual tasks they will set, the strategies they will adopt when going round to talk to individual pupils or groups while they are working, and so on. Part of the Committee's suggestion is that teachers should be more explicit with themselves and others about the teaching and learning processes that they are envisaging Especially when teachers are working as a team or a department, it should not be taken for granted that they all mean the same by such expressions as 'discussion', 'project', 'enquiry', 'making notes', and so on. The readiest way of finding out what one means by familiar educational terms such as these is by looking closely at what pupils and teachers actually do, and this is what I am recommending.

We can approach 'what teachers and pupils actually do' through what they say and what they write: in this case the writing would be considered not as a final product to be evaluated but as evidence of learning activities. (Teachers would also wish to look at non-verbal work done by pupils—models, art and craft, and so on—but that takes me beyond my present topic.) It is clearly possible to tape-record communication between the teacher and a whole class, and it should also be possible for a teacher to carry a lightweight cassette recorder and record his communication with individual pupils and small groups. Almost all teachers engage at times in this latter kind of teaching but we know very little about the range of strategies which they commonly use, though this is probably an important part of their work. A teacher who frequently organized small group work —for example in science practicals—might wish also to have information about the kinds of discussion which his pupils were able to engage in without his leadership. Thus teachers can have four sources of information about what they and their pupils do:

1. Spoken communication: teacher–class
2. Spoken communication: teacher–individual/group
3. Spoken communication: group without teacher
4. Written communication.

Let us suppose you are a middle-school teacher with a class of ten-year olds, and you are interested in finding out more about what happens in that part of your pupils' time which is devoted to social and environmental studies. Some of the time you are presenting new ideas and possibilities to the class and encouraging them to talk about them, but most of the time your pupils are working alone and in pairs on topics which they have chosen in the light of your presentation and suggestions. During this time you go round giving help and advice, and, when you have time, asking particular pupils to explain to you clearly what they are trying to do. Every now and then you plan a session in which pupils show the class what they are doing, and you endeavour to encourage general discussion of this so that they may learn from one another. Let us further suppose that you have tape recorded two presentation sessions, and have recorded yourself on several occasions going round the class giving individual advice. You have the written work done by pupils, and perhaps a recording of a 'report-back' session, and with all this bundle of material you turn back with the question: What should I be looking for when I listen to the recordings or read through the written work? There are some suggestions below, but in the end it is you who should decide what you are looking for—or you and your colleagues together, if you are working in a team.

What you should be looking for when you listen to tapes—preferably with one or two other teachers with similar interests—depends on the patterns of learning which you are aiming for. Thus one of the first benefits of discussing recordings with colleagues is that this is the ideal way of focusing discussion on the details of how children are learning and how best to support them in doing so. I am therefore not imagining that many schools will have a clearly-spelt-out policy document which describes the patterns of spoken and written communication to be adopted, but rather that deeper understanding of where you agree, and disagree with colleagues will come from looking closely at real examples. It is not a matter of achieving consensus—which is unlikely—but that after studying classroom communication you and your colleagues will be clearer about what kinds of talk and writing each of you values.

The best support I can offer for such debates is to suggest some questions which might start a discussion. These suggestions are far from exhaustive; indeed they may well prove unsuited to your values or to your situation. They are offered here merely as starting points.

Spoken communication: teacher–class

The central question to be asked is: Are you carrying out the teaching strategies which you intend? In answering this you might consider questions such as these:

1. Are you requiring your pupils to think for themselves or mainly asking them to feed back information from a book or from an earlier lesson?
2. Are you eliciting the pupils' existing experience and understanding and working from that, or does the way you are planning lessons tend to make their present knowledge irrelevant?
3. Do your responses to pupils' contributions include replies which use and develop what they have said, or are you predominantly evaluating replies as right/wrong, or good/bad?
4. When you present information, or give a demonstration, or read a poem, or discuss a visit, are you requiring your pupils to explain and hypothesize, or are you telling them what it means?
5. Do you ask pupils to expand what they have said, to respond to one another, to ask questions, to offer evidence, to consider alternative explanations, to plan lines of action?
6. Are your pupils in fact contributing at some length to the lessons, or answering merely in brief phrases?
7. Are they raising questions of their own, offering experiences and opinions, joining in the formulating of knowledge?

The way I have framed these questions tends to indicate what I consider to be good teaching and to contrast it rather crudely with an alternative view. If your own view of good teaching is different you will need to frame different questions.

Spoken communication: teacher–individual/group

The seven questions suggested above would be relevant here also. Indeed they are even more relevant, since in talking with one or two pupils a teacher is able to pursue such a teaching technique without her normal concern to hold the class' attention by keeping the discussion moving. The following may however be added.

8. What range of matters are you discussing with them? Are you mainly concerned with methods or are you asking them to talk about the meaning of what they are doing?
9. Are you succeeding in eliciting your pupils' thinking, so that you understand their idiosyncratic ways of interpreting things, their problems and misconceptions but also their strengths?
10. Can you sit in on a group discussion and gather how the work is

progressing without all the group addressing their remarks to you? Do you join in pupils' discussion as a participant rather than an evaluator?

Spoken communication: pupil–pupil

If a teacher asks a group of pupils to tape-record their discussion, what appears on the tape is unlikely to be exactly as it would have been without the recording, unless the microphone has been in place so long as to be virtually forgotten. What can be taken from such recording is an impression of what pupils can do at their best, and not necessarily an accurate picture of how they normally talk during group work. In listening to such recordings it is important not to bring in expectations drawn from written language. It is perfectly normal in conversation for sentences to be incomplete or to change direction, for much of the meaning to be left implicit and not put into words, for speakers not to make explicit the logical relationship of what they are saying to what has gone before, or for their contributions to overlap. All of this is perfectly normal; if you doubt it I suggest that you tape record yourself and your colleagues arguing in the staff room, and look at that. Once you have taken this into account, and listened to the discussions several times until you understand what is implicit in them, you are likely to find that your pupils have capacities which are not often visible in classwork. The questions which follow relate both to what the pupils are able to do, and to the part which the teacher plays in setting up group discussion.

11. Are your pupils really discussing the meaning of what they are doing? For example, in science are they talking about how their 'experiment' relates to the principle in question, or is their talk mainly at the 'Pass the matches!' level?
12. Can they find problems and formulate them, put forward explanatory hypotheses, use evidence to evaluate alternatives, plan lines of action?
13. Can they cope with differences of opinion, share out the jobs to be done, move steadily through a series of tasks, summarize what they have decided, reflect on the nature of what they are doing?
14. Have the topics which they have chosen or you have prescribed led to useful discussion? Did they succeed in raising valuable issues, or would they have benefited from some help in focusing attention? On the other hand, if you gave them questions to consider, were these helpful or constricting, did they lead to the kind of discussion you believe to be valuable?[1]

---

[1] Issues such as these are analysed in more detail in D. Barnes and F. Todd, *Communication and Learning in Small Groups*, RKP (forthcoming).

Written communication

The emphasis here should fall upon writing as one way in which a pupil increases his understanding both of the world about him and of what is presented to him in lessons. Since most teachers have traditionally treated writing as a way of storing information or of assessing achievement, the accent falls differently here, as a step towards redressing the balance. The central question is: Does the written work being done by your pupils accurately represent the kinds of learning you wish them to be engaged in? In answering this overall question you are likely to consider sub-questions very like the fourteen proposed above for Spoken Communication.

15. In what proportion of the writing being done is the pupil feeding back received knowledge to the teacher solely for the purpose of evaluation? (It has been said that this kind of writing is addressed to The Teacher as Examiner.[1]) Similarly, how much of the writing done appears in a complete and public form, and how much shows the incompleteness, discontinuity, tentativeness, and lack of full explicitness typical of exploratory work-in-progress?
16. How much of the writing is concerned primarily with the copying or paraphrase of information? On the other hand, how much of the writing which begins with such information shows that the learner is reinterpreting, applying, transforming, discussing and evaluating that knowledge?
17. When written work reports first-hand activities or experience, does the writing show that the pupil is interpreting and evaluating?
18. How far do the topics set for written exercises enable and encourage pupils to utilize first-hand experience, and to deal with problems and concerns which they see as urgent?
19. How has the teacher responded to the written work handed to him? Has he only evaluated it? Has he treated it primarily as an opportunity to correct misconceptions in pupils' grasp of subject matter, and solecisms in their use of spelling and punctuation? Is the teacher concerned about appropriate style to the extent of rejecting colloquial formulations? Does he respond to and comment on the ideas put forward by pupils? Is the writing published by being read aloud or displayed on a wall?

My final question relates to all the above, but also to teachers' communication with their pupils at other times than lessons, and in corridor, hall, playground, and street.

20. Do you treat pupils as rational human beings with viewpoints which are different but valid, even when you believe them to be wrong? Do you persuade rather than command? When commands are necessary, do you give them politely and supply reasons? Do you

[1] Britton, *et al.*, *The Development of Writing Ability*, Macmillan, 1975.

treat your pupils' viewpoints with courtesy and understanding, and
seek to strengthen their ability to think for themselves?

It would be difficult to supply evidence that answered this last group
of questions, yet this is not necessary. We all remember occasions
when we have failed to carry out this kind of policy. Teachers work
with boisterous young people, some of whom resent school control,
and at times talking for learning becomes overwhelmed by a teacher's
desire to keep control. It is important however, not to value control
for its own sake, to recognize the genuine diversity of children's
interests and perspectives, and not to allow 'controlling a class' to
become 'stopping young people from thinking for themselves'.

My list of questions implies informal discussions of recorded material
and of children's writing. Published systems for the analysis of classroom interaction are clumsy instruments, much inferior to the intuitive
understanding of intelligent adults. I am envisaging groups of teachers
who share responsibility for a course, and who trust one another
enough to collaborate in monitoring the progress of that course. It
would probably be best at first not to attempt to listen to enormous
stretches of tape or to read large piles of writings, but for one member
of the group to select in advance a range of shorter examples characteristic of various kinds of talk or writing.

It can be quite difficult to make sense of a recorded extract from a
lesson which one has not taken part in, and teachers will find it
necessary to spend considerable time on extracts of no more than a
minute or two. Nevertheless, the trouble taken to select an interesting
episode, perhaps to transcribe it, to listen to it several times, and to
discuss it at length, is likely to be well rewarded by the range of insights
and issues that the discussion will reach to. Discussion of these examples should make it possible to define the range of kinds of teaching
and learning which the teachers wish to take place and thus help to
guide future teaching.

Informal sampling of courses may be all that many teachers can
find time to do, but more systematic study would be possible. For
example, if special time were made available for this kind of monitoring, it would be possible to analyse recordings of teachers at work to
estimate roughly how much of their time was devoted to classroom
organization and discipline, how much given to low-level advice
about methods, and how much to theoretical discussion of the matter
in hand. This last category could then be broken down—again very
roughly—into sub-categories such as eliciting description and
narration, eliciting reasoning, giving information and explanations.
The teachers in the light of such an analysis could consider whether
they were carrying out their intentions and decide what changes
might be made in their teaching strategies. But it should be emphasized that such a sophisticated approach is far from essential. Every
teacher can benefit from even the most informal look at what goes on

in his lessons, both at the kinds of communication that his pupils engage in and at the way in which he influences this communication by the part he himself plays.

As a result of this a group of teachers might decide that individualized learning needed to be supported by group seminars, or that their science practicals needed to be accompanied by group discussions to ensure that pupils considered the meaning of the practical work done. They might decide to widen the range of written work to include more occasions when pupils were expected to 'think aloud on paper', or to spend more time in trying to persuade pupils to talk explicitly about what they are learning. They might decide to set up an experimental course with quite different patterns of communication from those currently in use. Thus I am envisaging the beginning of a process of developing new ways of looking at teaching, and not the kind of completeness that 'policy' would suggest. In our time it is beginning to be possible to be much more aware of how we communicate with other people; teachers should be in the forefront of such awareness since communication—in the sense of a two-way attempt by teacher and taught to reach and understand one another —is at the centre of their work.

6. Classroom Technicalities

To make the broader approaches of Chapters 4 and 5 effective, some measure of agreement is also required on what I choose to call 'classroom technicalities'. These are in some ways easier to tackle, for they are limited, instrumental, and technical. I am including a technical vocabulary of language, ways of introducing new vocabulary, approaches to spelling, phonics, punctuation, and the very important study skills. None of these on their own would be of a great deal of value, but they underpin the use of language in a school, and if attention is given to them, they help assure that language growth is effectively assisted by the school.

Language terms

The Report recommends that 'the teacher ought to ensure that in a given period of time the pupils cover certain features of language, and for this purpose he might find a check-list useful. We believe these features should certainly include . . . a knowledge of the modest collection of technical terms useful for a discussion of language' (11.21), and Dr Gatherer confirms that teachers and pupils require what linguists call a metalanguage for talking about language. Whilst it is important not merely to start a game of exchanging jargon, staff need vocabulary for their analysis and discussion. They also need a working vocabulary for helping pupils. This list could serve as a vocabulary for teachers to use with pupils, and thus to be taught systematically:

sound, letter, syllable, word
vowel, short, long, stress, consonant
prefix, root, suffix
upper case, lower case
italic, bold
ascender, descender
comma, semi-colon, colon, full stop, etc.
indentation, paragraph
skim, scan
numerals, Arabic and Roman

headings, sub-headings, running heads
table of contents, index, reference, cross-reference
accent, dialect
phonic
register

Introducing vocabulary

The whole process of education, however we may work to alter it, is a long process of learning more words. The teacher is frequently a supplier of vocabulary. Sometimes one feels the vocabulary is a mere frill, a barrier between the pupil and the understanding. Sometimes a subject like Geology seems to be just a matter of difficult names for easy ideas. If only one could sweep away the verbiage, one feels, one could teach so much more easily. To a small extent that is true, and much learning is made easier if we can work with the pupil's own vocabulary and not drive him too early into words that he cannot himself feel or possess, as I have discussed earlier. However, that aside, there will be a continuous need to work on vocabulary at three levels:

1. Slightly unusual words necessary to a topic and used in their standard sense. The humanities are especially full of such words, e.g. *development, growth, examine, civilized, establish, relations*—and a huge host of others, each used in its normal sense, but not part of the usual vocabulary of a school pupil, in many cases not part of the ordinary vocabulary of domestic and personal talk. These are the words glossaries don't gloss and teachers don't explain.

2. Common words used in special senses, perhaps in their original sense, or core sense, perhaps in a specialized sense, e.g. *veneer, series, contemporary, energy, rotate* (maths), *balance* (physics)—which are also frequently left unexplained. Particular problems, it seems to me, arise out of this second category. Indeed, sometimes the sense of a word can change from subject to subject, e.g. *volume*, which pupils can meet with a different sense in music, science, art, mathematics, and in the library!

3. Technical terms, more or less particular to the subject,. e.g. *ductile, ferrous, taper shank, contour, topology, enfranchize, pipette*. These words are usually explained fairly fully, but sufficient practice in using them may be unavailable.

The sheer size of the English vocabulary is daunting, and we do not seem to have faced up to this in schools. Webster's Third International Dictionary, according to Hunter Diack,[1] contains 450,000 words. If you take 'headwords' only (that is not compounds derived from

[1] Hunter Diack, *Standard Literacy Tests*, Hart-Davis Educational, 1975.

them), the *Concise Oxford* has some 36,000 (with a further 30,000 derived). The first 6,000 are known by an eight-year-old, a further 6,000 are usually learnt between nine and twelve, and a third 6,000 by the 'linguistically adept' between twelve and fifteen. This is a target which will not be met if it is left to chance. As well as the quantity, there is the problem of the unease so many feel with a large part of the vocabulary. We British have a dislike of words which sound unfamiliar and puzzling. Although often referred to as 'long' words, these difficult words are frequently not actually long. It is the unpredictability of pronunciation which puzzles people. They are usually words from Romance origins. Words of Anglo-Saxon origin, though not half so numerous, are used about five times as often.

Not only do others use them—so that we *must* understand them, but *they are the key words for further study, for the exchange of ideas, for debate, indeed for the learning of many school subjects.*

Often the sense of a word is simply hidden because its root is lost by pronunciation changes. 'Significant' is an example. Used in the humanities, literature, and commonly for the early stages in mathematics, it remains vague for many pupils because they have never have pointed out to them the simple fact that it comes from 'signify'—'to be a sign', that is, 'significant' is said of something that *points to* meaning.

The way into these less commonly used words is not merely extensive reading—especially as extensive reading usually means of novels, which have a considerably lower use of such words. Specific help must be given, and this must involve analysing vocabulary.

In a whole-school language policy, I should suggest agreement is reached on modes of introduction, on the technical terms used (as explained in the previous section), and on who in the school will give the basic theoretical teaching about words. There is then the knowledge available to help the introduction of new words, and every teacher is building up the pupil's understanding of how our vocabulary works, and thus making it easier for the pupil to absorb other words later. This again, is a combination of the contextual and specialized language teaching approaches. A policy might include a consideration of five aspects of advice.

Phonic approach and syllabification

If a new word is to be understood and used by a pupil, he needs to see it (I mean actually *see* the structure), hear it clearly, be able to pronounce it himself, and then be able to spell it. Most of us find it difficult to take in new vocabulary, and secondary pupils, struggling with so much at once, often have great difficulty with new words. The first aim is to make the word aurally and visually clear.

Some words offer difficulties beyond their conceptual level simply because of their pronunciation or spelling difficulties. In these cases special phonic care on introduction is worth while, with an opportunity for drilled pronouncing aloud. The 'rh' words are an example. 'Rhombus' is in fact phonically regular, but the 'h' always confuses, as do the other words transliterated from the Greek ρ (*rhetoric, rheumatism, rhinoceros, rhododendron,*—difficult, but all phonically regular). Also in mathematics 'ratio' remains foreign sounding, but need not if related to the other 'sh' pronunciation of 't' in *ration, introduction,* and many other words. I even find that the pronunciation difficulties of 'th' can cause problems, so that 'tenths' and 'hundredths', especially that last one, torture pupils.

A school drawing up a policy might like to consider an agreed procedure for all specially introduced words. It might be based on a list such as this:

1. The word is written on the board or in the individual pupil's book. (The pupil does not yet copy it.)
2. The teacher pronounces it, underlining each separate syllable, e.g. s y l l a b i f i c a t i o n. The word, therefore, is *not* broken up by lines or gaps.
3. A number of pupils read it aloud, perhaps even the whole class in unison.
4. The pupils are given time to learn it.
5. It is covered up, and the pupils asked to write it from memory.
6. They then check against the original.

In this writing out, reference is made to phonic expectations or irregularities. The pupils are being helped to grasp the sound structure of the word, and the phoneme/grapheme relationship. They are being given a chance!

Word building

In finding his way around the huge vocabulary I mentioned earlier, the pupil is helped considerably if he is aware of two things.

1. The way a word can be changed to give the sense a variety of uses (noun, adjective, adverb—though he needn't know the terms). I call this the family of words. Pupils frequently know only one from each family, and are not used to recognizing, yet alone using, the rest of the family.
2. The way words can come together with other words or special parts to create new compounds.

In other words, pupils need to be taught word building. Sean O'Casey was one of those who put the justification very clearly:

> Ella went over to rummage among the books left behind as unsalable out of her father's fine store. She brought back a Superseded Spelling-book

by Sullivan, who held that by learning affixes and suffixes, Latin and Greek roots, you could net words in hundreds, as against the old method of fishing one word up at a time. . . . (*I Knock at the Door*)

This should not become a fetish—it hardly justifies the learning of Latin, for instance. It also needs to be treated cautiously, for the clues can be misleading. However, the pupil should be taught how words can go together (*sometimes, upstairs*); then they should learn the idea of prefix, root, and suffix. Next, the most useful examples of these should be taught (see Appendix One) by the English teacher in general terms, and the specific ones by subject teachers. Pupils should be taught to tackle an unfamiliar word by examining it for familiar parts. If they know the meaning of that part, they apply it. If not, they deduce the meaning from the known word in which the familiar part appears.

The vocabularies of mathematics and science are rich in regularly constructed Latin or Greek compound words. If these subject teachers can know that prefix, root, and suffix has been taught, they can draw on this knowledge economically to help explain new words, and at the same time widen and reinforce the pupils' grasp of how such words go together. A few examples make the point clear:

divide, division, divisor, equilateral, quadrilateral
polygon, hexagon, diagonal
metre, centimetre, metric
subtract, subtraction
triangle, rectangle
rotate, rotation
convex, concave
energy, energetic
compare, comparison
electric, electrical
mechanic, mechanical
magnet, magnetic
oxide, dioxide, monoxide

The vocabularies of other subjects can be similarly examined by teachers, and vocabulary can be taught in two complementary ways: the basic systems of word analysis should be specifically taught by an agreed department (probably English), but the 'knowledge' must be constantly used and built upon by the range of subject teachers.

Word building is an important process in which all teachers work together to provide the pupils with the necessary knowledge, experience, and confidence. It has the great virtue of de-mystifying the most difficult parts of the English vocabulary, especially those parts used so much in the language of abstract thought and of technical explanation. The knowledge helps spelling, reading, and understanding.

Timing of introduction

One principle which can well be considered by the staff of a school is when special vocabulary is best introduced. At one extreme, the specialized teacher has a 'vocabulary' session. The craft teacher starts the autumn term with a list of tools, metals, and special terms: *ferrous, corrosion, alloy, anneal, ductile,* are listed, explained, learned, tested. Then work starts and the words are used in context. At the opposite extreme, mid-activity, the teacher explains 'And this is called the "drill chuck key"; don't forget that'. Because the demonstration is going on there is no time for explanation, clarification, or discussion of the term.

The first method risks unreality: 'malleable' is explained months before the quality of malleability can be felt. The second risks superficiality: the word is passed over so quickly that it is barely heard, never mind comprehended.

It seems likely that a mixture of approaches is required: the word should be introduced as near as possible to the point of use, but it should be part of a programme of methodical subject vocabulary building, with the word introduced, used, followed up, and then put into a growing subject list by the pupil. Subject teachers should have pupils build up their own subject dictionary. Thus the geographer's personal dictionary will grow during the two years, say, of a CSE option, helping the pupil *possess* the words for himself.

Establishing meaning

In establishing a language policy, a school staff can consider ways of revealing the meaning of words. One principle might be that prior to the teacher's explanation of a word there should usually be a deductive process, to help the pupil work towards the meaning of a word from his own memories of other uses or other parts. I have already spoken in Chapter 5 of the deductive approach to unfamiliar words in reading. I suggest something slightly different could be considered when new vocabulary is introduced orally—somewhat less deductive, more experiential. This both helps the present grasp of the new word and helps the general learning of how one can and should focus the past on newly discovered words.

Relationships of meaning

I pointed out that one of the difficulties for pupils is the special use of words familiar in wider or different contexts. A language policy should face up to this, and establish what can be gained from it. I should suggest that normally it is worth while *making use* of the relationship between the current meaning and others, both to assist·

the present apprehension of sense and to assist the general understanding of sense relationships. With many words which are used for subject concepts, the starting point should be the 'everyday' sense: with a word such as *cycle* used in religious studies or biology, for instance, or *series* used in mathematics, the teacher moves from the general to the specific sense, pausing briefly on other related specific senses (the bi*cycle*, the TV *series*).

The reverse process is also important, moving from specific uses to the wider metaphorical sense, for this also not only sharpens the understanding of the moment, but also deepens an understanding of the nature of language. Thus the craft teacher introducing *veneer* would move out to the metaphorical sense.

Conclusion

Certainly vocabulary grows by experience, but not adequately. A whole-school policy of mutual reinforcement, on the other hand, can combine the specific with the contextual approach with great power. Only *use* can help a pupil take possession of words, and the use must be in a variety of real situations. But a carefully co-ordinated series of approaches to the extension and explanation of new vocabulary will help the subject understanding and deepen the pupils' underlying grasp of how words work.

The phonics approach

Ann Dubs

In the English alphabet, letters and groups of letters represent different sounds. Phonics relates these letters to forty-six[1] possible sounds. Many people learn these letter/sound relationships through a non-conscious, seemingly automatic process. Others find this difficult and need to be taught the relationships to a greater or lesser extent.

Many children entering secondary school have acquired a large sight (or whole-word) vocabulary, yet are still unable to read a new word when they come across it. They have not learned how to identify the sounds of the letters or groups of letters in that particular word. This is even more apparent from their poor spelling performance. Nearly every eleven-year-old I have tested from amongst our poorer readers could for example spell the word 'big'; few could manage 'wig'. Both are phonically regular, but 'big' is a word which every

[1] Axel Wijk, *Rules of Pronunciation for the English Language*, OUP, 1966.

child would have known and used since infant school; 'wig' is far less familiar. To spell the word correctly, these pupils have to be taught formally the generalization that 'g' at the end of a word has a hard sound.

The majority of words in English are phonically regular, i.e. they conform to basic rules. The reader who has learned or absorbed these phonic rules does not then have to learn every word separately. Of course, some words do not conform to the basic code and they will have to be learned as sight words. But the phonic system does simplify the spelling and reading process by reducing the number of words that have to be learned. Experience has shown that the pupils whose spelling and reading performance has improved the most are those whose programme has included a very systematic phonic training in encoding and decoding sounds.

At first sight, identifying a word by its component sounds may not appear to be altogether straightforward. 'Cat' is sounded k/a/t/ only because the reader has the foreknowledge of what sounds the letters 'c' 'a' 't' make in that particular word. Yet the letter 'c' can make, amongst others, the sounds /s/, /k/, or /sh/ depending on the letters with which it is associated in the word in question. The letter 'a' can make, amongst others, the sounds heard in 'hat', 'hate', 'halt', and 'hart'. 'T' makes a /sh/ sound when it is followed by an 'i', as in 'patient'.

Nonetheless, the choice of which sounds to select for the letters in the word 'cat' is not an arbitrary one. The reader familiar with phonics knows that 'c' preceding an 'a' has a /k/ sound and that the vowel 'a' in a single syllabled word, with a consonant-vowel-consonant structure has a short sound.

The remedial reading teacher quite often has to explain this process in some detail. The subject teacher would not have time to do this. But, in order to clarify the system of word pronunciation for pupils who are not fluent readers it is helpful if the teacher is familiar with the broad outline of phonics instruction. That teacher is then able to do two things: (1) To identify the irregular words which cannot be sounded out or decoded, such as 'any' and 'does', and which have to be learned as whole words. (2) To indicate certain letter combinations within a word which give a clue to the pronunciation of the word.

Most teachers, as fluent readers, are unaware of the phonic elements of words. They never stop to question the ways in which the letters go together to make the sounds because they take them for granted.

But, an ability to recognize the combinations of letters which produce a particular sound is essential to anyone trying to teach a new word by this method. A pupil baffled, for example, by 'shingle' would be helped if told that the final sound is similar to that at the end of a familiar word like 'table'. He may, at first, need help in isolating the sound made by the letters 'le', particularly if he is learning French!

A large part of the teacher's task is to help the pupil use his secure knowledge of common words as raw material for interpreting less common words. Let us suppose that the word 'phalanx' has come up in Roman History. The teacher points out that the 'ph' is /f/ 'as in "photograph"' and the 'x' represents the /ks/ sound 'heard in "tax"'.

'Scutage' is another technical word which occurs in Longman's Secondary History *The Middle Ages*, a textbook used quite frequently in the lower part of the secondary school. Such a word would obviously first have to be taught in context and with reference to its derivation. It is an extra *aide-mémoire* for the pupil if the teacher can make an analogy with other '-age' ending words in the same course, like 'pilgrimage' and 'Carthage'

It is apparent that there are certain groups of sounds which can cause difficulty to all but the most competent readers. It is the aim of this chapter to indicate (a) some of these sounds, (b) certain basic aspects of phonics which it would be helpful for the subject teacher to be aware of when introducing new words or reading a text with a class. Examples are taken from the secondary school learning vocabulary.

With this purpose in mind, it is useful if the subject teacher lists, over a period of time, technical words or words which are giving difficulty to his pupils. It is not suggested that these words should be taught out of context or that the subject teacher should teach lists of words as such. Once he is aware of the phonic patterns within the words relevant to his subject, he can then make generalizations which will help the slower reader to learn and retain that word.

As some of the simplest identifiable phonic groups are found at the end of a word, a brief list of suffixes that are useful phonically is given first. Those suffixes that are primarily of semantic interest (such as '-by' in place names) are intentionally excluded.

Next, certain consonant groups are mentioned. Finally, there is some basic information about long and short vowels.

The principle of breaking up words into syllables which is essential to the process of phonic analysis is dealt with in the section on spelling.

Word endings

(a) *Examples*:

-*age* (idge sound)   language, mortgage, homage, vintage, hostage, average

-*er*   lawyer, thermometer.

   Note: the same sound can be made by -or, -our and -ar and mainly in the beginning and middle of words by -ir, -ur, and -ear. (For examples, see section 5, long vowels).

-ic democratic, epic, ethic, bionic, isometric, ironic, nomadic, Arctic, Hellenic.

Note: all these words have more than one syllable. A single syllabled word with this ending would be spelled -ick, e.g. trick. (See short vowel section.)

-le shingle, quadruple, portable, double.

Note: to represent the sound heard at the end of 'shingle' it is necessary to use the phonetic symbol /ə/, which designates the murmur or schwa sound, +l.

-y (/ee/ sound) colony, injury, philosophy, savagery, clemency, magistracy, monastery, philology, slavery, astronomy, yeomanry.

Note: the fact that '-y' becomes '-ies' in the plural does not affect the pronunciation.

-ous (/us/ sound) ferrous, ingenious, igneous, monotonous.

-tion (/shun/ sound) elevation, initiation, projection, construction. (These are just a few of the words with this suffix collected from the Longman's text *The Middle Ages* referred to earlier: constitution, population, destruction, publication, execution, Reformation, foundation, excommunication, occupation.)

-sion (/zhun/ sound) confusion, corrosion, division, precision, explosion.

-ssion (/shun/ sound) admission, fission, progression, accession.

-sion (/shun/ sound) pension, mansion.

-ture (/cher/ sound) conjecture, pasture, texture, fixture.

-sure (/zher/ sound) exposure, enclosure, measure.

(b) *Inflected endings* cause many pupils difficulty.

The most helpful generalization, clarifying the pronunciation muddle for children of West Indian origin in particular, is that '-ed' is pronounced /id/ when it is preceded by a 't' or a 'd', e.g. demented, added. In all other cases, '-ed' adds a /t/ or a /d/ sound to the root of the word; it does not add an extra syllable. If more clarification is needed, the rule can be amplified further

ed = /t/ after 'p', 'ck', 'f', 'ch', 'tch', 's' (as in 'sell'), and 'th' (as in thirty).

e.g. hopped, puffed, wished, watched.

ed = /id/ after the consonants 'd' and 't'.

e.g. abated, faded.

ed = /d/ after 'b', 'g', 'v', /j/ ('g', 'ge', 'dge'), 'z', 's' (as in pleasure), 'th' (as in those), 'l', 'm', 'n', 'r', 'w', 'y', 'ng'.

e.g. stabbed, hugged, trudged, clanged.

and following $\left\{\begin{array}{l}\text{vowels} \\ \text{vowels} + \text{'r'}\end{array}\right.$
  e.g. fried, stirred.

(c) *-s, -es endings*
-*s* = /*s*/ after the consonants p, t, ck, th, f.
  e.g. crops, currents, rocks, months, giraffes.

-*s* = /*z*/ after consonants b, d, g, m, n, -ng, -th, v, l.
    e.g. tubes, liquids, drags, diagrams, basins, filings, tithes, dissolves, levels.

  and after vowels + 'r'
  e.g. stirs.

-*es* = /*iz*/ when it has been added to a word whose root ends in a hissing sound:

-ss	e.g. compresses
-x	coaxes
-ch	dispatches
-sh	punishes
-ces	substances

and to
-ge e.g. abridges

Selected consonants

$\left.\begin{array}{l}\text{c} \\ \text{g}\end{array}\right\}$ (attached)
gh
  In a final position, 'gh' is sometimes pronounced /f/:
  e.g. rough, tough, enough
      cough
      but not in bough, Slough, through, thorough, borough, where
    it is silent.

-*igh* has a 'long i' sound:
  e.g. fright.

ph A not very frequent representation of the /f/ sound found in words of Greek origin:
  e.g. amphora, Euphrates, hieroglyphic, phalanx, chlorophyll.

qu Never separate in English. Together they represent the consonant /k/ sound heard in cheque, oblique;
  or more frequently the (kw) sound in equatorial, aquatic, adequate.

th has two main sounds:
  (a) as in *th*eme, *th*eorem;
  (b) as in la*th*e.

These sounds are so similar that there is no need to make the distinction explicit.

Its third sound, /t/, is one which many children of West Indian origin use in preference. The most helpful way of clarifying this is to present the relatively few words in which 'th' has this /t/ sound, e.g. *Th*ames, *Th*omas, Neander*th*al, *th*yme, disco*th*eque.

s   makes a /sh/ sound in sugar, sure, surely, insurance. (See also suffixes.)

and a /zh/ sound in usual, casual.

wh   sounds the 'h' alone in *wh*ole, *wh*o

and the combined letters /w/ or /hw/ sounds in *wh*irl, *wh*isky.

x   has a /ks/ or /gs/ sound in phalanx, paradox, exact.

Letter 'c'

The rules relating to the pronunciation of the letter 'c' are practically infallible. They are worth learning thoroughly as their application is very wide and relevant also to the pronunciation of 'c' in French, apart from the minor variation of the soft (ch) sound. (In any case, we have retained the French /ch/ sound in English in several borrowed words, such as 'ma*ch*ine' and 'cro*ch*et'.)

The rules are summarized as follows:

Spelling	Pronunciation	Examples	Exceptions
1. 'c' followed by the vowels 'e', 'i' or 'y'.	's' sound called 'soft c'.	*c*entimetre con*c*entrated *c*ircumference *c*itizen os*c*illate *c*yclone cal*c*ium	(a) Certain words containing letters 'ci'. (See 4 below). (b) Celt, soccer, sceptical (c) Several musical terms borrowed from Italian, e.g. crescendo, concerto.
2. 'c' followed by: (i) the vowels 'a', 'o' or 'u'; (ii) other consonants.	'k' sound called 'hard c'.	college Carthage carburettor collateral statistics crevasse classical clarinet	Soft /ch/ sound as in chur*ch*. /ish/ sound in words of French origin: chef, machine.
3. 'ch'.	'k' sound.	chemist stomach-ache mechanical technical	As above.

Spelling	Pronunciation	Examples	Exceptions
		characteristic chronicle Chrysler saccharine Jericho archaeology chlorophyll	
4. 'ci'.	'sh' sound.	precious ancient racial electrician musician association coefficient	(Most words conform to rule 1, e.g. deciduous.)

Note

(*a*) The pronunciation of words containing a double 'cc' conforms closely to 1 and 2 above.

    e.g. *soft c* —access, accident, success, accession
         hard c—occasion, occur, tobacco.

(*b*) (Rules 3 and 4) As with many 'rules', to over-teach them is to risk confusing the pupil by leading him to make false analogies. For example, a pupil who has practised a list of words of Greek origin with a spelling for the 'ch' (/k/ sound) like 'chorus' is liable to apply the same pronunciation to words like 'chimney'. By grouping technical words which contain a similar element, e.g. *ch*lorophyll, chloroform, chlorine, and teaching them in context, the subject teacher can try to avoid this phonic trap.

    In the case of 'ci' words listed in Rule 4, it should be noted that in every instance the 'ci' (/sh/ sound) never appears in the first syllable. It always occurs at the beginning of one of the subsequent syllables. An awareness of this might help to prevent the mispronunciation of a word like 'city'.

(*c*) When an oddity like the word 'circuit' is met, it is helpful to draw a parallel with the more familiar word 'biscuit', explaining the connection between the hard 'c' and the following 'u', which has no function other than that of preserving the /k/ sound.

Letter 'g'

The letter 'g' has two sounds, soft like /j/ or hard as in *g*un. Basically similar to the 'c rule', the 'g rule' works on the principle that the 'g' has to be followed by 'e', 'i', or 'y' to have a soft /j/ sound.

Not all words containing the letter 'g' conform to this rule. However, since the list of exceptions includes quite a lot of very familiar, over-learned words—e.g. get, girl, gift, begin, geese, give, etc.—it is still worth teaching the basic rule nonetheless.

Note

(*a*) If the /j/ sound is to be written in a word, the 'g' has to be followed by 'e', 'i', or 'y', e.g. *G*eorge, gorg*e*ous, pig*e*on, reli*g*ious, inte*g*er.

(*b*) The letter 'u' indicates a hard 'g' in a fairly large group of words containing the letters 'gu', e.g. *g*uarantee, *G*uardian, dis*g*uise, *g*uidance, *G*uernsey, *g*uest, *g*uild, *g*uillotine, *g*uilty, *g*uitar, demagogue. Once this is appreciated, the pronunciation of these words becomes much more logical.

(c) When the letters 'gg' appear in a word their sound is always hard before 'e', 'i', 'y', e.g. Rugger, Maggie, stagger, carpet-bagger; exceptions: suggest, exaggerate, Reggie.

(d) 'g' as a final letter is always hard, e.g. wig. (Reg is an exception because it is a shortened form.)

(e) For -age, see section on suffixes.

Consonant Combination

	Initial			Final		
br	bl	sc		-lb	-ft	-nk
cr	cl	sk		-ld	-lt	-lk
dr	fl	sm		-nd	-nt	-sk
fr	gl	sn		-lm	-pt	
gr	pl	sp		-lp	-st	
pr	sl	st		-mp	-ct	
tr		sw		-sp		
		spr				
		scr				
		str				
sh				-sh		
shr				-ch		
th				-ng		
thr						

Some pupils find it difficult to blend consonants together. Although the word *scratch*, say, might be familiar as a sight word the pupil could still have difficulty in reading *scree*. The stumbling block would most probably be the first three letters, and practice is required.

Many slower readers find it hard to articulate the different sounds in the initial blends group, such as 'cr'/'gr' and 'cl'/'gl'. This is confusing when they are attempting to read a word which is unfamiliar.

Silent consonants

Teachers will wish to devise their own lists of words which contain silent consonants. It is worth mentioning here, however, the fact that such letters are rarely silent in isolation.

For example, 'k' is silent when combined with 'n' in 'knowledge', 'Knaresborough', etc.; 'b' is silent before 't' in 'subtle' and 'debt' and after 'm' in 'thumb', 'catacomb', 'succumb'; 'p' is silent when it precedes 'n', 's', and 't' at the beginning of a word, e.g. pneumonia, psychology, Ptolemy. 'H' is an exception: honour, vehicle.

Stress

Before considering short and long vowel sounds, the effect of stress on the pronunciation of words must be mentioned.

The generalization many primary school children are taught that the final 'silent -e' has a lengthening effect on a preceding vowel (e.g. pine) is a very useful one to know. It does not, however, apply to multi-syllable words like reproduc*tive*, deter*mine*, clim*ate*, because the sounded vowel in these final syllables is unstressed and pronounced with the schwa (ə) sound. The long vowel effect is heard in multi-syllable words where the relevant syllable is stressed, or has a secondary stress, e.g. stam*pede*, consti*tute*, Constan*tine*.

In very broad terms, the position of the stressed syllable can be determined in these ways:

1. The first syllable of a two-syllabled word is frequently stressed, e.g. *mu*sic, *pic*nic.

2. The root of a word is generally accented, e.g. im*poss*ible, un*do*ing. Though if a two-syllable word begins with a prefix it is then the second syllable which is stressed, e.g. re*call*.

In longer words vowels tend to have a short sound in a closed syllable (i.e. one that ends with a consonant) and a long sound in an open syllable (i.e. ending with a vowel). The stressed syllable is underlined in the examples:

vol <u>ca</u> no ⎫
<u>u</u> ni form ⎭ (open syllables)

<u>clas</u> sic al ⎫
re <u>jec</u> ted ⎭ (closed syllables)

Of course, children cannot be taught to decode automatically by this method because there are so many exceptions. In many words, the vowel is in a stressed syllable with only one consonant following the vowel yet the vowel is short, e.g. *ra*dish, *li*nen, *me*rit, *vo*luble.

While it is important for a teacher to appreciate the distinction between open and closed syllables so that he can syllabify a word in the most helpful way when presenting it to a class, it is not necessary for pupils to be taught the distinction in these terms.

A simpler method of explanation is suggested at the beginning of the section on long vowels. (1b)

Some teachers might find it useful, in addition, to familiarize their pupils with the diacritical markings in a dictionary, emphasizing the role of the stressed syllable.

However obvious, it must be restated that the most important factor in helping children to decode apparently unfamiliar long words is the teacher's consciousness of the need to enlarge their listening and speaking vocabulary. The pupil who looks blankly at a word like *concentration* will decode it successfully by combining a little phonic knowledge with an oral/aural awareness of that word.

Short vowels

The short vowel sound is the sound heard in had, red, bit, pot, cup.

1. (*a*) In consonant-vowel-consonant (cvc) monosyllables the vowel is short. Such syllables are known as 'closed' syllables.
Exceptions occur when the vowel is followed by '-r' or '-w'. (See section on long vowels.)
(*b*) In words of more than one syllable all five short vowel sounds may have a schwa sound (ə) in unstressed syllables. This is the sound heard in: *a*lone, *be*tween, cann*o*n.

2. A vowel is short when it is followed by
(*a*) *a doubled consonant*, e.g. mammal, narcissus, pollen, mussel, buzzing, potassium.
Note: in a monosyllabic word or root after a short vowel:
   (i) The /k/ sound is spelled -ck, e.g. trick.
  (ii) The /ch/ sound is spelled -tch, e.g. pitching.
 (iii) The /j/ sound is spelled -dge, e.g. abridged.
     (Exceptions: much, rich, such, which.)
(*b*) *two consonants*, e.g. crank, cling, temper, pond.
(For exceptions, see long vowel section.)

3. *Stressed cvc forms + suffixes become cvcc + suffixes.*
In the following type of structure a doubled consonant marks the short vowel sound, e.g.

	Root + *suffix*	
-*ing*	drag + -ing	= dragging
-*ed*	stun + -ed	= stunned
-*y*	wit + -y	= witty
-*en*	trod + -en	= trodden
-*er*	dim + -er	= dimmer
-*est*	thin + -est	= thinnest

The same principle applies broadly to these suffixes:
-*le*   The short vowel sound is heard in batt*le*, sett*le*, preceding the doubled consonant, while the long vowel sound is heard in sta/ble, etc.
-*ow* e.g. bellow, follow
-*et*   puppet, bonnet
-*el*   kennel, funnel.

This generalization, though helpful, is far from infallible as exceptions like 'city', 'coming', 'model', and 'panel' show.

4. When the letters *wa, swa, qua, squa* are followed by '-a', that '*a*' generally represents the short *o* sound, e.g. wasp, wallet, wander, swab, swamp, quantity, quarry, squatter, squabble.
Exceptions: most cases where a + r is found, e.g. warning, quart, swarthy.

5. The letter 'y' is sometimes a vowel and sometimes a consonant. It is only a consonant if it is positioned at the beginning of a syllable, e.g. yeoman, youth, yacht. When 'y' is found medially it generally has a short /i/ sound, e.g. synthesis, cylinder, mythology.

In the Greek prefix forms hyper, hypo, the 'y' has generally a long /i/ sound, e.g. hypothesis, hypotenuse, hyphen, hydrogen, hyposulphite, though it is short in hypocrite and hypnotize.

Long vowels

1. (a) Where there is one vowel in a syllable and it comes at the end of that syllable the vowel is frequently long. The syllable is then called an open syllable, e.g. me, so/lo, mu/sic.

(b) There are so many exceptions to this rule in multi-syllabled words that it is more helpful to children decoding long words to tell them that a cvcv syllable may be either open as in *i*/vor/y, *i*/tinerant, or closed as in ac/*tiv*/ity, hos/*til*/it/y.

In simpler terms, the instruction, 'Try /ĭ/ (short i) then /ī/ (long i)' is adequate in most cases. By breaking down words syllabically the pupil will probably reach a more accurate version of the word than he would by guessing.

2. *Silent -e*

(a) A 'silent -e' at the end of a word makes the vowel in front say its own 'name'.

In cvc+e structures the first vowel is long, e.g. evapor*a*te, extr*e*me, ag*i*le, micr*o*be, cath*o*de.

The final '-e' is dropped when all suffixes except '-ly' are added,

    e.g.   hope—hoping
             shine—shiny
             ride—rider
but   time—timely

This generalization can be applied to a few cvcc+e structures, like *taste*, but usually the short vowel sound is heard as in *hinge*.

The most common exceptions to the 'silent -e' rule are well known as sight words to most secondary school pupils. They are:

    have, give, love, shone, above, dove, glove, come, some; done, none, gone, shone, lose, whose, move, prove.

(b) When a vowel is followed in a syllable by '-re' the sounds are modified in this way:

    -are   compare, share, rare, spare, scare, etc.
    -ore   sh*o*re, sp*o*re.

3. *Some vowel digraphs*

(a) *-ee, -ea, -ai, -oa.*

In these combinations, the sound is the name of the first letter, i.e. the long vowel sound,

e.g. ch*ee*tah, discr*ee*t, st*ee*l
    b*ea*ker, guin*ea*, sh*ea*ves, incr*ea*se

retain, appraise

groat, moat, approach.

(There is also a large group of words in which *ea* has a 'short e' sound, e.g. weather.)

(*b*)

'ai', 'ay' have the same sound in plaintiff and dismay, but the '-ay' spelling only appears at the end of the word or root.

'oi', 'oy' have the same sound in celluloid, rhomboid, and alloy, but the '-oy' spelling is generally found at the end of the word or root.

(Exceptions: oyster, royal, voyage.)

'au', 'aw' have the same sound in dinosaur, inaugurate, automatic and the *augh* group, trawler and sprawl.

'or', 'our' can also make the same sound:

e.g. storage, courtier.

'ow' has two sounds:

the '-ow' sound in owl and

the '-ow' sound in yellow, growth.

'ou', 'ow' have the same sound:

e.g. doubt and cowl.

'ui', 'oo' have three very similar sounds:

  (i) as in fruit juice, bruise, suitable, cruise, sluice,

     and stoop, harpoon;

 (ii) as in nuisance, pursuit,

(iii) as in partook, shook.

'ew', 'ue' have two closely related sounds:

  (i) as in clerihew and argue;

 (ii) as in shrew and glue.

'ie', 'er' have a 'long e' sound:

e.g. fief and plebeian.

4. '-y' in a final position in a one-syllabled word usually has a 'long i' sound, e.g. spry, by.

(Final '-y' in a word of two or more syllables generally has a 'long e' sound. See suffixes.)

5. *Exceptions to rule of short vowel in medial position.*

(*a*) When letter 'r' follows a single vowel in a syllable the combined vowel +r can produce one of three sounds:

  (i) /ar/ sound   as in Carthusian, argument.

 (ii) /or/ sound   as in swarthy, warden.

(iii) /er/ sound   as in burglar, Cistercian, emerge, girder, thir-

      tieth, donor, vector, carburettor, bursary, sturgeon, survival.

      Note: in addition to the five spellings in (iii) above the /er/

      sound can also be found in these forms:

      wor   as in Worthing, world, worship.

      ear   as in earth, early, learn, heard, pearl, search, rehearsal.

      our   as in vapour, labour.

(*b*)

$c+a+ll$, *ld*, *lt*, *lk*   e.g. enthrall, bald, malt, walk.
$c+o+ll$, *ld*, *lt*   e.g. poll, scold, bolt.
$c+a+ft$, *th*, *sh*, *sp*, *ss*, *st*, *etc.* e.g. craft, bath, surpass, task, clasp, cast.
$i+nd$ e.g. find, blind.
$i+ld$ e.g. wild, child.
$i+gh$ e.g. sigh, flight.
$i+gn$ e.g. sign, design.
$a+w$ e.g. law, crawl.

Although this chapter is concerned with the teaching of phonics it must be read within the framework of the general thesis of this book. Poor readers have to use their phonic skills in the context of cues provided syntactically or semantically by the text. To concentrate too heavily on word analysis is detrimental to comprehension. The purpose of phonics teaching as defined here is to simplify the pronunciation process for poorer readers and to help those who have difficulty in decoding and retaining unfamiliar and technical words.

Spelling

There is no doubt that spelling remains a bugbear, even if you try to avoid making an issue of it by playing it down. On the one hand it can be argued that it becomes more of a burden to the pupil when not enough attention is given to spelling, and on the other it is possible to argue that our society places too much emphasis on spelling. Many critics have attempted to demonstrate that concern for correct spelling is misguided, belonging either to class snobbery or to capitalism's wish to stratify people.

These arguments, I have found, convince neither parents nor pupils: they *know* that uncertainty over spelling embarrasses them at a number of moments in life. The examples of the words that can be spelt wrongly without impeding communication given by most theorists are irrelevant. It is true of a few examples a few times, but not logically true if extended to many words for a long time. To argue from some apparently non-significant variations to the low importance of spelling in general is weak. Those who argue thus do not seem to have in mind the real difficulties of the poor-spelling pupil, who is wandering amongst a forest of lost letters, and to whom writing is an agony.

I have little sympathy anyway with those who dub correct spelling merely the equivalent of literary table manners, to be fussed over only by the socially squeamish. These people overlook the contribution that a grasp of spelling makes to an understanding of *sense*.

The two are closely linked. The importance of helping the pupil's vocabulary growth depends heavily on the pupil's understanding of the way words are what they are. For many pupils, vague teaching for ten years has given the impression that words are chance collections of letters, with a vague meaning loosely attached. Attention to spelling, on the other hand, is attention above all to form and therefore to meaning. For instance, the pupil confused about the number of 'r's in 'interrupt' has lost, or never found, the relationships *inter— between*; and *rupture—to break*; hence *to break between or into*. The pupil missing the first 'a' in 'extraordinary' has lost the sense, of *extra— beyond*, hence *beyond the ordinary*.

The Report stressed not only the social disability of poor spelling, but the fact that 'confidence in spelling frees the child to write to fulfil his purpose' (11.43). Spelling is really part of the concern for vocabulary, which I have argued must be part of a whole-school language policy. The school must pay regard to the needs of a pupil's spelling because it helps him to write freely, it helps with an understanding of vocabulary, it gives a useful occupational and social skill.

The difficulties in spelling come from the diverse roots of our vocabulary, and the layers of confusion that they introduce:

1. Similar sounds from different roots have been transliterated differently, e.g. especially the Greek sources, where the different alphabet has led to the 'ph', 'rh', 'ps' combinations. Homophones are inevitable in a spelling that retains the etymological origins of words (e.g. *tied* and *tide*).

2. Pronunciation shifts alter the sound of root words, e.g. *phótograph, photógraphy*.

The result is a vocabulary in which there is a constant tension between phonic and etymological pressures on the spelling of a word. What should the school do? There are two extremes in teaching techniques, both impossible not to label pejoratively: (*a*) Issuing word lists, and requiring them to be learnt; (*b*) Leaving the learning to be 'picked up' as words are met over the years. In overall curriculum terms, there is also the choice of putting the responsibility on one Department, or leaving it to all. Virtually nobody who has done research into or written on spelling or vocabulary considers that either is adequate. Certainly the learning of de-contexualized lists has been shown to be ineffective, as has mere leaving to the chance of picking up. The latter seems almost impossible for most pupils given the comparatively small amount of reading and writing that they do.

Indeed, learning for recognition in reading is far from providing most people with the complete mastery required for writing, in which a complete recall is necessary. This is why, of course, contrary to much popular opinion amongst teachers of English, extensive reading is not itself sufficient to help pupils spell adequately, though it is a vital background and helps some children extremely well.

We do not know which pupils are likely to learn best by which methods, but it does seem that the less able and those from less educationally supportive homes are the most in need of specific teaching. Phonic analysis is necessary even for what seems to be sight reading, and those from less favoured homes have had less home training in the underlying skills, an idea which I suspect underlies the Report's survey results: the poorer readers increasingly come from the families of the lower socio-economic classes. It is for these kinds of reasons that the Committee said of spelling that: 'less favoured children need to be taught, and taught rationally and systematically' (11.48). A witness to the Committee from an EPA area stressed: 'An incidental learning approach (to spelling) is hazardous for all children, but particularly so for those from disadvantaged homes' (11.48). The Report therefore called for 'an agreed policy' between subject teachers (11.13), but did not specify in detail what this could comprise. However, a school planning a language policy would clearly wish to arrange a co-ordinated programme of specialized attention in the English class, and attention in the context of all subjects, especially as far as the special vocabulary of each subject is concerned.

What should that attention involve? Not mere list learning—indeed the sheer size of the task would obviously make that unsuccessful. A more careful approach is required, for the heart of helping a pupil to spell well is helping him to concentrate on the internal structure of words.

Children talk about 'difficult words'. It is helpful if they can be brought to think instead of 'difficult syllables'. For most words that offer difficulties there is a vague sense that the whole word is a muddle: the pupil just cannot embark on it. The first task, therefore, is to break it into its constituent syllables. Obviously to do this the nature of syllabification must be taught specifically and used generally.

Having syllabified a word, itself a phonic activity which concentrates attention on sound and structure, each syllable needs to be examined according to the phonic expectations. (Thus the simple phonic patterns of our language should be ready at hand for all teachers.) Then the phonically irregular or difficult syllables can be focused on, and the difficulty isolated, and, incidentally, reduced in size. Thus the teacher facing a pupil or a group having difficulty with the following words would syllabify them:

separate	separate
corridor	corridor
necessary	necessary
analysis	analysis.

Before asking the pupil to memorize the correct spelling, the teacher would indicate the syllable that needs special care. *This* is the one that requires learning, for this is the one that is phonically irregular or for which there are reasonable phonic alternatives. These syllables are then specified, thus:

separate   with an 'a' in the middle
corridor   with only one 'o' at the end
necessary   with double 's'
analysis   with a 'y' in the middle.

Many weak spellers in secondary schools simply have not got the knowledge of the basic regular phonic patterns. There are pupils in secondary schools who are vague about the sound possibilities of the single vowel sounds (e.g. they confuse 'i' with 'a' in short sounds) or blends (e.g. 'dr', 'spl', etc.). The teacher coming across spelling difficulties must (a) recognize the cause of the difficulty, (b) refer the pupil to the phonic generalization, and (c) if possible add other examples. *Merely to correct gives the pupil no power over the spelling: he cannot re-use the correction on other occasions.* Therefore a school-wide knowledge of simple phonics is vital. This involves being able to draw on a commonly agreed pool of phonic teaching. Again, taught specifically, and used throughout.

Phonic generalizations, however, rarely stand up to the full range of examples because of changes of pronunciation or because of alternative less common phonic patterns. The report quoted the letters 'calmbost'. This group of letters could be pronounced as 'chemist' by applying a set of sound values, each of which is used in English (candle, many, silent 'l' as in calm, harm, silent 'b' as in lambing, women, and so on). The simple phonic rules do not cover all of the vocabulary, for as many as 1 in 3 words may be irregular. America's experience of burdening children with a vast number of such generalizations has shown that it does not help, and after a point can be counter-productive. Furthermore, some of the rules are inevitably complicated in expression and use terms which are unfamiliar to the pupils. The rules are more difficult than the points being covered. It is therefore only the firm central phonic principles that should be taught and used, and a school drawing up a language policy should commission its own list, and agree it as a full staff.

Clues

Apart from this phonic analysis, clues can be offered to help the concentration on the key difficult syllables. The main ones are:

1. *Derivations.* Clues come from a knowledge of structure, and this means considering what a word comes from, and what it does not come from. For instance, 'corridor' seems to have something to do with doors, and many writers want to put two 'o's at the end. In fact it comes from an Italian word (via French) meaning a runner. The teacher would therefore point out that the word has nothing to do with doors and comes from quite a different word altogether.

2. *Patterns inside words*. There are a number of letter groups that are used often as alternatives to the simple regular phonic pattern. These should be taught, and when a subject teacher comes across a word that uses such a combination he should refer to the similar ones, such as the examples below:

'ph' is pronounced like 'f' sound (except in Clapham): photograph, etc.

'aught' group: caught, taught, naughty, daughter.

There are approximately 1900 words in English which end in '-tion'. It is useful to point out that this suffix is pronounced 'shun'.

'-uit' group: fruit, suit.

3. *Unstressed sounds*. One of the hardest parts of spelling is choosing the right form for the unstressed syllables in each word. Most errors occur in such places (e.g. sep<u>a</u>rate, poss<u>i</u>ble, opp<u>or</u>tunity). There are only three approaches:

(*a*) Pure visualization. Some people learn them best by learning the look of the difficult area.

(*b*) Artificially stressed pronunciation.

(*c*) Knowledge of etymology to trace the source of the indeterminate sound.

4. *Homophones*. With homophones, pronounced the same but having different meanings and different etymologies, research[1] shows that for secondary-age children they are best taught separately. It would seem wise to tie each word to its etymological family of words.

5. *Spelling rules*. The Report commended a comprehensive school that used a list of spelling rules. The trouble is, as I said of phonic generalizations, on the one hand there are often exceptions, and on the other hand some rules are extremely difficult to comprehend. However, those rules that are simple and fairly reliable should be known, agreed, taught, and used.

The maths teacher, for instance, should know the 'silent e' rule, and have that knowledge available if any of his pupils are having a moment's difficulty over any of the following words, all from a first-year maths syllabus:

rotate

divide

spike (a spike abacus)

prime.

To do this he must also be sure that the rule has been taught elsewhere specifically. Only if that is so can he call on the rule to help him, without risking having to embark on a full-length explanation of the rule. Of course, by making this reference in context, especially with a central word like 'prime', over which he is likely to linger, the maths teacher is reinforcing the pupils' knowledge of the rule and ability to use it readily as required.

[1] K. C. Harder, *The Relative Efficiency of the Separate and Together Methods of Teaching Homonyms*, Journal of Experimental Education, VI, 1937.

Methods

Because some people have less good visual perception and memory, much bad spelling results from not having ever really *looked at* the letter patterns. Thus mechanical copying is as bad as rote learning. The pupil given a written word to help him with his spelling should be encouraged by all subject teachers to follow the routine: look—cover—write—check. There is ample evidence that for most pupils if this drill is not followed, and if mere copying is allowed, the pupils will usually *use* the word, and as promptly let it go from their minds in the same way that most people promptly forget a telephone number recently looked up the moment they have dialled it.

Reading aloud has been shown to help spelling (as I believe it helps punctuation and grasp of argument). This is because a fuller articulation of the word is required for a vocalized reading, and this fuller articulation involves auditory analysis (e.g. in the words 'multiply', 'analysis', 'elasticity', 'corrosion').

The key question for the teacher is not 'Is this pupil a bad speller?', but 'What kind of mistakes?' does he make? A continuous professional curiosity is vital—the too-common attitudes of hopeful optimism or hopeless despair are useless. Teachers of English can not teach a general skill, 'good spelling'. However, they can give the familiarity with words, their structure, the phonic basis, and methods of analysing words which provide the necessary foundations. Each subject teacher then uses this in handling the vocabulary of his subject and the writing in it.

A school language policy might, then, involve attention to the following ideas:

1. Phonic introduction of all new, or specially important words in each subject.
2. Words always to be syllabified, to help the understanding of structure, and to make it possible to focus on the difficult syllables. Draw attention to the syllable to be specially remembered.
3. A school-agreed list of spelling rules to be drawn up and promulgated. When commenting on pupils' spelling these to be referred to.
4. A list of some of the main word patterns to be similarly drawn up. This is likely to be specially important in schools with less able intakes where many of the simple patterns (e.g. 'aught', '-uit', or '-tion') have not been learnt at younger stages.
5. A list of useful prefixes, roots, and suffixes to be used throughout the school for reference when introducing new words or correcting old.
6. Always giving a spelling in writing, never letter by letter aurally. Usually then have the pupil memorize it before writing it. Discourage copying.
7. Each subject teacher should produce a word list for a sequence of work, and these words should be tested and taught.

Punctuation

Punctuation is an integral part of writing, arguably the most important technical aspect, and one that has been a least successful part of formal education. The paradox is that if we are to help those that can take least theorizing, *our* theory of punctuations has to be so much better, so that what instruction we do judge fit to give is not only accurate, but also useful because it refers to fundamentals and can thus be applied on other occasions.

The teaching of punctuation has suffered from a number of fallacies:

1. *That as the teaching of grammar is out, punctuation should not be taught.* This rests on a misunderstanding of the definition of grammar and the arguments against teaching it. As Dr Gatherer has made clear in this book, punctuation is not part of grammar as taught, so that the arguments against the teaching of it are in most ways irrelevant to the teaching of punctuation. The available research shows that punctuation is used best by pupils who have been taught it.[1]

2. *That punctuation is all a matter of personal taste, and so cannot be taught.* It is true that there is considerable latitude for personal taste in, for instance, the use of the comma. In most sentences the absence or presence of one comma alone is unlikely to make that sentence either 'wrong' or 'right'. However, the fact that we could leave that verdict to personal taste judged against stylistic consistency with the rest of the passage should not obscure the vital fact that there is an underlying system for the use of the comma. There are thus frequent occasions when its presence, or absence, *is* indubitably wrong judged by the sense needs of the writer's intention, and all teachers will be able to think of examples from pupils' texts alone. Thus even on those occasions when we agree to differ, we differ only in our judgement of the effect of the application of certain aspects of the system on any particular occasion, not on the system itself. Whatever choice we make is not a matter of pure taste, such as whether you prefer Double Gloucester or Wensleydale cheese. The fact of there being a choice depends on our understanding of an underlying system of punctuation: thus the choice is better exercised if the system is understood.

It is also misleading to invoke reaction against the teacher's personal taste in the argument, since we do teach many matters in school which are aspects of personal taste. Clearly the approach and aims are different from the more objective parts of education, but we do not consider them beyond the scope of our work.

3. *That concentrating on mechanical aspects of language inhibits creativity, and therefore punctuation should not be taught.* Apart from the way the use

---

[1] W. G. Heath, *Library-Centred English*, University of Birmingham Review, 1962.

of this kind of metaphor preempts the argument, this is more a point about the method of teaching than against the need to teach punctuation.[1] Even the teacher least willing to explain a point of punctuation is eventually driven to object to eccentric punctuation, for eccentric punctuation inhibits not merely communication but the actual articulation of thought. The Report commented that: 'It was not uncommon to find the despairing comment "Your punctuation must improve" on the writing of pupils who seemed to have received little or no specific instruction in it' (11.21). *This* broadside and blunt criticism certainly inhibits creativity, and, what is more, it does not in any way help the pupil with his punctuation.

4. *That for the less able it should be 'first things first', and any consideration of punctuation is an excessive burden for such pupils.* This point of view has an honourable lineage, and, indeed, did a great deal of good, helping to get pupils away from pointless exercises (e.g. *Visual English*, all little cartoons and error correction) onto writing. David Holbrook approves of this realignment from exercise to doing (although it is worth reminding teachers who romanticize his approach that he includes 'drills' in punctuation in his philosophy.[2] This approach of putting writing before punctuating was well put by the Newsom report when it tartly commented:

> In practice many of the weaker pupils never seem to reach the point at which real English begins.[3]

However, this should not deny pupils the opportunity of sharpening their understanding and practice of punctuating, but merely ensure that the tuition is kept in its place—that is, learnt in sufficient depth and detail for the writing in hand. We can accept that less able pupils cannot be taken through a decontextualized systematic analysis of all aspects of punctuation (indeed, should any normal secondary pupil?). However, the more we argue for reduction the more important it is that what is brought before the pupil is both accurate and above all usable on other occasions, when the advice may come to mind. Now this patently has not been done so far. Inaccurate half truths, of little use for extrapolation, have been the sop for the less able: 'A full stop marks a big pause, and a comma a short one'; 'never start a sentence with "but"'; 'all paragraphs start a little way in.' These rough 'rules' are not 'ready' because they are neither accurate nor useful. They commit the first sin of curriculum building, losing essential concepts while accommodating ourselves to the less able. Indeed, I should argue that it is precisely by sifting out the essential concepts, clarifying them, and then concentrating our practice on those that one works with the less able.

---

[1] cf. Neville Bennett, *Teaching Style and Pupil Progress*, Open Books, 1976.

[2] cf. *English for Maturity*, CUP, 1961, and *I've Got to Use Words*, CUP, 1964.

[3] *Half Our Future*, para. 462, HMSO, 1963.

5. *That punctuation is unnecessary in any case.* Those who attack the need for punctuation ('Bernard Shaw didn't use the apostrophe') use phrases such as 'middle-class', 'only snob value for big business'. Their attack is usually illustrated by a lengthy diatribe against the pointlessness of the apostrophe – somewhat similar in my mind to attacking the value of the vital organs of the body by criticizing the appendix.

A theory of punctuation

The Report definitely recommends (11.21) 'explicit instruction' in punctuation. The Report's twin approaches of general use and specific intervention fit especially well. Within the writing policy, pupils should be given as many and as varied assignments as possible, but:

1. Some named sector of the school should be responsible for relevant explanation in context. This is likely to be the English teachers, but could be any Humanities Department.
2. Every teacher should work to the same principles, agreeing on punctuation priorities, and knowing the methods of explanation of others. This general support should concentrate on the fundamental principles.

There seem to me to be two problems—firstly of classification analysis and secondly of terminology. In other words, a theory of punctuation is required which is adequate to cover the complexities of real language, but simple enough for use in all subject classes. I know of nothing published to help us in the classroom, and I therefore offer my own approach.

Punctuation should be analysed by function, not by sign. The common analysis by sign (e.g. 'a capital letter is used to start sentences and for the names of persons or places') confuses quite separate functions. The full stop ending a sentence is quite different from the one showing an abbreviation. Instead of the uses of the semi-colon, we need to show seven ways of marking off a sense group, or the three ways of inserting interruptions (commas, dashes, brackets), or the three ways of indicating a word or phrase has been borrowed from a special use. In this analysis the emphasis would be on the way we have to group words to make sense. Ungrouped words are mere puzzles, and wrongly grouped words are nonsense. These ways of grouping are by use of:

the comma
the semicolon
the bracket
the full-stop with space and upper-case letter
the paragraph indentation (or the extra horizontal space)
the space or signs for section divisions
the chapter-ending space

These signs can be seen as a hierarchy of sense groupings from the phrase to the chapter.

I am suggesting that space should be seen as a sign, for it is used to signal meaning to the reader. The paragraph was originally marked indeed by a sign in the margin. Only in modern times was the indentation used instead (now frequently replaced by a wide horizontal band of space).

Another aspect of this functional analysis is that the full stop is never on its own. As a major, *the* major, sense-group marker it is always followed either by an upper-case letter or by space to the end of the line (to show the end of a paragraph). Thus the combination of full stop and upper-case letter should be taught from the first, and explained as a *pair* dividing off sense groups.

If punctuation is to be taught, both in a specialized and contextualized way, and if an analysis by function is to be used, the points made must be accurate and consistent. The theory of stops most commonly taught, and indeed the one which seems to rise to the teacher's mind when he is obliged to point out a failing and thus to explain, is surely inaccurate. It is often said to help young pupils in schools that the main punctuation marks (, ; : .) indicate pauses of varying lengths. This is so commonly said that you may well have come across it. It is a limited definition of their function, since the statement applies only to prose read aloud. Even then it is only partially true; experience shows that pauses are almost entirely left to the reader's own choice. The strongest pause signs are paragraph indentations but the others are flexible. If you listen to yourself or any other reader you will soon notice that the *length* of a pause has almost no relation to the punctuation marks. Pauses are part of a speaker's effect, but in prose read aloud do more to control the impression and atmosphere, than the sense, which is indicated far more by the intonation or pitch of the voice. Consider this remark and try reading it aloud as dramatically as possible.

I want you to realize this is your last warning. If you come late again, you're fired!

Where have you made your longest pause? It could be at the full stop after 'warning', but there are many other places where a speaker might make a long pause. One could occur at the comma after 'again', but is just as likely even where there is no sense break, e.g. after 'realize' and after 'you're'. It could be said like this:

I want you to realize [*long pause*]
[*very fast*] this is your last warning. If you come late again, you're
[*long threatening pause*]
[*slowly*] fired!

That would be a natural and effective way of reading it. The pauses would be for dramatic effect, and not for basic sense. If you listen carefully, you will notice that the sense groups marked by the punctuation marks (the full stop and comma) *are* used by the reader. *Punctuation helps control his phrasing and intonation, while the reader's speed and length of pauses are left up to him.*

It is also important to put across the idea that the 'signs' do not include only the familiar stops, but space, and the change of letter-shape to upper case, and italics or bold type.

Terminology

Finally, there is the question of terminology. When analytic grammar was taught, 'phrase', 'clause', and 'sentence' could be used, as could the remainder of the Latin terms. A school must establish its agreed vocabulary, what the report calls 'the modest collection of technical terms useful for a discussion of language'. 'Sentence' would no doubt be retained. I have already mentioned that I find the idea of 'sense groups' useful. Here are two other important things to teach when explaining punctuation conventions.

1. *Defining or non-defining clauses*, the correct use of which is especially necessary in transactional writing. Teachers will have their own methods for explaining these to pupils. A useful question is: 'Does the extra part tell you which or tell you more?'

A word or phrase in apposition would also be described as one 'that tells you more', or 'a second naming' and taught similarly in both reading and writing.

2. *Vocative of address*, very frequent in story writing, autobiography, and plays. It is best to say: 'Always put a comma before the name of the person you're speaking to, never before the name of the person you're speaking about.' Thus: 'Come here, John'; and 'I don't agree with John'. In all these examples the emphasis should be on punctuation as it indicates *intonation patterns*, not pauses.

Conclusion

A school, then, needs a theory of punctuation. It needs an agreed analysis and set of terms. A named department should have the explicit, specific teaching function, probably with check list and record system to ensure that opportunities are found for all aspects to be explained. The system should be agreed on by the whole staff, expounded, and circulated, with a list of priorities. Each teacher is then in a position to reinforce the teaching within the context of the writing requirements of his or her learning activity.

Study skills

We award the highest academic accolade to a student who can see a question, focus it into an enquiry, trace sources, find relevant information in those sources, collate the information, reorganize that information in a way that meets the question posed, and write up the reorganized material as a report. To those who achieve that pinnacle of scholarship we award a Ph.D. This same process is the one we have adopted as the main teaching method for the less academic and less well motivated school pupil, almost completely in the humanities, and extensively even in the crafts and sciences. Yet we often give no specific help. The 'project method' is felt to motivate inherently, and this motivation is supposed to solve all learning problems. No wonder projects are often so feeble.

The spread of CSE brought the spread of the project, sometimes even called the research project. From the earliest days perceptive teachers were worried about the quality of the pupils' work. What looked to a superficial glance like involvement, perhaps because of the cover and presentation, proved on a closer look to be undigested and uninvolved copying. In history it was reported that 'it became apparent that many pupils had copied sections from their source book, sometimes showing evidence of lack of understanding'[1] and examiners in geography similarly reported: 'A large number copied enormous amounts or made thinly disguised paraphrases, and this led to over-lengthy accounts'.[2] I came across one example of a page of pupil's project writing that included the words 'see Fig. 24' — but the reference was to the original, slavishly copied, text. Too often the pupil was not merely not understanding the subject matter, he was not getting experience in writing, for he was not sufficiently master of what he wanted to say to be handling the ideas in his own language. Indeed the project or research folder too often provided the antithesis of the writing approaches recommended in Nancy Martin's contribution to Chapter 5. Ironically some teachers, having recognized these weaknesses, have tried to avoid the problem by recommending that project topics should be less factual. In other words they have fallen for the temptation yet again of recognizing a linguistic difficulty, but, instead of facing it and attempting to solve it, are seeking to avoid it.

The process has slid down the years, because of a peculiar logical flaw of assumptive teaching. The teacher first conscientiously notes that the next stage of education is going to require some particular ability; he then decides to prepare for that next stage; then, instead of teaching *for* it, he merely presents the new situation, assuming that

---

[1] Schools Council, *The Certificate of Secondary Education: The Place of the Personal Topic – History*, Examination Bulletin No. 18, H.M.S.O., 1968.

[2] Schools Council, *The Certificate of Secondary Education: Trial Examinations – Geography*, Examination Bulletin No. 14, H.M.S.O., 1966.

the pupil will develop the required abilities to tackle it. Thus projects go further and further down the age group, with as little tuition in reference skills as ever. Many textbooks habitually throw hopelessly huge investigations at pupils, and many teachers accept from pupils hopelessly vague project titles. Typical assignments from a religious studies book, clearly designed for average pupils of fourteen or fifteen, include such bald statements as: 'Make a detailed study of Yoga'. Where would a pupil start? What kinds of things would be appropriate to include? Where might he find information?

As any school Librarian will tell you, usually pupils embarking on a project go to the library for a book. The famous 'use of initiative', 'discovery method', and so on, often consist of 'ask Miss', and 'Miss' is asked for a book of the precise title of the project. 'Please, Miss, have you a book *on* "Pollution Today"?' What knowledge of the library was taught in Junior schools is often lost in the early years of the secondary school.

The study skills are yet another part of the policy that requires both a specialized and a disseminated approach. At certain moments in the school, agreed in the policy, some department must be responsible for specific teaching of the basics. All subjects must then draw on this foundation knowledge, add the key data for their own subject, and give the study skills scope by guided experience in their subject field.

The study skills could be listed as:

1. Some idea of the range of kinds of sources available, which includes non-book sources.
2. Some idea of the kinds of books from which knowledge can be gained, that is, not only from full-length books on the subject being explored but reference books, encyclopaedias, compendiums, books ostensibly on other subjects, etc.
3. A growing understanding of how a library is organized, with special emphasis on the use of the catalogue.
4. Familiarity with the conventions of books, including table of contents, index, etc. It is especially important to understand the value of an index for freeing the reader from the author's organization of ideas, and allowing a different means of entry into the book.
5. Training in flexible approaches to books, especially skimming and scanning and searching for the points required.
6. Training in noting information and ideas.
7. Guidance in reorganizing and synthesizing—possibly the most difficult task.

Underlying all these sub-skills is the central need to focus the enquiry in such a way as to make it a definite enquiry and not merely a wander through any facts which come up.

It would help if more subject teachers gave specific lead-ins to any enquiries that they are mounting. Below, is an example of a worksheet prepared for third-year classes to help them handle an enquiry into a religion.

Report on a religion

These notes give you advice on how you might gather in information for, and write up a report. It is only *advice*, and you should use your own ideas as much as possible.

1. *Choose the religion you will study* (n.b. if you are yourself a member of a religion, it is advisable to choose *another* one.) Hinduism, Sikhism, Judaism, Buddhism, Islam.

2. *Sources.* You may use any of these ways of finding out. It is best to use a number of ways. When you are finding out, make notes as you go along. When you are using books, do *not* copy—put the ideas into your own words.

(*a*) Class book box.

(*b*) School Library.

(*c*) Public Library.

In libraries the classification numbers of books on religions are:

Christianity	230
Comparative religion	290
Judaism	296
Islam	297
Hinduism	294
Sikhism	294
Buddhism	294

You can also look up the religions under their alphabetical position in Encyclopaedias (classified as Reference). Books on peoples' lives are 920.

(*d*) Newspapers—cut out any news item from local or national papers.

(*e*) TV—note any news item, and watch any documentaries.

(*f*) People—ask friends, relatives, neighbours.

(*g*) Places—try to visit at least one religious building. Look carefully and make notes.

3. *Questions.* These are the sort of questions you might ask: When was the religion started? By whom? Where? What are the main beliefs? How do these beliefs affect ordinary life? How do they affect families? Could you make this clearer? What are the main rituals? What do they stand for? Describe one in detail. What are the main festivals? Describe one in detail.

Does worship take place at home or in a special building, or both? Is the home or the building more important for worship? What is one special building like from the outside? If you went inside, what would you find?

Is there a special person in charge of worship in the building? What is he/she called? What does he/she do?

All religions have stories (myths) about their god/gods or their founders. Re-tell one of the stories which plays an important part in the religion you are studying (e.g. if you were studying Christianity you might want to tell the story of the death and resurrection of Jesus).

4. *Writing it up.*

(*a*) Make notes as you find out facts, opinions, etc.

(*b*) List the main headings under which you will write. (For example: history; main countries; main beliefs; rituals; one in detail, etc.)

(c) Re-arrange the points in your notes so that you write about all you know on each part of the subject.

(d) When you have spoken to someone to find things out, quote his or her actual words.

(e) Only quote key phrases or sentences from books, and put them in quotation marks. (Put everything else in your own words.)

Use diagrams, drawings, pictures, photographs, to illustrate what you have written.

Previewing a book

Amongst the problems of individual study, possibly the hardest is how to get from a book what is wanted without a complete read from page one onwards. Colin Harrison has described in Chapter 5 how even quite advanced students start at the beginning of a book, and are unable to grasp its whole, indeed to establish whether it is likely to include the information being sought. It is helpful if they are specifically taught the clues which can be used in previewing. If a whole class is to spend some time using a main source book, the teacher would be well advised to preview it with the class, thus both helping the pupils use that book throughout the year, and giving a specific setting for the knowledge of book structure that will be taught specifically elsewhere. Such previewing involves considering:

1. *Title and sub-title.* Particularly the latter gives clues to the angle, focus, or purpose of a book.

2. *Blurb or preliminary summary.* The book jacket blurb, frequently reprinted on the half-title page is, as it were, an extension of the sub-title.

3. *Editorial details.* Almost always found on the reverse of the title page, these establish the date of publication, and any subsequent revision. (The difference between a new 'impression' and a new 'edition' should be taught.) Even the youngest pupils should learn to consider this for all information books.

4. *Table of Contents.*

5. *Introduction.*

6. *Summaries* or terminal aids. Many books have conclusions, summaries, or sets of questions that review the entire book.

As more and more subjects use individual enquiry as a teaching method, it is vital that the school as a whole helps pupils develop what have come to be called the study skills, as the ability to do this is of lasting value to the adult. The need is put clearly and forcefully by this American writer:

> What is the teaching of a particular subject such as social studies, science, literature, or home economics other than that of teaching the pupil or student to recognise and face issues, questions or problems inherent to

that body of content; to locate appropriate information content; and to devise from that content ideas, generalisations, and principles that will help him answer his questions, resolve the issues, or form valid bases for opinions or judgements? It would seem, then, we are saying only in another way that *the teaching of a particular subject is the teaching of the study of that subject*; and that makes inescapable the fact that every teacher is a teacher of reading and study.[1]

[1] A. Sterl Artley, 'Effective Study—Its Nature and Nurture', J. Allen (ed.), *Forging Ahead in Reading*, International Reading Association, Newark, Del., 1968.

7. School Organization

To be concerned with language development in the secondary school is to be concerned with the total school context, and that means matters of school organization. The classroom approaches outlined so far need backing up by a number of school-wide organization points. In this chapter we shall consider the main ingredients for a language policy which are aspects of school organization.

Liaison between schools

One of the romantic vaguenesses peddled frequently in educational exhortation is that we should create a closer liaison between educational institutions. In fact it is one of the hardest things to achieve, and can consume considerable time to little effect. Hadow in 1926, Plowden forty years later, and Bullock again have all echoed the need. Certainly the comprehensive school has usually built some form of liaison into its pastoral system,[1] but too often this is the responsibility of one Head of Year, and whilst something is achieved, it cannot be said that there is a functional continuity. Usually, even at its best, this is only a pastoral continuity; it rarely has a curriculum dimension, and frequently has only the sketchiest reference to language.

Where such pastoral continuity so often goes wrong is in its emphasis on a *personal* relationship between a limited number of teachers. This in practice must mean a relationship between a very small number of people, and thus very little real information is passed on to those who need it most. The records most transfer systems use are inadequate. Suspicion of measured reading data is made worse by the erratic and incompatible systems used even within one group of schools. From a language point of view this lack of continuity means work is not built on, needs are not prepared for, there are confusing conflicting explanations for pupils, and the language environment can change awkwardly and unprofitably from school to school. A secondary

[1] cf. Michael Marland, *Pastoral Care*, Organization in Schools Series, Heinemann Educational, London, 1974.

school needs to know what has gone before, generally and specifically. Whatever other reasons there are for policies of continuity, a
secondary-school language policy depends upon one. A good liaison
policy is likely to consider:

1. Shared knowledge of the learning activities, materials, and styles.
2. Specific information about individual pupils, their reading and
language skills (this will include the interchange of samples of
writing).
3. An agreed policy on at least some aspects of a language policy
across the schools.

In my view there is no harm in there being stages in education,
marked by distinct breaks. Rather than energy being devoted to
removing or smoothing over these breaks, the pastoral side of schools
should be devoted to helping the growing pupil *use* them. There is
therefore a need for preparation. However, the pupil needs to know
that he is known, and that his achievements have not been left
behind him. The receiving staff need to know what experiences he
has had, what his strengths are, and what special help he requires.
This information is ill-supplied by many current LEA transfer
systems. What is clearly required is four-fold:

1. A language 'profile', that is a description of each pupil's language
use.
2. Standardized reading data, measured by the same tests throughout
the group of schools, preferably in the form of informal reading
inventories or diagnostic test data.
3. Titles of books read.
4. Samples of various kinds of writing by the pupil.

Knowledge either of schools or of individual pupils is not itself enough,
unless it leads to action. Part of the action will be the adjustment of
the teaching process and learning materials to take cognizance of
the complementary approaches of the other school. I do not mean by
this a wholesale change, indeed it would be ridiculous to try to
reproduce, say, primary methods for thirteen- or fourteen-year-olds.
It is, though, possible to retain the differences between school types,
and between subject experiences within the secondary school, and
still to respect and react to this knowledge. This action is likely to
be on a number of planes:

1. Agreement about terms to be used amongst the community of
schools (see the first section of Chapter 6).
2. Agreement about definitions and methods of explanation (e.g.,
'What is a full stop?').
3. Agreed approaches to the hierarchy of reading skill.

4. Broad agreements about the language demands reasonable at various stages, and of the preparation that will lead to those stages.

Thus liaison would result eventually in a community of schools creating a broad plan, within which specific details were agreed, and individual pupils' work known. This would allow each of us to work at our specialism in its own way and within our own approach knowing what we build on, what we are expected to contribute, and the common terms with which to do it.

Testing policy

There is a tendency in education for crusaders to be left fighting enemies that have all but disappeared. If they stopped to consider, these crusaders would often find the battle has been won, and that the enemy they are now hitting at is not the original target, and does not deserve their animus. So it is with testing. Those who fought against selection and for the common school had in the course of the war to wage a battle against selection, which involved attacking and destroying the selection tests that were part of it. There are those who are still fighting tests as the agents of selection, even when selection has been defeated.

More sophisticated objectors to test programmes are those who have read about the labelling effect of testing. 'Teacher expectation and pupil performance' was the telling phrase that Douglas Pidgeon used as the title for his important study of the possible bad effects of the misuse of crude test data.[1] This was, and still is, an important argument: crude labelling of pupils' abilities can lead teachers to teach to and keep children to the levels declared by the labels, and at the same time can lead pupils to live up to, or down to, those label levels.

Thus educational testing and measuring of all kinds became discredited in the eyes of many teachers who were anxious to encourage high achievement, and who regarded themselves as progressive. In fact, however, such blatant condemnation of testing does not stand serious consideration, nor should the possibilities of mis-use of data logically lead to the abandoning of the data if it can have good uses.

The Report retains a healthy scepticism about much testing, and notes all the possible fears, even that testing time uses up precious teaching time. However, it establishes a new positive approach to testing, given the main point that 'Testing should never be carried out without a real purpose' (17.15).

[1] Douglas Pidgeon, *Teacher Expectation and Pupil Performance*, NFER, 1970.

The Report recommends testing programmes at three levels: national monitoring, local authority screening, and in a school. It is this last that is part, as I see it, of a whole-school language policy. However, it should be seen in relation to the first two. National monitoring by a rolling programme of light sampling based on frequently revised item banks is carefully worked out by the Committee as the only sane, reliable, and valid way by which the nation can know how its education is doing. The community is, quite rightly, bound to want an answer to that question. A method such as the committee recommended avoids the panic that blows up from time to time without it, and the inefficient measurement that results. The case for local authority screening is equally strong. By the use of appropriate measures at younger ages, pupils whose language deficiencies need attention can be identified.

My concern, however, is with in-school programmes. The argument I shall develop grows out of Bullock, but in some ways goes further than the Report, which does not go into great detail in the secondary phase.

The central purpose of testing is to obtain knowledge that can be used to help the pupil. There is plenty of evidence that we have insufficient knowledge to provide the help that is required. One interesting example was produced by the Committee's survey, and it is an example which could be replicated with teachers of older children also. For me it epitomizes one level of knowledge requirement. The teachers of six- and nine-year-olds in the sample were asked to estimate how many of their own pupils would be placed in the top 25 per cent ('Good') of the *nation*'s readers, the middle 50 per cent ('Average'), and the bottom 25 per cent ('Poor'). Obviously when totalled and expressed as a proportion of the total number of children in the whole sample, the number of children in each category should roughly equal the defined percentage of each category: 25 per cent, 50 per cent, 25 per cent. In fact the teachers of nine-year-olds over-estimated the ability of their children by putting no fewer than 41.1 per cent of the pupils in the top 25 per cent, only 37.4 per cent in the middle 50 per cent, and only 21.5 per cent in the bottom 25 per cent (Survey Table 43). My impression is that similar over-estimating of reading ability is common in many schools, though it is difficult to get firm evidence.[1] Secondary schools have a

---

[1] cf. the report on *William Tyndale Junior and Infants School Public Inquiry*, ILEA, 1976, p. 59. ILEA Junior schools are obliged to place pupils in similar percentiles (25, 50, 25) for transfer to secondary school. This table is interesting quite apart from the purpose for which it is quoted in the Inquiry Report (i.e. to assess the levels of the pupils' achievement). The figures show the teachers' assessments, in the centre column, as widely discrepant from the NFER-monitored test results for the school, shown in the right-hand column:

way of reacting with shock after the first screening tests that they administer—a shock that can be explained only by the inaccuracy of the previous estimates. I therefore believe a reading testing programme is necessary as part of a whole-school language policy:

1. To monitor the overall curve of the ability:
(a) to establish changes from year to year, or following alterations in the transfer procedure.
(b) to help consideration of the curriculum.
(c) to help consideration of pupil-grouping methods.
(d) to help the disposition of all forms of resources, teachers, rooms, money.
(e) to contribute towards the evaluation of the curriculum and teaching by comparison with follow-up figures.
2. To identify those pupils who seem to be deficient and who need help.

Clearly individual pupils would then require detailed diagnostic tests to establish what kind of help they require and to suggest a teaching programme in reading for them. (There seems no doubt that pupils who need such help can go unnoticed by class teachers without this kind of check.)

Ideally such a programme would be established over a community of schools. If, as the Report suggests, all contributory schools and the secondary school worked to a standard test programme, there would be no need for early testing, only for later follow-up testing. Such a co-ordinated programme, however, seems too difficult for most schools to achieve, and in that case I believe the secondary school must initiate its own programme.

	Authority-wide proportions	School assessment of 4th-year pupils	ILEA's banding of them
Above average	25%	25.8%	16.4%
Average	50%	38.2%	54.1%
Below average	25%	36%	29.5%

The differences between the centre and the right-hand columns are the measure of how far out teachers can be in their unmoderated assessments! Although there are reasons for believing that this group of teachers had greater discrepancy than most.

Planning a screening test of reading attainment at lower secondary level

Colin Harrison

The aim of conducting a screening exercise is straightforward—to identify at an early stage those children who urgently need extra help in reading. This aim is much more general than that of determining exactly what kind of help is needed, which can only come from a closer diagnosis. Individual diagnoses and specific remedial attention would then need to be made available, but initially for an intake of two or three hundred an individual diagnostic reading test would probably be impracticable and inefficient. What is necessary is to pinpoint those in need of extra help during the first half-term, and not allow a situation to develop in which nearly a year passes before a child who had been considered simply quiet or lazy is found to be a very backward reader.

The field of mental testing is a highly complex one, and many teachers who use reading tests are blissfully unaware of the fact that their method of administrating and scoring a test may totally invalidate its results. Most of us have very little understanding of the private world of the statistician and psychometrician, but this does not stop us from borrowing their tools. The kind of error we make may be comparable in magnitude to that of the child who tries to measure the length of a line with a slide rule, but we obtain a result—a number, a score, or better still a quotient, and we make the assumption that it has given us accurate information about the child's current level of ability. We may indeed put much more faith in the score, which seems objective, than in the evidence of our observation and experience, which are necessarily subjective. Every test ever published has weaknesses, and each test result gives only an approximation of the child's true ability. Most test norms have a standard error associated with them, which indicates the range within which the true score is likely to lie. This may be for example plus or minus two months in terms of reading age on a well-constructed test, which represents a range of four months. Even this range would only take account of 68 per cent of the results; the standard error concept implies that 32 per cent of true scores will in fact be outside that range. The need therefore is for great caution in interpreting test scores; the teacher must try to ensure that the results are used to help children, rather than simply to brand them.

The very concept of reading age, so cherished by teachers in their urgent need to classify those in need of help, is not accepted as meaningful by many of the most eminent experts on testing. The manner in which we divide reading age by chronological age in order to produce a reading quotient is similarly regarded as unsound. It presupposes that development in reading ability is linear, i.e. that it tends to follow a straight line, as in graph (a) of Table I. Such a notion is highly speculative, and would indeed be challenged by many teachers. Progress in reading probably conforms more to graph (b), or even graph (c), either of which would be wholly incompatible with the usual manner in which we obtain a reading quotient.

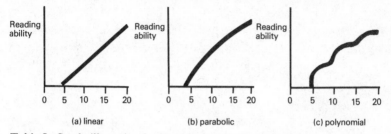

Table I: *Graphs illustrating three possible types of relationship between chronological age and the development of reading ability*

The fact that the field of testing is a complex one need not deter one from using tests, but rather should alert us to the dangers of misuse and misinterpretation. In the present case, where the aim is to carry out a general screening exercise, heeding such a warning may in fact save a great deal of time. In particular, if all we wish to do is to establish which children are not reading well, there is no real point in changing every child's raw score (e.g. 37 out of 53 items) into a percentage, then obtaining a reading age, and moving from there to a reading quotient. If the test has pinpointed the five poorest readers in a class it has done its job. If four of those children are younger than average, using raw scores has not made allowance for the fact, but this could be considered an advantage since they are still the children who are reading most poorly and this would have been masked to some extent by working from a reading quotient.

Choosing a test

An excellent and comprehensive review of the reading tests available in this country has appeared, which tabulates details of ninety-one British and overseas tests as well as offering an introduction to some of the theoretical and practical aspects of testing. This is a monograph in the UKRA Teaching of Reading series, called *Reading: Tests and Assessment Techniques*. Its author is Peter Pumfrey, and the book is in the Hodder and Stoughton Unibook series.

The tests in Table II overleaf could all be used at first-year secondary level. Those cited are necessarily a small selection of the ones available, but represent some of the most widely known and most easily accessible, together with one or two which are less well known

Table II. *Reading tests suitable for lower secondary level*

Name of Test	Chronological Age range	Test mode	Publisher	Skills examined	Time	Remarks
Burt Word Reading Test	5:0–12:0	Individual, oral	Hodder and Stoughton Educational	Reading single words aloud	⩽ 10 mins	Unreliable at upper and lower limits.
Neale Analysis of Reading Ability	6:0–12:0	Individual, oral	Macmillan	Oral reading and comprehension of brief passages.	⩽ 20 mins	Gives remedial teachers valuable diagnostic information.
Schonell R1 Graded Word Reading	5:0–15:0	Individual, oral	Oliver and Boyd	Reading single words aloud	⩽ 10 mins	Unreliable at upper and lower limits; used so frequently that it must be known by heart by some children.
Vernon Graded Word Reading Test	6:0–18:0	Individual, oral	Hodder and Stoughton Educational	Reading single words aloud	⩽ 10 mins	Unreliable at upper and lower limits; less widely used at primary level than Burt or Schonell R1, which could be an advantage.

Table II—*continued*

Brimer Wide-Span	7:0–15:0	Group, silent	Nelson	Comprehension (sentence completion)	≐ 30 mins	Gives diagnostic information; test booklet can be re-used.
Edinburgh Stage 3	10:0–12:6	Group, silent	Hodder and Stoughton Educational	Various subskills of comprehension	≐ 30 mins practice part 1 : 30 mins part 2 : 25 mins	Attempts to assess individuals' attainment on separate sub-skills such as comprehension of main points, vocabulary, etc.; time-consuming to mark.
Gap	7:0–12:0	Group, silent	Heinemann Educational	Reading comprehension (type of 'cloze' test)	15 mins	Easy to administer and mark; less well researched than most standardized tests. Easy to copy answers—teacher must separate pupils.
Gapadol	7:3–16:11	Group, silent	Heinemann Educational	Reading comprehension (type of 'cloze' test)	30 mins	Similar to Gap test; somewhat stronger in its statistical frame-work. Again, teacher must be sure to prevent possible cheating.
NFER DE	10:0–12:6	Group, silent	NFER (Ginn)	Various subskills of reading comprehension and vocabulary	≐ 45 mins	A relatively recent test (1967) which is similar in concept to Edinburgh 3, but simpler to administer.
Schonell R4 Silent Reading B	7:0–14:0	Group, silent	Oliver and Boyd	Reading comprehension (multiple choice)	15 mins	Straightforward to administer; quite widely used although supported by no details of reliability or standardization.

but which merit consideration. A point which must be made in these days of financial stringency is that some tests are very expensive. The Edinburgh Reading Test Stage 3 (at the time of writing) costs about £24 per 100 pupils, and this is by no means the most expensive on the market. It is not surprising that many teachers pirate tests or at least try to re-use the answer books. Generally speaking the cost of the test is proportional to the amount of diagnostic information gained from it; one should also note that longer tests (i.e. those with more items) tend to be more reliable. Nevertheless the word reading tests should not be dismissed out of hand, simply because they do not require the child to read a whole passage and answer questions on it. The point is that the ability to articulate single words on a list has consistently been found to correlate highly with overall reading attainment, and although they give very little diagnostic information such tests can be useful because they are straightforward and quick to administer. Finally, some warnings are offered.

Warnings

1. Any group test causes stress and anxiety for children, but this can be reduced to some extent:
(a) Do not give a screening test in the first fortnight of the school year.
(b) Ensure that so far as is practicable any group test is administered in an atmosphere and environment similar to that of a normal class lesson.
2. Make absolutely sure that each class or group does the test with the same instructions, and is allowed the same time.
3. Make absolutely sure that the results of each class or group are scored consistently. If the questions are multiple-choice, no divergence from the published answers can be accepted. If there is any element of subjectivity of interpretation in the scoring, then the only safe course is to have every child's answers marked by the same person. If a test has subtests, different teachers could share the load by marking every child's answers on one subtest.
4. Do not give children exactly the same test again for at least nine months. If you do, results may be enhanced by a practice effect rather than by any gain in the skills the test measures.

Pupil grouping

How pupils should be grouped is one of the technical issues of education which has become a subject for popular debate, not only throughout the teaching profession but in the general press and amongst parents as well. Its socio-political aspects have given it this status, and everyone feels qualified to opinionate. There are more assertions than considered arguments and many factors are omitted. 'Mixed-ability' versus 'streaming' is the popular form of the argument, an over-simplified polarity which blunts the points being considered. In many ways it was unfortunate that throughout the 'sixties the battle raged so long and so fiercely that the details of teaching method were too frequently lost sight of amongst the broader sociological arguments.

However, there are some issues which focus very sharply on language use, and although this would not be the right place for a full discussion I must try to outline the language learning aspects.

The outline arguments are now well known, but have a new look if you consider them for the moment purely in terms of language use: however careful you are, classifying pupils makes different pupils in the same group seem more similar than they are, and similar pupils in different groups more different than they are. The arguments for not attempting to separate (a formulation that I find better than 'for mixed-ability') are normally stated in the negative in that this, that, or the other disadvantage can be avoided. The positive point is a hope that the differences between people can be used advantageously.

The argument will have to consider the particular circumstances of the school: its intake curve, the local area, the size of a year-group to be divided, the size of teaching group, the classroom size, the resources, and the teachers. Some people speak as if the only problem is a resources problem, and that a mass of work cards, junction boxes, individual assignment cards, and the like will solve the problem.

There are various patterns of grouping for the remedial pupil, and from the language point of view each has its problems as well as advantages:
homogeneous remedial class;
full mixed-ability group;
partial mixed-ability group;
individual extraction from the mixed-ability groups;
visiting remedial specialist.
Obviously the first three can be used for part rather than all of the work in a variety of combinations.

The Report listed the criteria by which a school should make its decision, and gave a general view that mixed-ability work was likely to be most favourable for English as such (15.1). It did not debate the wider issue of pupil grouping throughout the school. The Committee did specifically worry about the less able reader—how would he or she get help?

There are two respectable philosophies—both have truth in them, and it is futile to think that debate will lead to any overwhelming agreement that all right is on one side.

One is that pupils need individual care and different treatment. Indeed, to give them all the same diet is unfair, and opportunities for specific teaching are possible only if the differences are recognized. As truly individual care is impossible with school staffing ratios (indeed pupil–teacher ratios are one of the main reasons why we have groups at all), some measure of grouping by needs is vital. This argument would have to include an analysis of teaching activity to show that extensive and significant individual teaching is not possible in school classes.

The other philosophy is that interaction is a key element in education, especially in language, and that there is a gain from keeping pupils together. This allows common humanity to be shared, and it allows language to grow more naturally.

The language situation of the backward reader in a fully or partially mixed-ability group needs thought. The conscientious teacher is usually anxious to supply a range of activities. To meet the needs of the less able, many of these will be non-verbal tasks: colouring, drawing, filling-in, modelling. If there is not very great care, the clever backward reader will weave his way through the tasks, going for the less verbally difficult time and again. Indeed it is possible for a pupil of twelve or thirteen with mixed-ability English, humanities, and science to go for weeks without reading—or even doing much writing. One count was 300 words read in six weeks!

Writing of mixed-ability work in Science, J. Dark, Science Adviser for Devon, recommends sub-groups of about four, which, he declares, is 'the best size of group to accommodate non-readers'.[1] What does 'accommodate' actually mean? Too often it means allowing the pupil shelter from having to read, and thus denying him practice in this setting. Such a pupil is probably extracted from his class to be given a couple of periods of reading teaching each week. Valuable as this is, it suffers from breaking the continuity of the lessons precisely for those who need the continuity most, and even the reading teaching is discontinuous. The worst fault is the isolation of the teaching of reading from the other learning processes. Dr Ruth Love Holloway, Director of the US Right to Read effort, shrewdly calls this the 'band-aid' approach.

A version of this for older pupils which we developed at Woodberry Down School is called Support Option. Pupils who require such help choose one fewer option in their subject choices. In the time thus freed they are given support teaching—reading and language work (as well as other skills, of course) through the medium of the materials they are using for their other subject choices. This is an attempt to produce proper integrated teaching for the less able. It is, however, very difficult to get the integration fully effective.

The visiting specialist is a tempting device, and seems to me

[1] In E. C. Wragg (ed.), *Teaching Mixed-Ability Groups*, David and Charles, 1976, p. 147.

effective where there are sufficient staff. I have for instance seen it
effectively used for immigrants when the LEA has specifically put
in additional staff for the purpose. The remedial or reading specialist
visits classes to a timetable. When there he assists those who need
help, giving reading and language tuition through the medium of
the materials actually in use. This point-of-need tuition can be very
effective. It suffers from three problems:

1. There is not always, or indeed often, time for the specialist to give
real tuition, only to offer short cuts.
2. The identification, which those who recommend mixed-ability
wish to avoid, is re-emphasized.
3. Usually the remedial specialist can visit for only a few of the timetabled lessons. Thus the help is sporadic, and sometimes hardly
worth it.

From the point of view of language development, pupil-grouping
should be looked at carefully, and the decisions based on the following
criteria: Are groups sufficiently often sufficiently mixed for language
interaction? Do those who need specific help get sufficient time with
sufficient concentration? Where separate specific help is given, is it
related functionally to the other subject teaching?

Print availability

I have stressed throughout that the Committee came to see growth in
language as requiring attention to the whole of school experience, and
thus involving school management. This is true in the provision of
books, what I would like to call a print-use policy. The individual
teacher cannot himself provide the range or integration of reading
material that is required.

Traditionally each Department selects, orders, and organizes
books, and more recently other print sources, in its own way, and
a library provides different kinds of books with a totally different
method of availability. The pupil himself, with no guidance whatso-
ever, is expected to integrate the various sources in his mind, know
where to go for what, and to make up the deficiencies himself—
presumably from public library or home. No wonder education is
class differentiated, for this burden is intolerable.

Apart from the question of availability to pupils, there is the question of the economics of supplying books. Are we making best use of
limited resources? Money for books is extremely tight, perhaps tighter
than staff-room complaints realize. An analysis I did recently showed
that the average figure available for spending per pupil per period

on learning material for the country's secondary schools was 1p![1]
Consider what materials you can buy for that money. How little is
likely to be left for books? Take the 1p per period for a secondary
school. A small part will have to be kept by the school for central
spending on circular letters home, exam papers, duplication for
school administration, etc., say £1.40 a pupil for the whole year or
0.1p per period. Some will have to be put aside for library books.
The Association of Education Committees recommend £2.25 as the
minimum for secondary pupils up to 16. That would require a further
0.16p per period. This leaves 0.74p to spend on all learning materials
for each lesson.

Look next at the costs of a few lessons. I have costed a sixth-form
dissection in biology at 69p a period for each pupil, a fourth-form
heat structure investigation at 9p, and a particular fifth-year physics
lesson at 1.65p a period. A school must run very many chalk-and-talk
lessons to save money for these. A page of an exercise book costs about
0.1p—so it is expensive if pupils are too prolific in their writing.

It is not usual to cost printed books on a period basis, but when
one does it is clear why schools feel short. Take, for instance, an
anthology of plays at £1. It might be read for six weeks for five periods
in each week, and three classes might do that in the year. If the books
last for six years (the Association of Education Committees' recommendation), the book would cost 0.2p for each period. Even the
book cost of an apparently cheap subject like mathematics works
out at hardly less. However large the global sum seems, the actual
amount of money to spend for every lesson is not adequate for the
materials required, certainly not to carry a stock of additional follow-
up material.

There is considerable evidence, what is more, that spending on
books is decreasing not as a result of conscious educational decisions,
but under the pressure of other insatiable needs.[2] Bullock put the
worry clearly: 'Since expenditure on books is part of the larger block
of non-teaching costs, it is in competition with other demands, and
books are in a particularly vulnerable position in times of financial
stringency.'

[1] Michael Marland and Ian Leslie, 'A Penny for All Their Thoughts',
Times Educational Supplement, 26.3.76.
[2] Details of book spending were given by the Secretary of State to Parlia-
ment on October 27, 1975. These show that in the four-year span 1970–71
to 1974–75 the ratio of cash spending on books to that on other materials
had steadily worsened from 1:2.1 to 1:2.3 in primary schools and from
1:2.3 to 1:2.6 in secondary schools. In real terms the worsening is even
greater. The same parliamentary answer showed that the retail price index
increase during the same period had been greater for books than for equipment by a factor of 1.16:1. This means that in 1970–71 schools were spending
about a third of the real value of their allowances on books, and by 1974–75
they were spending only a quarter.

A school studying its costs finds that home economics, needlework, science, and crafts require so much consumable material if the subject is to continue that book purchase in those and other subjects declines. Those subjects that can just about get by on old sets are forced to do so.

There are also problems of level. Many school libraries are sixth-form orientated. Many lack simple enough books on topics of interest and importance to pupils of the younger ages.

We need therefore to look carefully at schools' policies for books. Too often there is a muddled selection and ordering procedure, frequent changing of courses without adequate planning, and sheer inefficiency in stock control. A ratepayer seeing the losses, or the piles of disused books in jumbled corners in some schools, might well protest that he does not want his money spent on that kind of waste. Certainly an integrated print-availability policy could be part of a school's language policy.

In summary, then, a print-availability policy would look at: *relevance* to the pupils' lives and to the school courses; *suitability* in levels and style; *availability*; and *integration*, that is, stocks with stocks and stocks with publicity.

The first three are probably self-explanatory, but the last might need some expansion. The interrelated provision should consider each of the following supply sources:

1. *In the classroom:* full-class 'textbooks'; classroom small sets or topic books; classroom individual copies.
2. *The library:* the basic collection; special collections; reference books; non-book material.
3. *The school bookshop.*[1]
4. *Outside the school:* children's library; main library; local bookshops.

The stocking of 1, 2, and 3 should be considered overall. For instance, titles for further reading or research recommended in books available in 1 should normally be provided in 2 and sometimes 3.

Arising out of this is the question of publicity. Book publicity should have at least some measure of co-ordination. Library and bookshop should mount publicity campaigns that are related to topics or themes currently involving at least some of the classes. Displays should be built up in lockable glass cabinets and outstations of both. School and sectional assemblies should feature or refer to available books. (At Woodberry Down, for instance, the list of Assembly Themes always gives the appropriate Dewey classification numbers.) Special units within a school, like the careers room or music department, should have displays and collections integrated with the central library. The school should thus present books in a varied, vigorous, and inter-connected way to all the pupils.

[1] cf. Marilyn Davies, *The School Bookshop*, in Owens and Marland, *The Practice of English Teaching*, Blackie, 1970, also *School Bookshop News*, Penguin.

PART III

Putting It Into Practice

8. Initiating and Implementing a Policy

Throughout this book, whether in analysis or recommendation, my contributors and I have assumed the need for action; we have pictured a school which wished to act, to build on its earlier discussions and thoughts, and to start up a coherent policy. In this chapter we chart some possible ways of starting that action, and of keeping it going. For a school with a tradition of discussion, joint planning, and school-based in-service training the start should not be too difficult. For a school that has not such a tradition, the challenge of Bullock may be a way of stimulating staff discussion.

Initiating
Nancy Martin

Many teachers, of all subjects and at all levels, are extremely puzzled by what a language policy across the curriculum means. Gerald Haigh's parody of the situation in an article in the *Times Educational Supplement*[1] is not so far from the truth and lays bare the confusion with inspired mockery. Let us quote from him:

> *Monday*. Arriving at school in a decisive mood, I wrote on my 'Things to do' pad:
> 1. See the caretaker again about that funny sticky stuff behind the radiator in room three.
> 2. Remove the outdated notices from the board in the corridor.
> 3. Institute a language policy across the curriculum.

This could be a comment on the comic diversity of a head's responsibilities, but it is equally a reflection of the fact that many teachers and administrators and heads do not understand that getting a language policy going is a new, difficult and long-term job, not at all the same kind of operation as, say, a policy for school uniform.

---

[1] *Times Educational Supplement*, 26.3.76.

Monday (continued)

During the morning Marston, my deputy, came to see me. He wanted to know on behalf of the staff, what I meant by a language policy. If it means a crackdown on swearing, they are on my side.

Tuesday

Read Marston's paper on the language policy. It consists of various standardized symbols to be used by teachers in their marking.

One laughs, yet both points are concerns of teachers: what makes them ridiculous is that they are so remote from the major issue of the active role that language could play in learning.

Again Gerald Haigh's fictional headmaster writes:

. . . Johnson is not taking to the language policy. Several of his pupils are citing Bullock as evidence that they are allowed to talk in class, and he is now asking me to define the boundary between insolent and non-insolent talking. How difficult it all is! In my day all talking was impertinence; all argument rebellion. And we were all literate to boot!

Thursday

. . . Parents are beginning to complain about the language policy. Mrs Flotbury wanted to know why her daughter is being taught by a tape-recorder and a pair of earphones. 'I pay my rates and I demand a proper teacher,' she said. . . .

The confusions ridiculed here are painfully near the bone, and are characteristic of all of us when we half get hold of an idea.

Let us look at some reports from real heads of department and real teachers.[1] First from a head of Home Economics in an 11–16 comprehensive school.

Approach to head—interested, though not willing to help formulate any policy or discussion meeting at this stage.

Approach to head of English—agreed, with some doubts, to a discussion meeting with other interested members of staff.

Approach to deputy head—interested and sympathetic—organised an informal staff meeting for interested members of staff.

Informal staff meeting held. Report on the area DES/ATO Course on Language across the Curriculum from me. Discussion that followed mainly concerned with grammatical errors in pupils' work. Only two heads of department attended, therefore head of English suggested a formal heads of departments meeting to discuss their ideas on a language policy. Probably later this term.

Here is a classic situation. A head of department who has a good idea of what the Report is about in its most general educational implications, a doubtful head; a doubtful (at first) head of English; most other departmental heads not seeing it as anything to do with them; and a sympathetic deputy head who occupies the right place in

[1] N. Martin, B. Newton and P. D'Arcy, *Times Educational Supplement*, 26.3.76.

the power structure of the school to organize a meeting for those interested. What is significant is that, once someone organized a meeting, the head of English overcame his doubts and moved into action with a heads-of-department meeting—which would seem a crucial step. And how necessary it is that someone, like the head of home economics in this case, should be explicit about the real issues involved, otherwise the discussion might well stay at the level of 'standardized symbols to be used by teachers in their marking'.

Next a report from the head of English in an 11 to 18 comprehensive school.

> After the DES/ATO course, reported to head who fully supports the notion of moving towards the long-term goal of a language policy. The head feels this will best be achieved by a series of contacts between the head of English and other departments. I myself have come to feel that the process should be institutionalised in the form of a committee. Agreed to discuss the matter in a meeting of the academic committee and determine a strategy with other heads of department.
>
> Asked the director of studies for an extraordinary meeting of the academic committee. This denied, but the matter was placed on the agenda for the next regular meeting.
>
> At this meeting I outlined the concerns of the Course and emphasised that there was little recognition of such issues in the school, and that all departments were involved, not simply English. It was stated by some that departmental heads were aware of such matters as the need for a variety of written exercises and were capable of making appropriate judgements themselves. I replied that there were many matters of common interest, and my initiative must not be misinterpreted as an infringement of each department's autonomy, but should be seen as a search for solutions to school problems by group efforts. It was felt that methodologies were at issue as much as language. It was agreed to discuss the matter further at the next meeting.
>
> Since the meeting I have approached the head of Mathematics, who is interested in linguistics, and asked him if he would be prepared to chair a committee concerned with methodology and language. He agreed to consider the matter.
>
> It is clear that 'language' is a highly sensitive area where teachers are concerned. Perhaps it would be better to emphasise 'methodology' instead?

In this case the head fully supports the idea though there is some disagreement about tactics, but what about those heads of departments who say they are quite capable of looking after their own affairs, thank you very much? For them the Report clearly has nothing to say of any consequence. Furthermore the feeling at this school meeting is right, that 'methodologies were at issue as much as language'—and, of course, the theories that lie behind methodologies. The Committee is indeed asking teachers to look at what they do in the teaching of their subjects. It is true that the context for this request is that of language: 'What uses do you, in fact, make of language in teaching? How much do you talk? What opportunities are there in your classes for your pupils to formulate their knowledge in their own words? Do they have opportunities to reflect on their work in talk or in writing?' These are indeed matters of methodology, and methodologies reflect hypotheses about learning, so the recalcitrants at this meeting were in effect saying, 'you are asking us to examine our professional expertise and we object to that. It is an infringement of our specialist autonomy'.

What was interesting and sensible on the part of this head of English was to try to get the head of another department (Mathematics) to chair a committee concerned with 'methodology and language'. Until heads of subject departments come to see that language is a major instrument of learning and is therefore their concern, initiating moves from a head of English inevitably appear as interference (or empire building) from a subject with a vested interest in language.

Finally, a thumbnail sketch by an English teacher of the situation in his school which expresses another common misapprehension.

> Since the Bullock Report the head, and heads of departments are committed to some kind of language policy. So far this has taken the form of the sort of support that the English department can give to the less able in other subjects: remedial staff support in mixed-ability lessons; encouragement to the less able to bring written work to remedial group English periods; the formulation of a common correction scheme. The school has a good academic tradition.

Because of the context in which the Bullock Committee was set up—problems of literacy, extended to include all aspects of the teaching of English—a great many teachers see the Report as concerned only with English teaching and remedial problems, and of course, these are its central concerns, but behind them lies its major theoretical contribution (Chapter 4 'Language and Learning') and its attempt to foster the implications of this by its recommendation that schools should establish language policies across the curriculum involving all teachers. This is not a matter of getting all teachers to cooperate in raising the literacy level of the backward, *but of increasing the quality of learning at all levels and in all subjects*. This is what it means.

One of the difficulties in implementing a language policy is that the operation has two directions—towards the classroom, and towards collective decisions by the staffs of schools. And both directions throw up very different kinds of problems. In the first, a teacher makes his own decisions about any changes he may want to make in his own teaching and classroom procedure; in the second he is initiating discussion, meetings, and decisions with his colleagues where the pressures and problems are different from those he encounters in the classroom.

The Report asks something new and difficult of teachers—not only that they should each as individuals foster children's reading and writing, but that they should *collectively* organize language policies for their schools. Here the pressures and problems are different from those of an individual teacher in the classroom. Here the problems arise from the organization of schools and the hierarchies within them. Who has the right to call a meeting? Whose responsibility is it? What are the attitudes engendered by this kind of activity? What unperceived questions lie behind the actual questions raised by the Report? No previous Government Report has required of teachers that they engage in collective action to achieve reforms, and there is therefore little tradition in schools to guide this kind of professional work.

Since the Bullock Report was published in February 1975 meetings and activity of all kinds have been taking place and a momentum slowly building up. What I shall try to do in this section is to document some attempts to implement the Report, choosing those which reveal both the nature of the problems and the kinds of changes which can (slowly) occur.

The very first steps have often proved the most difficult. Three teachers from different schools reported their initiating strategies as follows.

1. Get headmaster's support.
Work through some body already established? E.g., Academic Board of Studies.
If anything concrete agreed on, put to staff council (which consists of heads of departments, year heads+headmaster, deputy heads).
Some constructive ideas of what it *means* and what it has to offer as an educational policy would have to be formulated by somebody, and offered as a first step before any action taken.
Get interest and support of own department.
Get some evidence to present of value of such a policy.
Suggest books to read? Take Bullock Report as starting point?
Get advisers interested?
2. *School situation.* Small (500) rural grammar school, joining with local secondary modern school (at present $\frac{1}{2}$ mile away, 400 children) to form one-site comprehensive. Traditional approaches to most subjects. Little will to innovate (from top downwards).
Report back to Head, emphasizing Bullock. Ask permission to make following moves.
Begin arrangement of meeting (with two neighbouring schools) for Science or Maths teacher (outsider) to describe his attitudes.
Talk to own department (English) and describe course. Ask for follow-up suggestions since they have all been in the school longer than I have.
Approach those members of other departments with whom I have already had 'education' talk. Ask how they view English (ought I to say 'Language'?) in school.

Get them to complete questionnaire—possibly criticizing work of English department.

Collate these remarks and invite contributors to meet and discuss their views.

3. First approach the Head of Department who, happily is a member of the English Curriculum Study Group and in charge of Curriculum Development in the school.

Approach to Headmaster who is already interested in this area of thought.

Notice in staff bulletin—invitation to members of other departments to attend an informal 'talk-in' on this subject. (This approach may appear formal but as we are housed on a split site is necessary to ensure that all staff are aware of meeting.)

Informal approach to people known to be interested.

Meeting of interested staff (possibly 12–15) to discuss their requirements and how they would like to take action.

Possible (almost certain) visit from outside speaker to underline work started.

How difficult it all seems—and how time-consuming. How open to rebuff. It is not surprising that teachers who have not thought about the place of language in learning wonder what it is all about.

One of the recurrent tensions in trying to promote language discussion and action in a school is between short-term and long-term aims. Although there may be no end to the journey—in the sense that schools and their ways of working will continue to evolve—nevertheless it is encouraging to notice the odd milestone. Both long-term and short-term goals are needed and the relationship between them will need constantly to be reconsidered. So a short-term aim might be to get teachers to tape-record groups of pupils talking in their lessons so that there is material for group study and discussion on the role of talk in learning situations. But this really needs to be related to a long-term aim which might be something like this: 'teachers of all subjects should be aware of the importance of talk in making sense of new ideas and information—and find ways of facilitating it in their lessons'. A long-term aim like this might influence the discussion of the tapes so that the emphasis shifts from evaluation to a consideration of more fundamental issues. So the questions asked might be: 'What kind of relationship do you need to have with your pupils to enable situations like this to occur?' or 'could the teacher usefully intervene in this discussion?', rather than just 'how articulate are these children?' and 'how successfully have they answered the teacher's questions?'

A long-term aim should enable teachers to become 'active interrogators' of the material, rather than passive commentators, because they have a commitment to act.

Mike Torbe, writing from his experience as an advisory teacher says: 'The only profitable way in is action research. But the only profitable action research is the one that has visible consequences for tomorrow's teaching *as well as* long-term consequences. Thus, exploring teachers' questions ought to produce not just critical comments on existing questions which imply yes/no answers, but should also suggest questions which *don't*—such as, 'which part do you remember?' or 'did it make you think of something else?'. Exploring ways of structuring writing, rather than criticizing sterile ideas, should suggest alternative modes (log book, running records, branching diagrams) and how they might be introduced. Thus the working group can be seen as making a direct input to the major problem of teaching—*what do I do tomorrow?*

We have received many reports of school meetings to discuss action on the Bullock Report. We quote here one written by the deputy head (a science teacher) of a big high school—it is a personal report of the discussion on language across the curriculum in the Academic Committee.

1. The use of language—which means *learning*—is not the sole responsibility of the English faculty. They will lead, advise, inspire but each faculty must play an important part.

2. Pamela will produce a draft set of proposals for a common marking policy—spelling, punctuation etc. But more important, how do we encourage students to learn from their mistakes? Common errors fed back through the English faculty perhaps?

3. The 'thinking-it-out' which we adults tend to do with our 'inner-voice' (but not always) has to be rehearsed in a more overt way in childhood. And so we should be encouraging the exploration of ideas in oral work and expressive writing. How nice it was that nobody suggested it was the middle school's job and not also ours to do this, although I think we were all looking towards our third year.

4. How can we encourage more oral exploration of ideas? Is it more difficult in mixed-ability classes? (*a thought*: surely the oral mode of communication is less differentiating than the written). Are we too concerned with keeping our 30 quiet in our classroom so as to avoid upsetting our neighbours? All too passive?

5. Can we in our different subject areas look at ways of encouraging 'expressive' writing. How should we treat it when we get it, so as to avoid the teacher-as-examiner role?

6. So much gets committed to paper (exactly *why* is not always clear, but often in the name of examinations) that has not really been learned at all—copying from the board, out of a book, dictated notes. The process of mental digestion is not occurring. Surely, this is the rule of the whole business: receiving an idea, breaking it down and then reconstructing it individually in a way that fits within each person's mental framework. And this is precisely what language achieves.

7. Let us not forget how little we actually assimilated before which the person concerned cannot accept an idea; the experiences which construct the framework are simply not there.

8. Reading: we tend to think that (slow learners aside) there is no problem here, but there are important ways in which we can help: e.g., skimming and scanning.

9. I think we probably all went away with two feelings:
(a) I could devise more valuable language (and thus learning) experiences in my lessons, with all age groups and all abilities.
(b) I want to look in more detail at different examples of oral and written work: talk about it, criticize it and try it out.

10. To this end I propose that we ask Pamela, David and Trevor to organize, say, 3 workshop sessions in June/July (taking advantage of the slack period when many fifth-years will have left). One representative from each faculty to attend.

Let's hope that we shall see language in the curriculum appearing on more and more Faculty meeting agendas.

From the head of science (Drewry, 1976) in another school came the two questionnaires printed below, one for pupils in the second year and one for members of the science department.

A. *To pupils*
1. Write down the meaning of the following words.

Living	Distinguish
Animal	Similar
Dissolve	Concentrate
Refer	Temperature
Compare	

2. How do you know if you have learnt anything in Science?
3. Which of the following techniques help you to learn?

	Always	Often	Sometimes	Rarely	Never
Talking with teacher					
Talking in pairs					
Talking in groups					
Answering questions					
Asking questions					
Copying from board or books					
Writing up experiments					
Completing charts					
Writing in your own words					
Tests					

B. *To staff of science and maths faculty*
1. Please indicate how frequently you use the following techniques.

Discussion	Always	Often	Sometimes	Rarely	Never
Class—Teacher					
Group—Teacher					
Individual—Teacher					
Class—class					
Group—class					

Children only	*Always*	*Often*	*Sometimes*	*Rarely*	*Never*
Discussion in pairs					
in threes					
in three +					

Questioning
  for factual recall
  for development of ideas
  for reasoning
  to discover background
    knowledge

Writing
  Completing charts and tables
  Graphs
  Traditional experimental
    write-ups
  Free prose in paragraphs
  Copying from the board
  Copying from books
  Notes
  Dictation
  Calculations
  Sentences
  Essays
  One-word answers to
    exercises/tests

2. Do you assume that the children will understand the following words?

	Always	*Often*	*Sometimes*	*Rarely*	*Never*
Example					
Living					
Animal					
Dissolve					
Refer					
Compare					
Distinguish					
Similar					
Concentrate					
Temperature					

3. How would you introduce a new technical word, e.g., *Leibig condenser*?
4. How would you introduce work on a new concept, e.g., solution?
5. How do you know if learning has taken place?

Not only did this provoke considerable talk in the Science Department, but the idea was taken up by other teachers in the working party, and similar questionnaires were devised for other faculties.

About Westerhope Middle School, Durham, the Project team wrote:

We think it highly significant that we were not, in the first instance, given a language policy document. We were given a 'Statement of Intent' which set down in three pages the objectives of the school and the agencies by which those objectives might be carried out. This 'Statement of Intent' had been produced from many discussions between the headmaster and 'teaching staff who were to be the nucleus of a larger and changing staff of the new Middle School'. A rider was added that if any teacher having joined the staff was unable to accept the underlying educational philosophy of the 'statement', he should discuss this with the headmaster so that 'an acceptable solution to the dilemma' could be found. Accompanying this statement of intent was a document headed 'The Language Policy of a School'. With the language policy document went a video tape of a mixed ability class aged 12 to 13 recorded throughout three days and covering all the activities that this class engaged in, all lessons including drama, PE, craft and library, and occasions such as Assembly, school dinner and play time. The language policy document is meant to be seen as part of the school objectives and contains 11 aims. The first sentence reads: 'We hope that the video tape recording will illustrate as many of the following points as possible'. Clearly such a way of producing a visual language policy involved all the staff, disposed of the notorious gap between statements of objectives and actual practice, opened all that was going on to public discussion, and located the language policy firmly in the more general aims of the school.

The examples quoted above have focused on the practical—on what can we *do*? I now change the focus and quote from letters the Project has received which not only deal with the actual steps taken but which comment on the nature of the process involved—the changes in attitude and thinking which happen and the problems these give rise to. It also seems to me that these letters highlight the particular role of teachers of English. It is part of their professional expertise to know something about language, and to give a lead in implementing the Bullock Report, yet the paradox of the situation is that such a lead can be counter-productive.

Getting started on a language policy across the curriculum (by the Head of English in a Midlands Comprehensive School)

I suppose it was my own fault really. I first made notes about a whole-school policy on language in the Summer of 1972 sitting in the garden drinking bottled Whitbread and reading *Language and Learning*. I hadn't read *Language, the Learner and the School* at the time. Then the head retired unexpectedly, the Authority introduced a chaotic scheme of reorganization, and everything but survival got shelved for the best part of two years.

One of the first things the new head did was to ask for departmental reports, and when I sent in my first one about Christmas 1974 I spent some space on outlining the responsibilities of other departments for the language development of the children. He wrote on it something like 'I agree, but English Dept. must give a lead. Consult with DH'.

On 18 February the Bullock Committee Report was published amid such a blaze of publicity that within a week at least five of our 75 staff had heard of it. I'm not joking: an event in the educational world has to be pretty stunning to make that much impact on the staff of a Midlands Comprehensive School.

As a result, just before the end of the Easter term, the Deputy Head and I got notes from the Head asking us to look into this curious 'Language across the Curriculum' business. I lent the Deputy *Language, the Learner and the School* and my copy of Bullock; he hefted it thoughtfully in his hand. 'We ought to get one of these for the staff library', he said. 'How much is it? Christ, five pounds.'

A week or two passed. Then, ten minutes before a meeting of heads of department, the deputy asked if I would speak about LAC. Summoning up an ostentatious show of diffidence, stammering and mumbling like Brando ('I coulda been a contender, Charlie') I introduced the topic: it wouldn't do at all to let on that I or anybody else had *thought* about this beforehand, that it might actually affect their lives, or be dangerous in some other way. Even so, or maybe *because*, it stirred a surprising amount of interest. The Heads of maths and science got quite excited and started talking about spelling, always a good sign. Several others said, 'What? a spelling purge throughout the school? Good idea' and gave it their blessing. The craft, domestic science, art and geography departments ignored it completely. I lent out my last few copies of 'Gnat Killers'. A Committee was set up: deputy, head of maths, head of science, head of lower school history (we're hierarchy-mad in our place), head of craft and myself. We met in the autumn term (late September) to decide on action. In the meantime I had talked casually to perhaps 20 staff, including members of the Committee (I think this is probably the most important preparatory work). The most significant remark came from the head of science: 'They're not learning anything by the present methods we're using, so we might as well give this a go'. From a very Tory middle-aged Welshman, head of science since the school opened 16 years previously, this indicated the first stirrings of an almost overwhelmingly daring spirit of exploration and enlightenment.

First 'working' meeting of Committee: 26 September 1975. I had photocopied part of a tape transcript of a Nuffield Science lesson in a primary school. This was far enough from home, I felt, to allow fairly free criticism. I also had two sets of the pamphlets from the Schools Council project, a few quotations from Barnes, and a list of possible projects in areas of concern, something on the following lines:

1. The over-insistence of the use of technical vocabulary by insecure/ unaware teachers; this seemed fairly safe. Only the probationers would admit to being insecure and nobody would admit to being unaware.

2. The suitability or otherwise of textbooks in use in the school, paying particular attention to their language; similar consideration of duplicated material produced in school—was it better tailored to the children's needs, or did the teachers fall into the same traps?

3. A look at the extent to which talk is used as a means of learning in *our school*. They shied away from this a bit. We all know that teaching in many departments, from first year onwards, is by dictation of notes.

Open/closed questions came up here; I was censured for using jargon, and had to explain the term. Even the Deputy—three years in a College of Education before coming to us—had never heard of it.

There followed the usual teacherly talk about bad pupils/eccentric teachers I have known, spelling, whose fault it was if the kids write poorly, standards, and so on; but at the end of it we had agreed to produce examples of textbook work for a proposed seminar, plus a list of 'technical vocabulary' under the heading 'Things we all do wrong', most of the items to be unnecessary use of technical terms, undeclared use of technical terms and textbook phrases, unwillingness to abandon safe ground of subject language, and so on.

Next meeting, 6 November. The head of craft's list of 'Things we all do wrong' began:

1. incorrect stance before the class—we are inclined to loll about on the desk instead of standing up straight

2. incorrect dress: even in the workshop we should wear ties

3. use of colloquialisms and local slang.

In fact, he didn't produce this list at all in the meeting where he said practically nothing. He only showed it to me when I tackled him afterwards about his lack of involvement, explaining that when he heard what we were saying he realized he'd got it all wrong. In fact, many of his other ideas were very good.

An encouraging aspect of the business was the way teachers not on the Committee kept coming up and speaking about it. The head of biology borrowed the latest issue of 'English in Education' (9.2) to study the transcript of the biology lesson (pp. 52–58), and the head of history showed me two pieces on the way of life of North American Indians written by children of putative low ability. It's interesting that the teacher concerned commended them for their unusual length from these children, and for the extent to which the children were involved, although I'm not sure there's a lot of expressive language: I suspect that they had learned to 'do' Indians or 'do' days-in-the-life-of, or something, just as the top O-level streams are learning to 'do' the Stuarts.

Later the head of biology borrowed a cassette recorder and recorded some lessons; so did I and a history teacher. I already have a fair amount of teacher/pupil talk on tape, but for everyone else it's a whole new idea.

At the end of this meeting I was a bit worried when the deputy indicated that he saw the Committee's work as a sort of 'awareness purge', a bit like the periodic purges on smoking in the bogs. However, subsequent events lead me to think that he was just passing through a necessary transitional phase.

There was a long break before our next meeting, ostensibly to allow for the collection of material, and really because of work pressure and the mock exams, marking and reports; but we met again at the end of January to plan our first open event, a staff seminar, which took place on 12 February 1976, almost the anniversary of Bullock. The meeting was fixed for 4.20 p.m., ten minutes after school finished, and was, of course, voluntary. Twenty-two people attended, including the headmaster, but some of the younger staff stayed away because they had been offended by receiving notes from the head asking them to explain their absence from assembly that morning. However, it's difficult to see how such a seminar could have been much use if more had attended. The meeting lasted precisely one hour, and after a brief introduction from me (more Steve McQueen than Brando this time, but still not Cary Grant), discussion revolved around two of the three duplicated papers attached: we never got on to open/closed questions. Discussion was quite lively, at least a dozen people spoke, we even managed to avoid getting bogged down in spelling. I won't go into the discussion in detail, partly because it was a bit diffuse at times, but mainly because I recorded the whole thing, and hope to make an edited transcript soon. I outlined the next items in the programme: two more seminars between now and Whitsun, one on talk, and the other on writing. I hope that later meetings will enable us to look in more detail at textbooks, with the suggestion that certain criteria ought to be followed when making a choice; and, even more important, to consider the production of written and other source material by departments—some of the units currently being produced by, for instance, the history department, are depressingly like some of the less inspiring textbooks.

As part of the preparatory work for the talk and writing meetings, I announced that I would be badgering people individually to record their lessons (the PE dept looked amazed and horrified) and to provide examples of children's writing, with notes on the conditions under which it was produced.

A few comments.

You have to walk delicately. When I hinted that learning in science might be more effective if the excitement of discovery and exploration could be fostered and maintained, the head of science replied: 'But science *isn't* exciting; science is *dull*. It's our job to take any excitement out of it. We don't *want* people getting all excited about it.'

The head of craft said much the same thing about his own subject. His comment on 'Gnat Killers': 'This wouldn't do for us—it's just the sort of thing we *don't* want.' But he's mellowing a bit.

A great deal of work is likely to fall upon the head of the English department in implementing such a scheme—try at least to get secretarial assistance, which is something not normally available to staff in our school.

There was a strong feeling of the blind leading the blind to begin with. None of us knew where to start; and my main worry was that too definite a lead might produce a strong rejection by influential members of staff, hence the mumbling and shuffling.

Further along

A year later, the head of English in a Yorkshire Comprehensive School wrote this letter.

When I reread the piece I wrote last Easter about what I was trying to do in my school and what I felt were the guiding principles, I cringe at the easy way I accepted the long-term nature of the task of implementing a language policy. I still think that it is long-term; but having carried the process on I realize that I was, if anything, underestimating the complexity and difficulty of what I had undertaken.

I feel uncomfortable, too, when I compare my basic list of principles with what I have actually found myself doing. Again, I feel that if there is to be a real language policy, it is still imperative to begin with the present unacknowledged language 'policy'. Careful slowness still seems to me to be the appropriate strategy, small-scale discussion the basic tool. What I underestimated was the natural pressure to follow existing procedures and the extent to which this would become irresistible.

I was, if I was to prove my seriousness, compelled to go along with the ways serious business is conducted in this school—the matter is discussed with headmaster, aired at a meeting of heads of department, laid open at a staff meeting. These are unconvincing media for development here and I preferred to work in other ways. However, I was asked repeatedly to address the various groups; my reluctance had no meaning in this context and I certainly wanted to show my seriousness.

A sub-committee on curriculum development had seemed an appropriate place to begin. The discussions were exploratory, open, encouraging. The general attitude outside the committee was that our discussions would be futile and would change nothing. The pre-emptive attitude has turned out to be the crucial factor, covering as it does deep-seated ideas concerning the role of subject autonomy, and most particularly the fears of what change will bring. If we were to examine the reasons why most people teach a particular subject, the most frequent reason would be interest at school and college. As a basis for asking the question 'why?' about a subject, that is not a promising start.

As part of our discussions I have come to recognize more about the assumptions upon which schools operate through the teachers, teachers being the main element in the composition of the ethos or character of a particular school. There is no necessity for a subject teacher to question the subject. Thus, I have been unable to ask questions, however tactfully, and however pleasant the relations, without causing discomfort—and there is an easy place for any teacher to hide from discomfort—the teaching situation.

I don't know whether it is the same thing but I have sensed that the questions I have been asking are felt to be irrelevant to the process of teaching. For example: what is happening when a pupil takes notes? Does a pupil actually record what he sees and understands when he records an experiment in traditional form? Is discussion the same thing as question and answer?

What I have found most dispiriting has been the low level of thinking about education that has been typical of the discussions. Alongside that is an apparent lack of any feeling that anything is wrong.

What I am documenting of course are *exactly* the reasons why the pursuit is long-term. I foresaw them in general but I am nevertheless worn down by them in their endless particularity. I do not believe that I have the answer; I have not found that other subject teachers are often aware that there are any questions.

The last two terms have been dispiriting but in trying to evaluate what has happened, I have returned to firmer belief in my sense of the difficulty of the task and the possibility of change. Certainly a few people have indicated interest in talking about talk. When I am tempted to be depressed about the tiny step forward, I need to recall that I know of no convincing examples of actual cohesion on language in a school except those training children solely for examinations and employment. Now there's a thought.

Language policy across the curriculum

The head of English in a central London Comprehensive School wrote the following revised questions for departmental discussion.

1. Can you define the language skills demanded by your department in terms of demands on:
listening
talking
reading
writing?
2. To what extent can your department help in the teaching of reading?
3. Can your department make more use of work in small groups?

4. Can your department make more use of talk as part of the learning process?

5. How much does the work of your department encourage teachers to talk to individual pupils?

6. What attitude does your department have to non-standard English in speech and writing?

7. What sorts of questions should we ask, what sorts of assignments should we set to produce the most effective *learning* situations?

8. Are we asking for too narrow a range of writing from our pupils; in particular when we neglect poetic and expressive writing in favour of transactional writing are we asking children to run before they can walk, to parrot the language of teachers and textbooks, regardless of whether or not that language means anything to them? (I am sorry about the complexity of that question and its jargon—examples of expressive, poetic, and transactional writing are appended—see also Section 3 of the language group report.)

9. What can we do to get away from the banda worksheet and to improve the quality of our home-made resources? Do we need more sophisticated reprographic equipment?

10. What areas has the language group not yet discussed which it ought now to turn its attention to?

11. How has mixed-ability grouping affected your answers to the above questions?

These questions, which are an attempt to communicate with the rest of the staff, do not represent the thinking of any one member of the language group but were devised by those who attended the two meetings. In other words members of the group were happier with some of the questions than others. It should also be remembered that, as I stressed in the first article, each school situation is unique and what may be relevant in one school may actually be harmful in another. At our school members of the language group will be offering departments help with their discussions on the questionnaire—particularly with rather off-putting questions like 1 and 8.

Language across the curriculum talk has in fact featured very little since last summer (apart from one refreshing and encouraging report from a biology teacher who went on a one-day children's writing course) and we are now pinning our hopes on the response to the questionnaire and on the interest that is being aroused by ILEA's follow up to Bullock.

Dr Birchenough, in his letter to schools, quoted a piece from Bullock: 'each school should have an organised policy for language across the curriculum, establishing every teacher's involvement in language and reading development. . . .'

A policy document does not, in practice, 'establish every teacher's involvement' and I feel increasingly that, while it may encapsulate the views of a particular group at a particular time and even give guidance on specific issues which will outlive that group of teachers, it can never really be more than a point of reference. There is another quote from the same chapter which gets us, I feel, closer to the problem: 'The effort a child needs to apply in learning language must derive from the satisfaction of evolving from helplessness to self-possession.'

This is an enormous undertaking and the truth is that language is at the *centre* of any educational system we may devise. It is not just another aspect of school life like uniform, books, or afternoon games. When we make statements about language we often expose the heart of our educational philosophy. Language across the curriculum discussions aim to bring about increased understanding of how learning takes place and how best to bring it about. That is a *continuous* process and that is why it is so important that each school should appoint someone with specific responsibility for this language development with plenty of school time made available for working with staff (ensuring, amongst other things, that they come to meetings!)

Certainly, in our school, given the latent and manifest interest of many teachers (not all of them, by any means, in the English department) we *could* make much greater strides. As it is we are still dealing far too often with those already converted.

Teachers' ideas

We conclude this section by quoting from a teacher in the London comprehensive school referred to above who had worked hard in getting the language policy discussions started. He draws attention to the influence of the individual perceptions of the teachers involved in the discussions.

Bullock on language and learning makes the point that,

> It is a confusion of everyday thought that we tend to regard 'Knowledge' as something that exists independently of someone who knows. 'What is known' must in fact be brought to life afresh within every 'knower' by his own efforts.' (4.9)

If that is true for school students it is no less true for their teachers. As discussion progresses each teacher in his or her classroom or as a member of a team is going to have something of a personal approach to matters to do with language, whether writers of policy documents wish them to or not. Moreover, language is so much at the heart of the learning and knowing done by teachers as well as students that very strong feelings are generated whenever discussion of such matters moves beyond statements of personal opinions to a genuine questioning of our classroom practice. As we attempt to establish the sort of systematic policy that Bullock recommends we are immediately confronted with the same complex of knowledge, experience and relationships that we find in our classrooms.

The questions that Andrew (the head of department) has included in his article were originally circulated with a summary of the discussions from which they arose. As I read them in isolation now they appear a very mixed collection indeed. This again reveals something of the complex situation which produced them.

Each question relates to an area of concern amongst the teachers at our school, but they also reveal the different approaches to language that are current at the stage of development we have reached. The first question is a good example, particularly as we place it alongside question 8. Looked at together they may reveal a divergence of opinion within the school. The first question represents a behaviourist strand in the thought of some members of our group. Behind it lies I feel, an idea that, if only we can get it straight in our minds what we want the students to be able to do, we can go ahead and systematically teach them to do it. Along with that goes a notion that the performance of our students can be measured against these goals and the effectiveness of our teaching can be assessed. By contrast, the inclusion of question 8 in the list suggests a desire to change our attitude to the learning process so as to centre our approach on the students' experience of learning rather than on our perception of what they need to know.

If we are to be true to the spirit of the quotation from Bullock in my first paragraph, we must be prepared for both approaches to exist even if neither of them reflect our own opinions. It may well be that in the changing situations that exist in schools, particularly in inner-city schools, some sort of final policy document should not be our main aim; continuing discussion may well be more useful.

I conclude by a return to the practical—who can help?

The Bullock Report asks something new, and difficult of teachers— not only that they should each as individuals foster children's reading and writing, but that they should *collectively* organize language policies for their schools. This is proving particularly difficult in secondary schools because these are mostly organized in subject departments with nearly every teacher a subject specialist. Within this structure the English teachers are seen as being the language specialists. Many subject teachers feel that their concern is with teaching their subjects and do not see language as having much to do with this. Others, however, see children's language development as an important instrument in learning history, science, geography, etc.

Taking any kind of collective action is a very different kind of activity from taking individual action in one's own lessons. From our work with teachers over the last six months we have set out the following suggestions about who can help in getting some of the recommendations of the Report alive and active in schools.

Inside school

1. *The Head.* As the person directly responsible for the administration of the school, the head is very important to the success or failure of any innovation. The head can provide help—as we have seen in section 2—by:

(a) supporting teachers in their purpose by taking an interest in it and by making it clear to all the staff that he/she is interested and supportive;

(b) allowing opportunities for the teachers involved to inform their colleagues about what they want to do;

(c) being willing to explain the work to parents, governors and other interested people.

2. *Senior Staff.* Deputy heads, heads of departments, curriculum co-ordinator—if there is one—are important in the same way as the head is, and without the help of the senior staff it will be difficult to get a language policy really working.

3. *The Pupils.* It will generally be desirable to talk to pupils about any experimental scheme. Ideally there ought to be some facility for children to participate in a critical way about the courses they are following and the problems as they see them. We have found the children acutely aware of language and its problems and transcripts of their discussions or their writing on these topics can provide good starting points for teachers' consideration of these same problems (the difficulty of 'book' language for instance).

Outside school

1. *Local education officers.* The chief education officer and other members of his staff, the secondary, primary and subject advisers or inspectors are responsible for all the administration of the area in the same way that heads are responsible for schools, and their influence is therefore very wide. They offer a great deal of support to teachers in the form of short-term or long-term in-service education and very varied kinds of assistance. In addition, some authorities have an officer specially responsible for in-service work with teachers, and he/she often works in conjunction with a University Institute of Education. Many of the starting points described in the previous sections of this Pack were initiated by or in conjunction with such local education officers. They will organize meetings or courses and, where possible, duplicate and circulate material for discussion. Some authorities, for instance, have made their own summaries of sections of the Bullock Report and have circulated these to schools; they have also, in co-operation with heads, arranged joint meetings between local schools and follow up activities of various kinds.

2. *Teachers' centres.* Teachers' centres are, of course, the responsibility of the local education authority, and the scope of their activities varies

a great deal. At best, the teachers' centre warden would be the first person to approach for help in getting a meeting outside school organized, and the facilities of the centre should be available for any discussion material needed.

3. *Parents.* Most parents are keenly interested in their children's progress but they often have very vague ideas about what goes on in schools. We had a report of a meeting in one school where the English department had approached the Parent Teacher Association and arranged for one of the education meetings to be on the Bullock Report. Most parents have little opportunity to discuss educational matters, and PTA meetings would seem to offer an opportunity of getting a wider understanding of the aims of the Report.

4. *Subject associations* (the Association for Science Education, the National Association for the Teaching of English, for instance). If subject associations could be persuaded to see the Bullock Report as one of their concerns they could be more influential than any small group within a school. It is perhaps worth noting that some twelve months ago *Mathematics Teaching*, the journal of the Association of Teachers of Mathematics, carried a long editorial on the importance of language in learning mathematics; and the National Association for the Teaching of English through its annual conference, branch meetings and publications has actively campaigned. These activities must have reached many more teachers than could be reached by a school or teachers' centre meeting.

5. *The Schools Council Project 'Writing Across the Curriculum'.* The Project team of three with a fair number of teachers working with it has provided discussion pamphlets, Packs of 'outcomes' from schools, lists of relevant books, speakers for meetings, and a book of outcomes from the Project (*Writing and learning : across the curriculum*, Ward Lock 1976, £1.35).

Ward Lock has now taken over the distribution of materials and enquiries should be addressed to them at: 116 Baker Street, London W1, or to the Schools Council at 160 Great Portland Street, London W1.

Implementing

Introduction

It is not the British way for 'authorities' outside the school to either prescribe, as in continental schools, or to demand, as is common in American school boards. In California, for instance, there is a state-

wide Framework in Reading, a general syllabus, as it were. Within
that each district draws up its programme, the San Francisco State
Board, appointing a Director of Reading. He in his turn issues guidelines, which oblige the schools to draw up *their* programme. The
demand is quite clear: 'The Director of Reading expects to have on
file in his office as of September, 1973, a brief outline statement
describing the Site Reading Programme in each school.'[1] Even the
most energetic of LEAs have not done that, with the possible exception
of ILEA, whose initiative was courteously but firmly sent to all
schools, in the form of an invitation from the Chief Inspector:

> I believe it would be helpful if heads, in consultation with members of
> staff, would prepare written statements of the language and literacy policy
> of their schools, as has already been done in some cases. Such statements
> might contain descriptions of present approaches and ideas for further
> action. If these statements were given to the Inspectorate they would
> provide a source of ideas and information which could be made available
> to teachers throughout Inner London. I am therefore writing to offer the
> help of the Inspectorate in preparing such statements of policy and to
> invite you to send your statement to me at County Hall.

Elsewhere, however, the British tradition of school autonomy has left
the initiative to the schools. The very way in which these two requests
contrast reveals both the strength and the weakness of our system:
the San Francisco demand is limiting compared with the broader
request of ILEA. Yet the second could be dangerously vague for
schools in doubt (as Nancy Martin shows some are) about what a
policy concerns.[2]

In fact, surely no school could, or would want to, buy in a ready-
made language policy. This book has tried to cover the possible
ingredients of such a policy. Each school will want to make its own
selection of ingredients, study them, and develop its own approach
to each. Then it will want to put the ingredients together in the combination and with the relative strengths suited to its own situation.
Each school will have to establish its priorities. It is not often realized
how widely different these situations are. In some schools notions of
appropriateness are a tense and complex issue, requiring careful
analysis and really rather painful debate. In others there is an
accepted approach that offers no serious problems. In some schools
the initial stages of reading present difficulties to so many pupils that
here will be a central issue. In others the crucial task will be to open
up the range of writing tasks. Yet others may need to concentrate
their debate on pupil talk. It is likely that the central issue of communication will be common to all, but the balance of drive will and
should vary widely.

[1] San Francisco School Board, *Guideline for the District-Wide Programme*,
undated, p. 4.

[2] In fairness it ought to be added that ILEA supported the request with a
careful series of meetings, as have other LEAS such as Avon.

One difficulty has already been indicated in the previous section: some colleagues may over-simplify, and overlook the really important issues in favour of the relatively minor technical points. The opposite difficulty is to presume that it's all too difficult to understand, discuss, and put into practice. For instance, the underlying theory of Nancy Martin's account in Chapter 5 clearly is of considerable intellectual depth. Yet, on the one hand it is perfectly comprehensible to any teacher who gives it thought, and on the other hand the practical implications are not so daunting. At root it is a matter of considering the purposes of writing, and encouraging the use of the expressive category as the core out of which other forms will grow. It is also a plea for real communication purposes, which means a range of real audiences. Such considerations should not be presented as too complex.

The most hopeful first step is to set up a working party to look into Recommendations 138 and 139 in the light of the particular position in the school, and to make recommendations.

Running a working party

Presuming, following the kind of action Nancy Martin has described, that a decision has been made to set up a working party, is there any advice that can be given?

It is preferable if the very setting up of such a group can have wide backing, perhaps by submitting a general statement of the need, the purpose of a proposed working party, and its proposed composition to the heads of departments meeting or equivalent central planning group of the school. The composition of such a group needs care. Leaving it completely to volunteers is dangerous. In some schools this will mean a group who represent only some subject areas, or only one age-group of staff. In other schools it will mean a dominance by a few who are very knowledgeable in linguistics, frighten the other members into confused silence, and eventually draw up a statement which is far from acceptable to the staff as a whole.

Reports and observation, and general experience in staff decision-making, suggest that the group should include some volunteers, but should have a careful representation from a range of subjects, from a range of staff ages and seniority, and with a definite pastoral representative. It is vital that the pastoral role is not overlooked. I have tended to use and prefer the phrase 'whole-school language policy' precisely because it is not only the curriculum that needs attention. The quality of communication in tutor group, counselling, assembly, and interview needs attention equally.

The working party which we set up at Woodberry Down (actually to revise and expand the first attempt at a formal language policy) was chaired by the head of the remedial department, and included a pastoral representative, and the heads of the geography, craft, and maths (the last of whom was also Advisor for Recently Appointed

Teachers), a member of the English department (as a representative), one of the science department, the head of reading centre, and the curriculum co-ordinator. This is an example of a range of interests; there was also a range of teaching experience. For some schools the membership would have been too senior, and fewer responsibility holders would have suited better. However, as a general rule it is vital to have sufficient heads of departments to ensure that the voice of experience and seniority is heard early, and does not merely block later. Similarly, it is most important that the group is not ostentatiously composed as a progressive or any other clique, for if it is any recommendations will have less chance of being acceptable across the curriculum.

There are various possible starting activities for the working party:

1. *Basic reading.* All members would probably want to read a little in the subject—perhaps some of the books in the reading list, certainly substantial sections of the Report.

2. *Specialized reading.* Various members might volunteer to read one each of the more specialized books, maybe one each on writing, reading, and talking, and to report back to the group the main conclusions.

3. *Lesson observation.* Visits might be made by the working party members, initially maybe only to other members of the same departments, to observe what language difficulties and opportunities arise.

4. *Consideration of existing test data.* Any figures, e.g. from primary schools or the remedial department, already available might be collated and reviewed to establish what they show.

5. *Establish the staff's views.* A questionnaire has been used by a number of such working parties.

6. *Establish present practice.* Again, in some schools questionnaires have been used. Nancy Martin quotes one, and I have included that from Woodberry Down as an Appendix. Obviously no such questionnaire is ideal, and all drawn up without the benefit of professional planning, piloting, etc., suffer from technical flaws. Nevertheless, such a device has two advantages: on the one hand it informs the Working Party, and on the other it involves most of the teachers from the start.

7. *Visit other schools.* It is helpful if knowledge of progress towards a policy in other schools is acquired early on.

The Working Party will soon want to start reviewing possible recommendations: if it spends too long on the research stage the patience of the less committed, whose views are especially important, will run out. Where to start is a tricky tactical decision. If a school staff works in the order of my contents, from Chapter 4 onwards, for instance, it risks getting lost in disagreements about fundamentals; if, on the other hand, it opts for modest technicalities it risks getting stuck in simple agreements on the trivia—and, what is worse, believing the job has been completed. I recommend taking some sample areas, maybe writing (where the recommendations are likely to be fairly straightforward) and one technical aspect (such as study skills, which is obviously likely to be of real help in many subjects), and drafting initial observations and tentative recommendations fairly soon.

Experience suggests that these first drafts of preliminary sections should be discussed widely fairly early. This not only encourages the working party to be practical and consider its consumers from an early stage, but it allows an interchange of views at a formative stage. Without some such exchange, a working party can toil for a couple of years, getting farther away from the needs and atmosphere of its parent school, and eventually offering something which is entirely unacceptable and useless. As the working party should be trying to respond to the felt needs of the staff (even if it comes to consider that there are other needs not yet articulated), opportunities for the staff to express their problems are valuable. For instance, the Woodberry Down working party circulated the results of the questionnaire for full staff discussion at Departmental Meetings scheduled for the purpose, and devised the recommendations partly out of the staff's reactions.

The drafting of the report is a tricky business. Many I have seen are too long and off-putting. One school's was virtually a book, half an inch thick, an amorphous collection of material, which was difficult to find one's way about. Others are off-putting because of their pretentious and complex tone. Whilst it would be wrong to sacrifice accuracy or depth for the sake of an easy read, it is pointless to be obtruse. The most common danger is to include all the working party's *homework*, that is many items that were useful preparatory stages for the working party, but which are not necessary for the reader.

There is likely to be a statement about language, the result of the working party's consideration of the fundamental issues of language and learning. This is vital, but must be fairly brief, and drafted modestly and simply. It can consist of quotations if preferred, e.g. from Chapter XX of the Report, or from such writers as Professor Britton.

In my view the report must include actual recommendations for classroom practice, resources, and school organization. These recommendations must be suitable for all subjects, or suitably limited by qualification. They should not be too numerous or too strident in tone. Ideally, I consider that they should be grouped in such a way that the main points can be readily extracted. Finally, it is vital that the framework of the report is clearly tentative, and that the scope for later extension or amendment is made clear.

The draft report should then be submitted widely to those concerned—perhaps to heads of departments or maybe to the full staff in small groups. The governors should also be consulted at this stage, partly because this indicates the centrality of the issue to the curriculum, and partly to enlist their support. It must be remembered that they have a responsibility for oversight of the curriculum, and their views on some of the issues will be valuable. In some schools the parents will also be consulted.

Leadership

A policy needs institutionalizing. It must not die; it must not be overlooked. Its implementing therefore must be someone's responsibility, and it must be clear that the person whose responsibility it is has the personal knowledge, experience, and responsibility in the school to carry it out.

This leads to a strong recommendation that every secondary school should have a senior teacher, experienced and eventually suitably qualified, to lead and co-ordinate the school's overall language strategy, a Language Co-ordinator. His or her responsibilities should include: advising, leading, and co-ordinating teaching approaches across the curriculum; he should become expert in the grading of printed material (by the applying of age-level tests, for instance) and its suitability; he will have oversight of the diagnostic tests; he will lead the staff in-service training. In short, he would be the linguistic leader of the school. As the Report says, such a Language Co-ordinator should not always, or even usually, be an *addition* to the existing hierarchy. Our recommendation is that a senior member of staff should have those school-wide responsibilities. A number of organizational models seem to be open to schools. Each has its advantages and disadvantages, and only the individual school can decide which would be most likely to suit its particular conditions.

Nostalgic readers might with some justification say: 'But that is precisely what an old-fashioned Headteacher of a small secondary-modern school did.' Often, but not always, and usually without the wider qualifications now seen to be necessary. I concede though that I found the nearest to what I have in mind in two very small secondary modern schools. One head, in a small Midlands industrial town, had the reading ages of all his pupils in the top right-hand drawer of his desk. The other, on the outskirts of a small Derbyshire mining town had just finished hearing a boy read when I arrived. In the larger school, or in the grammar school, there is no equivalent. I am aware of the complications of a plea for yet another member of the senior staff, or of adding yet another task to those undertaken by the present holders of such posts. But if a language policy, including a reading policy, across the curriculum is to work it must be the stated task of someone, clearly described in his job specification, and well understood by his colleagues.

I could see that holders of each of the following posts could take on this responsibility:

Holder of role	Advantages	Disadvantages
The headmaster	Has overall vision and necessary status	In any but the smallest school is likely to be too busy to give detailed co-ordination
The deputy with curriculum responsibility, Curriculum Co-ordinator, or Director of Studies	As above. Additionally this responsibility would fit his overall curriculum concern	As above in the larger schools
The head of English	Likely to have necessary knowledge and interest	Difficult to have a HOD who is 'equal but extra' to the other HODs
	Likely to further broaden his experience into related and relevant fields	Already has a very heavy burden
Head of remedial department	As above, although not many have knowledge of the teaching of the higher reading skills	As above
A separate Language Co-ordinator	Given proper qualifications and status could be best placed to look at all aspects of the school	Relationship with the rest of the hierarchy could be difficult
Teacher responsible for in-service training	Has experience and facilities to organize and lead teacher development	Is not actually responsible for departments' syllabuses

The logical choice for many schools might be the second person in the list, for this would clearly link the work with leadership of the curriculum and the departmental syllabuses.

As many schools have started consideration of their policy by setting up a working party, some have embodied the leadership responsibility in that committee. My view is that it is probably valuable in some cases for such an initial working party to continue in existence to overhaul, and update, the original school statement, and to oversee in-service training in this field, but committees are not normally very successful at leadership.

Various combinations of responsibility are also possible. A working party can continue to develop the thinking behind the policy, whilst a deputy head in charge of curriculums is responsible for implementing it, and a teacher in charge of in-service training for promulgating it. What is certain is that it is not possible to establish a policy and leave it to work. Leadership is required.

The English department

The Report dealt in great detail with the teaching of English, and the staff and resources necessary for that. I have deliberately avoided straying into the wider field of the work of an English department,[1] wishing to focus only on the department's possible contribution to the whole-school policy. It must, however, be stressed that the whole-school policy requires from the English department both that the team do contribute in the agreed ways, and that there is a vigorous exploratory teaching of personal language, of literature, and of the imagination. Because I have needed to stress those uses of language that have not hitherto been extensively taught should not give the impression that I overlook the importance of good contextual teaching of English.

Those outside English departments should also know that the committee found disquieting deficiencies in the provision for English. Staffing was often random; a third of those teaching English having 'no discernible qualification' (15.14), many devoting only a part of the week to English. Timetable resources were frequently poor, that is, English was used to fit in round those subjects which more strenuously claimed blocking or had special period demands (singles *or* doubles). Rooms were frequently inadequate, again showing that English was fitted in to the rooms timetable after the needs of other subjects. This involved a large amount of split-room teaching, with not only teachers dispersed around a number of rooms, but the work of one class's English similarly distributed: 'A substantial proportion of English teachers—over one third—are itinerant within the school, carrying their books about with them from one lesson to another.' (15.21)

Storage space in general was shown to be poor, especially that vital equipment for English teachers—storage for books and papers in the classroom itself. Headquarters or Departmental bases, so vital for materials, were rare, and compared with other subjects the teachers were less likely to work *en suite*. The Committee also found internal deficiencies, of which weak planning, poorly worked out or non-existent syllabus or 'instruments of policy', and unbalanced range of

[1] Apart from the Report, this is a very well written-up subject. A short list of books is included in the last part of the reading list, and my own views have been developed in *Towards the New Fifth*, Longman, 1969, with Graham Owens in *The Practice of English Teaching*, Blackie, 1970, and in Denys Thompson's *Directions in the Teaching of English*, CUP, 1969.

activities were the worst. Clearly an English department must be well set up and well run if it is to provide the core of language development and if it is to meet the school's expectations in specific tuition.

It is clear that some part of the work of the department, or any faculty in which it is placed, must deal with skills of broader application than merely required by that department. In other words, there must be confidence in the staff as a whole that the specific teaching required as an element in the whole language policy is actually firmly in some department's hands. It is also recommended in the report that the English department should 'lead, inspire, and encourage' the policy across the school.

There are many problems with leadership coming from the English department, and many ways in which the conscientious wish of teachers of English to help is made difficult. On the one hand teachers of English may know 'too much' linguistics, and find it difficult not to over-complicate and make too many learned references. They may also be simply too confident in language and adept in debate, thus failing to allow other language perspectives to be described. They can also be extremely ill-informed about how other subjects work, rather presuming that the language activities in a subject such as the crafts must be less good than that in English. They can, as I have implied in Chapter 5, also be very inexperienced in teaching reading outside literature, especially the initial stages and advanced non-fiction.

Even should they have none of these difficulties, the magnitude of the triple task is great: to give good learning experiences in their own subject, to teach specifically the agreed core of language knowledge and skills, to assist with the overall language policy. This last requires tact, as well as knowledge, experience, and energy.

In-service training

Like all curriculum development, a new language policy has in-service training implications. A school will no doubt want to encourage some teachers to attend courses; indeed it might manage to have a suitable teacher seconded for a year's course on language, such as that at the London Institute, or on some aspect of reading. It might persuade the LEA to send one or two more on 'short courses'. However, although such additional expertise would be valuable, especially if fed into the school as a whole by membership of the working party, such piecemeal action is insufficient for a whole-school policy clearly requires whole-school attention. This is clearly a subject for a coherent in-school in-service plan staged over a number of terms, at various levels, and on various aspects. The staff might well be asked which aspects they feel that they would like most help on. One might feel the need for basic phonics (say a recently reorganized Grammar School) and another might ask for work on language theory.

Schools have found the following activities useful. They have been initiated by working parties, the Headmaster, a senior teacher with responsibility for language, or the staff association:

1. *Listening to a visiting speaker*, on use of language (e.g. writing), an aspect (e.g. class and language), or teaching techniques (e.g. small group discussion).
2. *Study and discussion of existing documents*, e.g. the Writing Across the Curriculum's Discussion Pamphlets.
3. *Joint meeting with feeder schools*. There have been many useful discussions planning a continuous policy on such an aspect as reading.
4. *Departmental meetings*, to consider the detailed working-out of recommendations in the particular subject area.
5. *Seminars*. On the whole seminars are most successful when there is 'evidence' to consider, so that discussion is based firmly on actual material. Possible seminar topics:
(a) How do we talk in the classroom?
    Tapes of teacher talk can be analysed and conclusions drawn.
(b) How do the pupils write?
    A selection of writing from various subjects, or all the writing of one pupil a week can be studied.
(c) Accent and dialect in the area.
    A meeting with parents can be valuable.
(d) Reading demands of subject texts.
    Extracts from a variety of commonly used books can be duplicated to establish firstly whether they are suitable and secondly what help could be given to pupil readers.
(e) Punctuation explanations.
    How do we explain a point to a pupil who does not understand?
(f) Graphic demands of subject texts.
    Examples of the graphic support from a variety of commonly used books could be photo-copied for study: maps, diagrams, flow-charts, graphs, picture-charts, etc. Is adequate teaching given at the right point in school to prepare for these?

The major aim of the programme of in-school in-service training would be to share across the curriculum the present expertise, and to help especially those teachers with useful experience or expertise to offer it to others.

When the initiative for developing a language policy has come from the English department, there are serious dangers likely to come from the feeling of other teachers that the teachers of English are frankly getting above themselves and in the process knocking their colleagues. Indeed this is sometimes so. Those teachers of English who feel superior have used the movement for a whole-school language policy as a way of pushing themselves. Even modest and collaborative teachers of

English have sometimes found it difficult not to find themselves in unhappy postures of preaching to the unconverted. If they are the sole possessors of linguistic knowledge that has suddenly become prestigious this is not surprising—but it is usually counter-productive.

Many other parts of the school have relevant skills which they have developed to a greater extent, because of a greater need and more opportunity for practice:

1. *Exposition*. Mathematics and technical drawing teachers have had to face difficult problems of clarity and precision.
2. *Initial stage of reading*. Frequently only the remedial teachers have this knowledge and experience. Very few teachers of English have. It needs to be shared with all.
3. *Pupil discussion*. Craft and science teachers have often developed techniques for establishing and encouraging functional pupil communication.
4. *Reading for meaning*. Sometimes historians have battled with the use of expository print sources for so long that they have faced the problems of how to help.
5. *Bibliographical skills*. Chartered librarians or teacher librarians obviously are fully confident here.
6. *Discussion*. Social Studies and Religious Education teachers have frequently been obliged to develop modes of work helpful here.
7. *Reading aloud*. Drama teachers have useful skills and tips to pass on.
8. *Graphic aids*. Geographers have possibly the widest experience of using a range of illustrations in study texts, and of relating these to the total reading experience.

These skills and experiences can be shared. Members of each of the specialisms I have mentioned can be asked to prepare brief expositions of their experience for the benefit of others. Sometimes there is actually high-powered linguistic knowledge hidden in a teacher of another department, who, such is the tradition in departmentally run schools of specialists, has kept quiet about it. In one school I was in, by far the most knowledgeable student of linguistics was a mathematics teacher. Processes such as I have described break up the apparent linguistic monopoly of the English department, and work towards a true collaboration across the school.

Finally, it is, of course, helpful to have a staff library, and to make sure that a good selection of books on language is available. When all is said, however, the implementation of the policy depends on the head teacher and his or her senior colleagues. Only their continuing interest will ensure that an initial policy is actually carried out, that practice is thus altered, and that the policy itself is reviewed and revised. There can be fewer compelling tests of the leadership of a head teacher than the Committee's recommendation of a language policy across the curriculum.

9. Conclusion: A Language for Life

The title of the Report is no mere publishing expediency. It embodies the two overwhelming complementary truths, that the language we are working with in our schools is the language of the pupils' lives, and that we are helping them develop a language that must serve for life. Indeed, it has jokingly but truly been said that if we fail we have imposed by neglect a life sentence.

The task the adolescent faces in developing his language during the secondary years is immense. John Dixon has given one measure of the immensity when he says of the learning of the scope and range of writing is perhaps equal to the original learning of the mother tongue by the young child—except, of course, that the adolescent does not have the motivation or constant encouragement that the child has. Even in growth of vocabulary the challenge is huge, and the ways of moving from the childhood language to the full adult range complex and largely unknown. In reading, the growth from the average eleven-year-old's competence to that of the adult able to engage with most forms of print is a task so daunting that few manage it. Yet the ability to read at the highest level is essential to the individual's personal growth in the modern world, his ability to benefit from most of the learning opportunities at school and beyond, and his ability to take his place in society. Indeed, behaviour and adjustment problems not only lead to difficulties in learning to read, but, and this is less widely realized, the reverse is also true: reading difficulties are a frequent cause of difficulties of behaviour. And yet too often we are forced in schools into creating the paradox that those who need most help with this formidable adolescent task are given the least help, and are allowed to avoid language challenges and are given less language tuition.

There is no real question of those of us who teach content subjects arguing that we cannot afford the time, nor that the English department ought to get on with the job. In the first place a school language policy *saves* time in that it makes learning more effective, and the use of print sources more rapid and more thorough. In the second place, when we come into teaching we must recognize that we have entered a profession that is dependent on language: the curriculum depends on communication. We must therefore be willing to consider the language which is a large part of our professional task.

More than that, anyone looking to a single department, English, to tackle the whole of the task should be invited to look at the question from the other point of view: what right have teachers of English to teach the most fundamental aspects of the learning of each subject? Surely historians and scientists must want to keep for themselves the tasks of teaching the language of their subjects and the language skills special to their subjects. Such teaching is likely to both be more effective, because not dependent on the transfer of skills, and more realistic, because grounded in a real communication need. Certainly the new coherence of the comprehensive school, which I spoke about at the beginning of the book, depends on overall curriculum planning, which means relating the work of departments to each other, and this will be at its most important in language.

It is worth noting that mixed-ability grouping, favoured now by a large proportion of the schools for their younger classes, creates a special need for a language policy. The central thesis of a mixed-ability teaching organization is that pupils should work in the same setting and at broadly similar tasks. Further, it is presumed that where possible they should collaborate, learning more deeply through that collaboration. This thesis involves a careful consideration of the language aspects of the environment, for the ambitions of the pupil-grouping system can be made impossible by language demands that exclude some, or which cause further divergence. This is notably true of the teaching of reading. If no effort is made by specific individual or small-group tuition to improve basic skills, the least able will not be able even to begin to join in. They will be forced either to choose non-reading tasks (thus getting even less practice), or to choose considerably easier tasks. Similarly, but less often realized, if no tuition in the higher skills of reading are given, background, verbal reasoning levels, and earlier educational experience will push the pupils apart and defeat the grouping that is designed to bring them together. On the other hand, specific tuition in the reading requirements of the particular subject, and specific preparation for the reading tasks involved, help the full range of pupils to benefit from the reading tasks, thus allowing the mixed-ability group to be brought together rather than driven apart. Otherwise the naturally more literate pupils pull even farther ahead, leaving the less able reader to flounder more than they would in homogeneously organized groups.

We are at the early stages of applying the fundamental findings of linguists and psychologists of learning to actual schooling. Those of us who work regularly with a range of ordinary pupils in school urgently want more knowledge, and a more detailed working-out of the procedural implications of that knowledge. There is a real need for further study of the relationship between language and learning in the adolescent stages, and of actual classroom techniques. In particular, I should like to see three kinds of study:

1. Subject-based. Intensive study of the language requirements of each of the subject fields.
2. Micro-aspects. Intensive study of an aspect of language, such as the growth of vocabulary, to fill out the broader studies that we have had so far.
3. Institutional. Case-studies and action research on policies and their effects in particular schools.

In the meantime we must make workable what we do know. In this book I have tried to gather together sufficient of the components of a policy for a school to consider its own situation and to build its own policy to suit. It will be obvious to readers that such a policy cannot be drawn up and applied mechanically, and that the detailed technical aspects will be useless if there is not a constant attempt to create language contexts in which communication is genuinely stimulated and genuinely required.

There remains the importance of something rather more intangible, the need for the entire staff to value language in all its manifestations and in all its modes of communication. If a group of teachers care for communication and care for language, this will help the pupils through the intangible but powerful hidden curriculum as well as through the ostensible teaching curriculum that this book has covered. This concern has to be a positive one for enrichment and extension, not a negative one for fault-finding. It starts with a real concern for what pupils have to say, and goes on to suggestions for reading, listening, and writing. The older tradition of schools depended on a less specialized teaching staff. It seems that with the somewhat more professionally segregated specialist staff of today's subject departments, there may well be a tendency to equate language with English, and this with one department. Within this, there may be less sharing of each teacher's interest in books. In an ideal school, every teacher would be sharing his particular interests, formally and informally, in reading.

Edward Blishen puts the most important single simple point persuasively: 'I do believe that, within limits, with qualifications, a teacher with a passion for a book can touch those he teaches with that passion. . . . The main hope most children have of being turned into readers is that they will somewhere along the way meet an adult, and in the nature of things it probably has to be a teacher, who is himself or herself a true reader, and lays on a demonstration, naturally or with some aid from the teaching arts, or the theatrical arts if needs be, of what it is to be a reader, what you get from it, the excitement of it.'[1]

A language policy is a learning policy. To consider carefully the ways in which our pupils learn the subjects and skills we offer them, we find that language is at the heart of the learning process in each

[1] Reported in the *Times Educational Supplement*, 20 August, 1976.

of the subjects, even, or especially, in the apparently non-linguistic subjects like mathematics. To plan ways in which we can effectively improve our pupils' learning is inevitably to consider how we use language, the language environment of our school, the language expectations we have of our pupils, and the tuition and encouragement we give in language. If we do all this, that is if we establish a whole-school language policy, we shall not only have helped the subject learning of our pupils, we shall also have helped them with their own language for life.

Appendix One

Word Building: A Sample List

A school might wish to produce a list of roots, prefixes, and suffixes which would be available to all teachers. Such a list would be contributed to by all subjects, and would include the vocabulary for each. It would grow out of the school's subject needs. The following list is offered only as a sample to show what such a list might look like. Prefixes are easier to recognize than roots, but unfortunately some have more than one meaning. Also the final letter often changes into that of the first letter of the root. It is easier to consider them *not* in alphabetical order, but according to their sense.

Prefixes of direction

In, On, Upon, Into, Within
in- (or il- and im-)
en –
intro –
To, Toward
ad –
pros –
Away, From, Out, Of
ab –
e –
ex –
ec –, ex –
Below, Down
de –
cata –
infra –
sub –
hypo –
Above, Over, Beyond, Outside Of
extra –
ultra –
trans –
sur –, or super –
hyper –
Across, Through
per –
dia –
trans –
inter –

After, Behind, Back, Backward
re –
retro –
Before, In Front Of, Forward
ante –
pre –
pro –
Around, About
circum –
peri –
be –

Time and age

neo –	new
ante –	before
pre –	before
pro –	before
post –	after
re –	again

Size and number

bi –	twice, doubly, having two
maga –	great
micro –	small
multi –	many
poly –	many
omni –	all
semi –	half, or less than

Negative

a –	not
in –	not
non –	not
un –	not
anti –	against
contra –	against
with –	against
dis –	apart, away
ob –	against
mis –	badly, wrongly
hetero –	unlike
pseudo –	false

Positive

com –, con –, co –	together with
syn –, sym –	together
bene –	well
philo –, phil –	love
homo –	like

| ortho – | straight, right, true |
| rect(s) – | straight, right |

Suffixes

Suffixes do not control meaning as much as prefixes. They more usually alter the function of a word, e.g. change the way in which it can be used. Here are some useful ones.

showing capability or fitness	– able, – ible
a disease	– osis
a man who	– ary
	– ard
	– er
	– ent
	– ian
	– ist
	– or
dimunitives—that make smaller	– cle, – cule, – le
	– ette
	– kin
	– less
feminine	– ette
	– euse

To make into verbs:

– ate	ameliorate
– esce	effervesce
– en	lighten
– fy	rectify

To make into nouns:

– age	montage
– ance, – ence	appurtenance
– ion	redúction
	(thousands of others, all indicate the action)
– ism	communism
	('ism' means a doctrine or system)
– ity, – iety	sobriety
– ment	escarpment
– mony	parsimony
– ry	mimicry
– tude	turpitude
– ture	aperture

To make into adjectives:

– al (– cal)	inimical
– an, – ane	germane
– ar, – ary	sanguinary
– fic	soporific
– ic	didactic
– id	insipid

– ine	bovine
– ish	childish
– ive	furtive

There are also a number of combining forms, mainly from the Greek, which are frequently found at the end of a word, although not strictly suffixes:

– arch, – archy	ruler	anarchy, oligarch, monarchy
– cide	kill, killer	homicide, suicide, regicide, genocide
– cracy	form of government	plutocracy, meritocracy
– iatric, iatry	healing, treatment	psychiatry, geriatrics
– nomy	law, rule, system of knowledge	astronomy
– ology	study, science	entymology, biology, geology
– phile	loving	bibliophile, Anglophile
– phobe, phobia	fear	agrophobia, xenophobia
– tomy	slice, cut, cut away	tonsillectomy

Roots

The following roots are examples of those that might be taught:

Root	Meaning	Words using the root
fact	make	factor
		factory
		malefactor
		benefactor
flu, flux	flow	effluent
		confluence
		fluctuate
		flume
		flux
		influence
		influx
		superfluity
lat, from latus	to carry or bear	collate
		dilate
		dilatory
		elation
		relate
locut, loqu	speak	circumlocutory
		colloquial
		grandiloquence
		interlocution
		loquacious
		obloquy
		ventriloquist
mit, miss	send	remit
		remiss
		mission

reg –	rule	regulate
		regale
		regency
rog, rogat	ask, ask for	abrogate
		arrogance
		arrogate
		derogatory
		prerogative
		prorogue
		supererogatory
		surrogate
ven	come	venture
		adventure
vert	turn	vertebra
		vertex
		vertical
vol	wish, want	volition
		volunteer

Appendix Two

Example of a Working Party's Internal Questionnaire

Language in Education can be divided into four broad areas: Writing, Reading, Talking and Listening. The paper below is divided into these four sections, on which we request your views. At the end is a series of general questions which may require extensive discussion. There is no space on the sheets for answering general questions, so please number your answers carefully, e.g. A.2.i., etc.

A. WRITING
Below is a list of many of the forms of writing expected of our pupils. Please indicate which ones apply to your subject.

		APPLIES		
	A lot	*A certain amount*	*Not very much*	*Not at all*
i. Copying from the board or a book.				
ii. Making notes from a book or a film.				
iii. Making notes from teachers' talk.				
iv. Taking dictation.				
v. Transactional writing, i.e. typical language of science, intellectual enquiry, planning, reporting, instructing, informing, advising, persuading, etc.				
vi. Expressive writing, i.e. in which the personal views or opinions of the writer play an intrinsic part.				
vii. Poetic writing, i.e. writing to be shared rather than corrected. Creative writing.				
viii. Answering questions.				
ix. Answering questions in an expanded form.				
x. Filling in blanks in worksheets.				
xi. Collating information from different sources.				
xii. Lists and other condensed or 'incomplete' forms of writing.				
xiii. Translating or interpreting from one form to another, e.g. Languages or Maths.				

	APPLIES			
	A lot	*A certain amount*	*Not very much*	*Not at all*

xiv. Map work, labelling, copying or creating diagrams, etc.

xv. Other—please specify.

2.   i. Would you say that the types of writing demanded by your subject are mainly ones that can be marked as either right or wrong?

ii. To what extent do you think the intended audience for a piece of written work can affect its quality?

iii. Who, in the main, is the audience?

iv. How important do you think it is to offer pupils a choice of kinds of writing or kinds of topics?

3. Assessing writing:

i. Do you correct most of the errors of spelling, punctuation and grammar in a pupil's writing?

ii. If so, do you write in a correct version or simply indicate that an error has been made?

iii. How do you find out if your method is effective?

iv. If you mark the pupils' writing, is your assessment numerical or a written or spoken comment?

v. If you make a written comment, are you mainly concerned with content or presentation, and does the pupil know which your specific concern will be?

vi. Are there times when your concern with content and presentation clash? How do you deal with this?

vii. What do you see as the role of the English and remedial departments in relation to the written work of your pupils?

B. READING

Below is a list of the various types of reading activities that may go on in your lessons, please indicate which ones apply.

	APPLIES			
	A lot	*A certain amount*	*Not very much*	*Not at all*

1.   i. Reading aloud round the class.

ii. Reading aloud to a teacher.

iii. Reading aloud to a friend.

iv. Following while the teacher reads.

v. Individual self-chosen reading.

vi. Individual reading for information.

vii. Reading instructions from board.

viii. Reading instructions from worksheet.

ix. Reading instructions from textbook.

x. Personal research in libraries—from a variety of sources, etc.

xi. Reading one another's work.

xii. Re-reading their own work.

xiii. Other—please specify.

2.   i. What methods do you have for finding out whether or not the pupils
        have understood what they have read?

      ii. How appropriate in general do you feel is the output from educa-
        tional publishing for the needs of our children?

      iii. If you feel that the language of educational textbooks is not appro-
        priate, how does your department deal with the problem?

      iv. Are you able to find a way by which non or reluctant readers are
        able to take part in the lesson?

      v. How much individual reading in and out of class do you expect
        from the least and most able? How hard are these expectations to
        realize?

      vi. How much help are you able to provide for the less able readers and
        of what kind?

      vii. How far do you find that backwardness in reading hampers your
        pupils' mastery of your subject?

C. PUPILS' TALK

Below is a list of the different kinds of pupils' talk that take place in the class
room. Please indicate their frequency in your lessons.

	APPLIES		
	A certain	Not very	Not
A lot	amount	much	at all

1.   i. Silence
      ii. Answering teacher directed ques-
        tions.
      iii. Asking questions.
      iv. Asking each other for help.
      v. Arguing/shouting.
      vi. Informal gossip/chatter.
      vii. Discussing work in hand inform-
        ally.
      viii. Discussing work in hand in groups.
      ix. Discussing work in hand formally
        as a class.
      x. Expressing opinions and feelings.
      xi. Thinking aloud.
      xii. Memorizing.
      xiii. Taping.
      xiv. Asking teacher for help.

2.   i. To what extent do you find it useful for children to talk about what
        they are doing with (a) each other (b) you?

      ii. Which kinds of talk do you find most difficult to set up?

      iii. What constraints do you feel that you need to put on talk and why?

      iv. What improvements could your department suggest in order to
        make talk a more central or useful tool in learning?

      v. What are the most effective ways your department has found to
        utilize the value of talk?

D. TEACHERS' TALK

Below is a list of some of the different kinds of talk which we, as teachers,
use. Please indicate the frequency in your lessons.

	APPLIES		
A lot	*A certain amount*	*Not very much*	*Not at all*

1. i. Giving instructions to the whole class.
    ii. Demonstrating with explanation.
    iii. Talking to individuals.
    iv. Reading.
    v. Dictating.
    vi. Giving information.
    vii. Explaining.
    viii. Discussing.
    ix. Questioning.
    x. Encouraging.
    xi. Nagging / negotiating / reasoning / bribing.
    xii. Shouting/haranguing.
    xiii. Lecturing.
    xiv. Telling stories/anecdotes.
    xv. Praising.
    xvi. Criticizing.
    xvii. Joking.
    xviii. Chatting.

2. i. What is the department's feeling about a class's attention span in listening to a teacher?
    ii. What ways have your department found to cope with the mixed ability reception of teachers' talk?
    iii. What are the problems in modifying your language to communicate the same ideas to different pupils?

E. LISTENING
    i. How do you help children to value one another's verbal contributions—and how do you help them to listen to you?
    ii. How important do you think is the role of teacher as listener?

F. GENERAL
    i. Does your subject have a specialized vocabulary which children need to master in order to do the work?
    ii. What problems arise in trying to teach this vocabulary?
    iii. How great an emphasis do you put on technical accuracy—written and spoken in your subject?
    iv. Do you think that your subject (or the speed at which a syllabus demands you should move through it) poses real comprehension problems for the pupils that you teach?
    v. What are the methods developed by your department to find out whether or not the children have understood the lesson?
    vi. Do you have any specific provision for coping with the range of ability in the classroom (i.e. for the least and most able)?
    vii. What are the problems in general, that the children bring to the lesson in terms of written and spoken language ability?

G.
    i. Bearing in mind the points raised in the language document,

'Reading to Learn . . .', what does your department feel can be done to support its work in relation to language and learning?

H.

    i. Corridors, Tannoy, Playgrounds, Assemblies, Tutorial and Pastoral care.
Any comments . . . in relation to language only please!

With thanks:
Language Policy Working Party
February 1976.

Appendix Three

Part of the Abbey Wood School
Report and Policy

Foreword

By the Headmaster, Mr C. E. Stuart-Jervis, Abbey Wood School, London.

This document came about because of the Chief Inspector's request for information from schools as to what they were doing, or about to do, as a result of the Bullock Report and its explicit concern for language development in schools.

Dare I say that Abbey Wood, largely due to the efforts of Brian Coxall and his colleagues in the English department, had been pioneering this work for some years, in a manner that predated Bullock. There had already been meetings in the school to discuss the problem. Heads of department and heads of faculty and house had all been involved to a greater or lesser extent and the topic was fresh in their minds.

Still, it is fair to say that we had not made as much progress as we would have liked. Bullock, perhaps, provided the spur needed to progress beyond discussion towards a more positive approach.

What emerges from the massive amount of work that Brian Coxall has undertaken is the need for all teachers to take responsibility for language development with their pupils, for all teachers to ask themselves somewhat searching questions regarding the type of language work involved in their discipline and for all teachers to return, to a greater or lesser extent, to the idea that we are all teachers of English.

This document, however, is also representative of the work of all at Abbey Wood, as it is also representative of their skill and thoughtfulness.

But though the report is an answer to the Chief Inspector's request, it is also a policy document and its content will occupy much time on agendas for many months to come, since one of its main aims is to develop a logical and coherent language policy within the school, one that will be fully understood and to which, eventually, all sections of the school community will be committed.

Introduction

1. These proposals are made in the light of the following:
(a) the work of the 'Language in the Curriculum' working party (Part 1) and Discussion Paper No 7 (Appendix 2);
(b) the Staff Meeting of 23 April, 1975, when it was agreed that 'all teachers

shared a responsibility for language teaching'. (Minutes Staff Meeting);
(c) Senior Staff Conference of 25 February, 1976 (Minutes quoted in Part 1);
(d) reports from Faculties on which Parts 2, 3 and 4 are based;
(e) our own conclusions.

Though writing, reading and talking are considered separately it should be remembered they are not discrete, but as the Bullock Report states: 'Language competence grows incrementally through the interaction of writing, talking, reading and experience, the body of the resulting work an organic whole'. (1.10)

2. There are several reasons for a language policy at Abbey Wood. When our children are in Junior Schools all the work is largely under the control of one teacher. At Abbey Wood they have a 'specialist' curriculum and they are under the direction of a number of teachers, all of whom make demands of language. One of the problems arising from a specialist curriculum is that teachers may make language demands which the pupils in any year are not equipped to meet, as subject teachers may assume their pupils are being prepared for these demands elsewhere. Development within each subject in the curriculum may well depend on coping with language in all its forms. The Language in the Curriculum working party came to the tentative conclusion that:

> For our young people, a week's experience in school may not be viewed as a time-table of various subjects, but as a mass of writing, talking and writing... development across the curriculum may depend on their skill in coping with a wide variety of language and finding language to make sense of new experience. (Appendix 2)

Whether this is true or not, we still have to ensure that our pupils can meet the language demands made on them. We should give particular attention to the part language plays in learning, for as the Bullock report says: 'The pupils' engagement with the subject may rely upon a linguistic process that his teaching procedures actually discourage' (12.1). It is hoped that such a language policy as the one proposed here will ensure that our pupils may be able to meet the language demands we make on them and, by directing our attention to the place of language in our teaching, ensure that pupils develop well in our particular subjects.

Proposed policy

Writing
1. Before presenting any written task to pupils an attempt must be made to establish the kind of writing expected. A check list is given below of the different kinds of writing which the Language in the Curriculum working party found were used in the school. There is considerable overlapping of these kinds within pupils' actual writing. But, once it has been established which kind is broadly required, it must be each teacher's responsibility to ensure that pupils are equipped to perform their task.
Check List
2. Expressive Function:
(a) Description of Personal Experiences
(b) Imaginative
The term 'expressive' means a personal language used in writing or speech. In writing expressive language closely approximates to speech at certain

stages. It is permeated with the self and the pupil's relationships, and is the personal voice of the writer. Expressive language is a matrix from which other language functions develop. The implicit function of words assumes great importance as expressive language depends largely on a shared context.

Transactional Function
(a) Communication of Facts and Information
(b) Summary
(c) Objective Description
(d) Argument, Opinion and Persuasion
(e) Translation from other means of communication, e.g. statistics, maps, diagrams
(f) Note Making.

The term 'transactional' means language of direct instrumental intent, from one person to another. The referential function of words assumes importance in transactional language, i.e. that property of words which enables them to summon up ideas of an object or class of objects or relationship between objects.

Poetic Function

A highly ordered and patterned language used at an advanced stage in play, novel, short story, poetry and some other kinds of writing.

3. Pupils should be allowed to write about new material in their own words before attempting the adult, mature, perhaps objective language required by the subject. The personal language of the expressive function is a foundation upon which the more difficult transactional forms may be built.

4. No pupil should be required to copy out long extracts from books. Many projects are unsatisfactory because they are directly copied and the pupil has not understood the content nor, indeed, the language copied.

5. In correcting pupils' written work we need to be aware of the following:
(a) A writer needs to have an audience—no one will sustain written work if he feels he is writing for himself alone. The range of audience should be extended to include, besides the teacher, the class and others by displays, and publication in magazine form.
(b) As much reading of the pupils' work with the pupil present as can be managed is helpful.
(c) Pupils generally want to write correctly and marking should include attention about the mechanics of spelling, punctuation and grammar.
(d) Too much attention to some pupils' mechanical correctness may inhibit fluency, so it might be necessary to select one aspect for correction at a time.
(e) Comment by the teacher on the pupils' work should be specific and clear; repeating such phrases as 'excellent', 'could do better', etc., will not give the direction that a particular judgement will.

6. New vocabulary required by a subject should be carefully introduced and discussed with pupils.

Reading

7. In presenting reading material, teachers should ensure that the material is appropriate to the reading abilities of their pupils and, where anyone is unable to meet the demands, it is the responsibility of subject specialists to help improve reading skills. Where the problem is serious the Head of the Basic Studies Department should be consulted.

8. Staff should be aware of the three different levels of reading skills— Primary, Intermediate and Comprehension:

(a) Primary skill: where a child perceives individual letters, groups of letters and individual whole words.

(b) Intermediate skills: where a pupil needs the ability to handle sequences of letters, words and larger units of meaning.

(c) Comprehension skills: where a child who reads fluently is extracting meaning from the reading material.

In mixed-ability groups, particularly, there will be a wide range of these skills exhibited. The teacher needs to be aware of the level of skill in each pupil and be responsible for the development of reading required by the subject. (The background to reading process is described in the Bullock Report, Chapter 6.)

9. The reports from departments and faculties generally indicate that in the curriculum the main purpose of reading is to gather information—using the word 'information' in its broadest sense. Of all the ways of gathering information—by observation, personal experience, listening and discussion—reading is by far the most difficult. Where pupils need to read to gather information, they must be helped in how they are to record the information they need, to avoid copying whole sections from books.

10. Where subjects need pupils to consult various books in the Library or within the classroom, pupils need to be taught how to find the relevant material.

11. The Bullock Report sums up the responsibility of subject teachers when it states that they need

> to be aware of the processes involved, able to provide the variety of reading material that is appropriate, and willing to see it as their responsibility to help their pupils meet the reading demands of the subject. (12.7)

Oral

12. The reports which formed the basis of Parts 2 and 3 indicate that the importance of spoken language in the educational process is clearly recognized. Learning requires making knowledge personal and understanding requires the pupil to come to grips with new material, firstly in his own language.

13. Staff should give time in a variety of ways for pupils to talk about the material that is presented to them, whether in small groups in a structured situation or the more formal class discussion. In preparing lessons, situations need to be devised to give pupils the opportunity to explore the particular topic in their own expressive language.

14. The reports from faculties indicate that there is considerable difficulty experienced in enabling children to use the specific technical language of a certain subject. This needs to be introduced carefully. The bridge between personal language and impersonal language should be given serious consideration in lesson planning.

15. Teachers need to structure situations, both formal and informal, in small groups and whole classes where demands are made on pupils spoken language, and to encourage pupils to speak appropriately in these different situations.

16. The kinds of questions staff ask are also important. There is a difference between the question for which there is but one answer and the open question which invites exploration and speculation.

17. More than any other aspect of language, oral work needs further investigation and faculties should document useful practice for the benefit of other subject areas.

Worksheets

18. Worksheets are now in fairly common use, particularly since the school changed to mixed-ability teaching. Subject areas are aware of their advantages and disadvantages and time is ripe for a thorough evaluation of their use.

19. Presentation of worksheets needs careful consideration. They may be constructed in some haste and there are indications that many are poorly presented. With the developing Media Resource Centre and secretarial assistance, there should be no excuse for inferior presentation. Worksheets need to be prepared well in advance of the lesson.

20. Modern methods of examining in several subject areas reduce the demands made on pupils language skills. Many worksheets, perhaps reflecting this, may also carry the danger that these demands are being avoided in the classroom. Consequently the content of worksheets needs to be evaluated, so that we make similar demands of reading and writing on pupils as the former teaching methods did.

21. The levels of ability to which the worksheets are devised needs to be seriously considered. One worksheet for a whole mixed-ability class may mean that only the average pupil is being provided for.

22. The place of worksheets in subject teaching; the need for them to make language demands on pupils; and their presentation needs to be considered further.

Conclusion

This Language in the Curriculum policy has these purposes:

1. to make teaching staff more aware of the language demands made on pupils;

2. to propose that staff should teach the particular language skills required by their subject;

3. to suggest the place of language in the curriculum;

4. to improve the quality of teaching;

5. to implement the recommendation in the Bullock Report that: 'Each school should have an organized policy for language across the curriculum, establishing every teacher's involvement in language and reading development throughout the years of schooling.' (Principal Recommendation 4)

Appendix Four

Part of the Woodberry Down School Working Party Report

Headmaster's preface

There is no doubt that a great deal of learning is by means of language, both because access to ideas, knowledge, and explanations is largely through words, but also because we come to understand ideas by putting them into our own words, by thinking them through. Equally, there is no doubt that a great deal of an individual's growth in language is by means of his or her learning in the subject areas.

Thus the heart of a whole-school language policy is a simple common-sense pulling together: success in the subjects is likely to be greater if we all consider the use of language and our teaching of it; conversely, the pupils' own language, which they so desperately need for their personal, intellectual, and occupational lives, is likely to develop better if we all consider the part language plays in our particular subject area.

At Woodberry Down the number of issues discussed across the whole school and the tradition of inter-departmental meetings (e.g. the house staff Meetings and the lower school pastoral conferences) have put us in a good position to explore how we can, whilst very much retaining our individual subject variety, work together in a concerted approach to and through language. Nevertheless it is a daunting challenge, and I and all the members of the Woodberry Down staff are grateful for the thorough care which our working party have put into considering the question, sounding out our views, researching, and drafting their recommendations. I am personally grateful to each of the members of the working party, and especially to its Chairman, Chris King.

Throughout their deliberations, I know that the working party were anxious to consider each one of us teaching in our classrooms; to respect our personal approaches; to help our subject specialisms; and to reflect our individual wishes. They therefore set up a dialogue with us all, as the Chairman outlines in his introduction. Their final recommendations were then open to scrutiny both individually and at a full heads of departments' meeting. The full staff voted unanimously that the recommendations as amended by this heads of departments' meeting would be accepted. Here, in a revised and polished form, then, are the results of this careful exercise in collaboration and consultation.

Like me, each member of staff probably feels that he or she would have altered a point here, or added an idea there. Opportunities for continuing collaboration will continue, for in accepting the recommendations of the working party, I am also accepting the recommendation that there should be further staff study and in-service work, and that the working party should continue to stand. I have therefore asked Mr King to chair a continuing working party, whose terms of reference are: to assist the Senior Teacher: In-Service (Mr Phipson) with the dissemination of the working party's recommendations; to monitor the implementation of the recommendations; to further consider the language policy, with special regard to language in the mixed-ability group and the use and teaching of reading across the curriculum.

Individual teachers, departmental teams, or house staff groups are invited to contact Mr King with ideas or suggestions.

In the meantime I ask every member of staff to study the recommendations carefully and to implement them vigorously. This document is as near as one can get to a policy for all the teachers actually by all the teachers. Let us make it work, and contribute to its further growth.

Michael Marland
August, 1976

Membership of the Working Party, June 1975–July 1976

Simon Clements, Second Deputy and Curriculum Co-ordinator
Margaret Despicht, Careers Advisor
Ann Dubs, in charge of Reading Centre
Judith Hemming, representing the English Department
Chris King (Chairman), Head of Remedial Department
Joan Nicholson, Science Department
Tom Peryer, Deputy Head of Keller House, representing the House Staff
Christine Peters, Head of Geography
George Phipson, Head of Maths and Advisor to Recently Appointed Teachers
    (from 1 September, 1976, Senior Teacher: In-Service)
Keri Priddle, Head of Technical Studies

Terms of reference

The working party was set up by the Headmaster in June 1975, with the following terms of reference:
    'To consider the present whole-school language policy, "Learning to Read and Reading to Learn", and to recommend any additions or modifications, including any strategies for in-service-training.'

Chairman's Introduction

The following report is the product of three terms' work towards a whole-school language policy.

Following initial staff discussion in 1972–73, Mr Marland wrote 'Learning to Read and Reading to Learn' in January 1974, which was open for discussion and was finally agreed in June 1974. Bullock reported in February 1975 and it was apparent that the whole-school language policy document was not being operated by the whole school.

A working party was set up late in the summer term of 1975 to consider the whole-school language policy as embodied in 'Learning to Read and Reading to Learn', and to make recommendations. The original intention was to draw on as wide a range of curricular experience as possible by involving subject teachers from all major departments. Pressure caused by other commitments made this impossible, and the majority of working party discussions have involved only a small 'nucleus' of members.

The first term was spent largely in defining our own terms and attitude to the matter and the second was spent in producing, distributing and collecting responses to a wide-ranging questionnaire, which was discussed by all departments. From our discussions and the collation of departmental opinion a draft report was circulated for further departmental discussion in May. Observations from these discussions have been included where appropriate, including those from the heads of departments' meeting in July, and the whole process forms the following report.

This report is not a consensus view; neither does it contain only majority views and common ground. It is democratic in the sense that it embodies views held by many staff, which have arisen in response to local necessity and practice. For this reason the working party thought it important to retain the main body of the survey because it is rooted in the reality of our experience and will be valuable for all future discussions. It is therefore included as Part Two.

It is the working party's view that this paper is not definitive. We consider that it is not possible to be absolute in this situation, and we recommend strongly that the paper should be further discussed by departments in relation to their work. The process should be on-going and to this end we further recommend that the working party should be made into a standing committee with the aim of stimulating staff thought in this area as an aspect of internal in-service training. A standing committee of this kind would produce occasional papers, organize seminars, and invite outside speakers.

The first part of the report lists our recommendations in four sections: Writing, Reading, Talking and Listening, and General. The second part is the report on our survey. We also include a short list of books for further reading.

Chris King, Chairman
August, 1976

The Recommendations

SECTION A: WRITING
A.o GENERAL
A.o.o Writing is very important in our education of our pupils, both as a mode of learning and as a useful skill for adult life.

    A.o.1 All teachers of subjects in which writing can be encouraged and all tutors should devote time to the development of the pupils' writing, even if at first sight this seems to be at the expense of the subject. However, the total educational diet of the pupil must be watched, and teachers should also ensure that there are times when there is no pressure on the pupils for writing.

    A.o.2 The less able should not be encouraged to avoid writing, and, equally important, the more able must have the stimulus to write at length whenever possible.

A.1 TYPES OF ASSIGNMENT

A.1.0 Writing skills grow by a gradual differentiation into the specific requirements of special forms. Pupils are less likely to master these forms both if they are forced into them prematurely or if they later have inadequate practice in them.

Writing can be classified into three function categories: expressive, transactional, and poetic. (These are defined at the end of this Section.) Of these 'the expressive is a kind of matrix from which differentiated forms of mature writing are developed'. (Britton, *et al.*, 'The Development of Writing Abilities', Schools Council, 1975, p. 83.)

A.1.1 In the first two years, the expressive function should be the most frequent one, and pupils should not be forced to develop transactional writing out of it too rapidly. However, they should be encouraged to move towards other modes whenever possible.

A.1.2 Teachers should provide considerable variety and choice in the writing assignments that they set.

A.1.3 As pupils get older, especially in year 3, all subjects in which writing is used should provide opportunity for expressive, transactional, and even poetic writing.

A.1.4 Departments should discuss how writing in each of these categories can be encouraged in their subjects.

A.1.5 Questions for writing should be formulated as far as possible so that they invite the pupil to give an expanded answer. There should therefore be very little reliance on worksheets which require one- or two-word answers or which use multiple-choice questions unless there is a special reason.

A.2 AUDIENCE AND RESPONSE

A.2.0 Writing develops better if the writer is aware of a real audience, whose response he values and can know.

A.2.1 Teachers should talk about the pupils' written work with them, or give a written comment. Despite the time involved, teachers should not rely on only a grade or figure to provide the pupil with an assessment.

A.2.2 Opportunities for creating pupil audiences should be developed as much as possible, and all departments should explore ways of doing this, such as displaying written work in subject rooms, having regular displays in tutor rooms, reading work to the class, duplicating pupils' work, producing small magazines.

A.2.3 House heads and heads of schools should also be utilized as readers by sending pupils with good work to see them as a supplement to the entering of commendations in the diary.

A.2.4 Parents should be encouraged to look regularly at their child's books, and this idea should be put across at parents' meetings, etc. Opportunities should be devised for parents to see and discuss their children's work at school.

A.3 TECHNICAL HELP

A.3.0 Responsibility for technical accuracy should be carried by all teachers who expect pupils to write. Although one of the main aims of the English department is to help children achieve technical accuracy, and therefore tuition is given in English time, this must be reinforced by the attention and support of all other teachers.

A.3.1   The most important aspect of technical accuracy is the division of sequences of words into 'sense groups', especially sentences, which should be marked off by full-stop followed by upper-case letter. All teachers correcting written work should make this a top priority amongst technical aspects.

A.3.2   When a pupil makes a great number of technical errors only one or two points should be corrected in each piece, and pupils should be made aware which particular errors are being corrected.

A.3.3   When errors are picked out, the corrected version should be written out by the teacher.

A.3.4   In commenting on technical aspects of writing, teachers should use the technical language: word, space, letter, syllable, stress, vowel (short and long), consonant, upper case, lower case, paragraph, indentation.

A.4   HANDWRITING AND NEATNESS

A.4.0   Neatness, careful presentation, and good handwriting should be encouraged by all teachers.

A.4.1   First-year pupils should have some provision for practice in hand-writing and other aspects of work in the curriculum.

A.4.2   All departments which include writing in their work should spend some time encouraging a legible style of handwriting, and should give priority to the correct use of upper- and lower-case letters (especially the letters 's', 'w', 'b', 'd', and 'r').

A.4.3   Parents should be encouraged to help their children with hand-writing and spelling, although this should not in any way diminish the school's responsibility. The Head of Lower School should find appropriate times to raise this matter.

DEFINITIONS—(A.1.0 ABOVE)

Expressive   This kind of writing may be very close to talking—but on to paper—with the same sense of being a conversation, free to offer personal thoughts and feelings whatever the topic happens to be. The 'writer' is very much part of what he is saying/writing and feels confident that his opinions will be of interest to the reader. His sense of audience is likely to be himself, a friend or 'trusted adult'.

The Writing across the curriculum project sees expressive writing as the core, or central function out of which the following two functions emerge:

Transactional   The job being done here is one of communication, the task of the writing is either to pass on information of one kind or another, or to persuade or command. There is always an audience other than the writer involved—and the more clearly the writer can envisage his audience the more effective the writing is likely to be. The writer's personal views are only a feature of transactional writing in so far as they are strictly relevant to his main topic.

Poetic The job here is to handle language creatively—to *make* something with it. It presents an experience, rather than passing on information, and shapes it into some kind of verbal art form (poem, story, play, film script, etc.).

SECTION B: READING

B.0 GENERAL

B.0.0 The ability to read at the highest level is essential to the individual's personal growth in the modern world, his ability to benefit from most of the learning opportunities at school, and his ability to take his place in society. The school must therefore take the teaching of reading very seriously. Behaviour and adjustment problems not only lead to difficulties in learning to read, but, and this is less widely realized, the reverse is also true: reading difficulties are a frequent cause of difficulties of behaviour.

By 'reading' we do not mean simply the basic decoding of print, but reading for understanding.

B.0.1 There is no point at which a pupil can be said to have 'mastered' reading. Reading development is a continuous development, which is always incomplete. It must therefore be taught at all levels.

B.0.2 Reading involves language, and therefore is best taught in an overall context of talking and writing.

B.0.3 Subject teachers have reported that their pupils are set back in their work in their fourth and fifth years by their reading. It is therefore important that the first three years are used to prepare pupils for the kinds of reading in subject areas demanded by the middle-school curriculum.

B.1. OCCASIONS FOR READING

B.1.0 Pupils should encounter and be helped through print, and they should not be encouraged to circumvent it. Teachers should ensure that there are a variety of suitable occasions for reading as an integral part of the study of most subjects. (We were worried at the interim report of the Schools Council's Effective Use of Reading project, which indicated that reading took very little time in many subject areas with younger classes.) Our survey suggested also that it is possible for a pupil to avoid reading for a large proportion of the week. The problem is partly related to the efficiency of mixed-ability teaching, and also to the view taken by some departments that subject knowledge rather than literacy level should be the main forms of assessment. Obviously there is a need for a balanced approach.

B.1.1 Where possible subject teachers should set aside time for individual reading as a class for reasonable lengths of time. (The same School's Council project also found reading tended to be in brief intermittent bursts.) We feel that as a school we should be aiming for more continuous reading. This reading must be relevant to the subject concerned. The least able can be given individual assistance in this context. The problem of the more able marking time in this situation should be considered by departments.

B.1.2 In certain circumstances and for specific purposes, it is good for pupils to read aloud to the rest of the class, or in groups, or to the teacher. (Teachers should be aware of the problems involved in asking poor readers to read aloud; reading to a larger audience will require the support of proper and adequate teacher intervention.)

B.1.3   Subject departments should, where appropriate, consider with the senior-sixth-form tutor the use of sixth-formers to help lower down the school. A formal structure should be devised to enable this to proceed with the greatest effect and continuity.

B.2   TEACHING READING

B.2.0   Every teacher should be a teacher of reading in his or her own subject.

B.2.1   Staff should use the phonic method of reading words, and should teach syllabification. 'Difficult' words should be approached in this way even with older and more competent pupils. (See Appendix.)

B.2.2   It is good practice to ensure that a child sees a word as well as hears it.

B.2.3   When worksheets are distributed to a whole class, they should be read aloud in advance, either by the teacher or pupils or both, at least at the beginning.

B.2.4   When a passage is given to a pupil to read, the teacher should normally prepare for the reading by (i) putting it into context, (ii) explaining the general aim of the passage, so that the pupil knows what to expect, and (iii) new ideas or concepts should be explained.

B.2.5   Pupils should have their attention drawn to the logical structure of the argument, and to the key words which carry the argument forward, e.g. 'since', 'as a result of', etc.

B.2.6   Pupils should be encouraged to isolate and read out key sentences which convey a particular idea or piece of information.

B.2.7   Whenever possible pupils should be encouraged to comment on the clarity or effectiveness with which a point is made in whatever is being read.

B.2.8   Pupils should be taught the study skills and their way round a book (e.g. use of table of contents, index, etc.).

B.3   RESOURCES FOR READING

B.3.0   Departments must ensure that reading resources are sufficient, suitable, and varied.

B.3.1   The librarian, Education Library at County Hall (via the librarian), and local libraries will provide special collections, given adequate notice, on short-term loan.

B.3.2   The practice of providing book boxes for classes, containing suitable books at a variety of levels, may be exploited by many departments.

B.3.3   When departments produce their own material, they should consider how appropriate it is, not only in the level and kind of reading, but in the quality of reprography. We recommend, therefore:

(i) The use of improved versions of past worksheets, rather than producing afresh on each occasion.

(ii) The maintenance of departmental libraries of worksheets for reference and improvement.

(iii) A central library of individual sheets. (*Note:* The Headmaster has acted on this recommendation: cf. Standing Instructions on Reprographic Facilities.)

B.3.4 The ILEA through its inspectorate should capitalize on and co-ordinate the individual production of materials in schools with a view to producing more of its own material. The SMILE, MRC, English Centre and others have begun to work in this direction, but we consider that the great amount of time spent in production of materials would be reduced if this could be continued in all subject areas. Further liaison between LEAs on a reciprocal basis might increase the materials available at a cost less than that of purchasing through educational publishers.

B.3.5 Representations should be made to the ILEA to discuss with educational publishers the suitability of their products specifically in maths, science, history, geography and humanities, and reading books for the older less able pupil.

B.3.6 Subject departments should encourage the use and understanding of the library in conjunction with the librarian.

SECTION C: TALKING AND LISTENING

C.0.   GENERAL

C.0.0 Spoken language is the basis of all other language activities, yet creating an appropriate situation for constructive language development is one of the most difficult objectives to achieve, since small group work is not always possible.

C.0.1 In the long term, each department should consider its criteria regarding both spoken language and vocabulary development. Material and references to encourage discussion should be made available.

C.0.2 The drama and English departments should consider their joint and linked role in this area.

C.0.3 Informal contact by children with staff in school should be encouraged. Individual contact with pupils offers a better, more natural chance for development in the pupils' spoken language. It is often difficult to achieve in a full classroom.

C.1   PRACTICE

C.1.0 A child has to 'use' a word, concept or idea in speech many times to make it his or her own.

C.1.1 Although children should be helped to extend their vocabularies and develop their spoken language structure we should be careful not to make any of them scared to open their mouths in formal situations.

C.1.2 A pupil's contributions should be valued—he or she should be listened to in the same way that we as teachers expect to have our contributions listened to. Pupils should also be encouraged to value each others contributions.

C.1.3   If a teacher has an 'expected' answer in mind to a verbal question in class, he/she should nevertheless be prepared to find unexpected answers interesting in their own right.

C.1.4   Practical work provides a shared focus for talk to take place. Where practical work is involved pupils should be given every opportunity to use talk to organize themselves, to talk through what they are discovering and to reflect on and explain what they have done and learned.

C.2   LISTENING

C.2.0   Listening is a difficult and important skill.

C.2.1   Positive training in listening should be the responsibility of all departments. Comprehension passages, formulated within subject framework should be given regularly in the lower school. These should be oral but require written answers whenever possible so that progress may be monitored. A standardized oral comprehension test should also be given in the first year.

SECTION D: GENERAL

D.0   VOCABULARY

D.0.1   We recommend that each subject department should draw up a list of its specialist words. It may be helpful to consider two categories—words specific to the subject (*pipette, contour, glaze*) and words given a specific meaning within the subject (*power, divide, perspective*).

D.0.2   Departments should set aside time to teach this vocabulary in whatever way each department finds appropriate. Lists should be distributed to staff for information.

D.0.3   The teaching of new words and their subsequent retention could be helped by a subject 'dictionary' drawn from the list mentioned above. Where the word describes a physical object this could be in the form of a 'picture dictionary'; however, this idea does help to highlight a problem in teaching vocabulary.

D.0.4   Some works are the names for objects or activities and can be learnt as such (*countersink, test tube, vertex*); but for some words their full meaning is only assimilated from contextual use and may differ from subject to subject (*revolution, improvise, moral*). Thus a word should be taught and its meaning understood in a context.

D.0.5   Even when the pressures of time and pupils make the ideas outlined above seem idealistic we would suggest that an ordinary dictionary is available and its method of use known.

D.1   MIXED-ABILITY TEACHING

D.1.1   The benefit to pupils with poor reading and writing of being in a group with all abilities will only accrue if the provision for coping with such a group is equal to that which they would receive under a different grouping principle. A particularly worrying element is when the main body of work or text is the same for all pupils and only at the end is there extra work or more difficult questions.

D.1.2   We would recommend that where a department has not got suitable material for mixed-ability teaching either the lack should be remedied or the mode reconsidered.

D.1.3   As a subject for further debate that of the efficacy of mixed-ability teaching in extending the most able and helping the least able while ensuring that those in the middle are suitably taught should be considered. The view has been expressed that in this situation everybody suffers, and it seems appropriate that the question should be raised at some future date.

D.2   RESOURCES

D.2.1   A selection of books dealing with the study of language across the curriculum should be held in school for staff reference.

D.2.2   The library should include more taped resources.

D.3   GENERAL PRACTICE

D.3.1   Teachers should consider starting some of their lessons by recapitulating what was learned in the last lesson.

D.3.2   In the giving of formal tests, the questions could be read out loud so that poor readers are tested on what they have learned of the subject matter and not penalized by their reading difficulties.

D.3.3   It is valuable not to rely on any one method of evaluating what the pupils have learned from a given body of work. There are times when this can be equally well done orally as in a written form.

D.4   REPORTS

D.4.1   More consideration should be given to the language used in the writing of reports.

D.5   SOCIAL COMPETENCE

D.5.1   All pupils should, by the time they leave school, be able to cope with being presented with all types of forms—e.g. application, tax, union registration, insurance, holiday booking, HP, cheques, and documents such as vaccination certificates, pension statements, mortgages, tenancy agreements, bills, record-player instructions, etc.

D.6   ENGLISH DEPARTMENT

D.6.1   It would be helpful if the aims, policies and practices of the English department could be disseminated so other departments could see their own requirements and efforts in a context.

D.7   TOPICS FOR FURTHER STUDY ARISING OUT OF THE REPORT

D.7.1   Woodberry Down departmental analysis of reading and writing as in the Schools Council report, Writing across the curriculum 11–18.

D.7.2   Staff familiarization with phonic method of teaching reading.

D.7.3   Whether sixth-formers, parents, etc. could and should be involved in helping backward readers, etc.

D.7.4   The efficacy of mixed-ability teaching in ensuring that all abilities are properly catered for.

D.7.5   The structuring of talk as a medium of learning and its 'dual', listening.

D.7.6   Also listed in document—seminars on Study Skills, Vocabulary Development, Comprehension Technique, Spelling Rules, Oracy, Social Literacy.

D.7.7 A collection should be made of the range of Woodberry Down pupils' writing.

D.7.8 A series of lectures and/or seminars should be arranged on pupils' and teachers' language as an important aspect of in-service training.

Appendix Five

A Policy Document for the School-wide Reading Programme in Culverhay School

Section 1

(a) *Why read?*

Some of the ways in which reading is an aid to children's development.

(1) information from reading used in work with other people.
(2) understanding of oneself and others through reading.
(3) behavioural changes as a result of reading.
(4) therapeutic effect of reading.
(5) building a personal philosophy from reading.
(6) understanding of the natural world and society.
(7) meeting personal needs with reading.

(b) *What is reading?*

Reading encompasses so many aspects of human behaviour that one definition could only be inadequate. The list below, of some of the many activities associated with reading, gives an indication of the complexity of the subject with which this booklet deals.

At secondary level reading involves:

1. *Vocabulary development.*
   (a) learning new words through wide reading.
   (b) learning of key words and concepts in various subjects.
   (c) learning of technical abbreviations, symbols and formulae.
   (d) consulting of dictionaries.
   (e) studying of words in various contexts.
   (f) study of word origins.
   (g) recognition of common words.
2. *Word recognition.*
   (a) division of words into syllables for pronunciation.
   (b) use of phonetic approach.
   (c) knowledge of prefixes and suffixes.
   (d) recognition of 'overtones' of words.
3. *Comprehension and organization.*
   (a) comprehension of sentences accurately.
   (b) comprehension of main idea of a paragraph.
   (c) recognition of the organization of an article or chapter.
   (d) summarizing what has been read.
   (e) learning to read critically—distinguishing essential from non-essential.

    (f) examining truth or correctness of statements.

    (g) recognition of fact and opinion.

    (h) bringing own experience to bear on what has been read.

    (i) noting of cause and effect.

    (j) drawing of inferences and conclusions.

    (k) reading 'between the lines'.

    (l) integration and organization of information from various reading sources.

4. *Reading interests.*

    (a) voluntary reading.

    (b) use of school and public library.

    (c) finding a personal value in reading.

    (d) appraisal of quality of reading material.

    (e) development of particular reading interests.

    (f) reads more for personal information.

5. *Study skills.*

    (a) sitting still long enough to read.

    (b) using 'skimming' for different purposes (to obtain facts, a general impression, main ideas, possible questions, plot).

    (c) reading of maps, charts, graphs, diagrams, formulae.

    (d) reading of 'out-of-school' material.

    (e) location and selection of information on a particular topic.

    (f) familiarity with a variety of sources of information.

    (g) learning how to take notes.

    (h) use of Survey Q3R method when appropriate.

    (i) reading more rapidly with adequate comprehension.

    (j) application in other forms of ideas gained from reading (making pictorial or graphic records, solving problems, entertaining, teaching).

    (k) forming of a study habit.

6. *Approaches to reading.*

    (a) setting of specific objectives before beginning to read.

    (b) use of a variety of methods and rates of reading.

    (c) reading with intent to organize, remember and use ideas.

    (d) relating of reading to circumstances outside the immediate environment.

7. *Personal development.*

    (a) meeting personal needs with reading.

    (b) use of information from reading in work with other people.

    (c) understanding of oneself and others through reading.

    (d) understanding of the natural world and society.

    (e) behavioural changes as a result of reading.

    (f) using of reading to build a personal philosophy.

    (g) therapeutic effect of reading.

From this greatly abridged selection it is apparent that reading can never be one teacher's task or even one department's responsibility.

(c) *Why a school-wide reading programme?*

Reading permeates the curriculum and is a major source of knowledge in every subject field. Therefore, instruction in reading should be an integral part of every reading experience in every subject. ('The Reading Curriculum', Amelia Melnick and John Merritt (eds), The Open University Press, 1972.

The level of reading skill required for participation in the affairs of modern society is far above that implied in earlier definitions of literacy. ('A Language For Life', The Bullock Report, HMSO 1975.)

Every school should devise a systematic policy for the development of reading competence in pupils of all ages and ability levels. (Bullock Report.)

All subjects are involved with reading and this booklet is intended for information and as a check-list for all teachers concerned about the reading abilities of the students they teach.

Section 2 : The school reading programme

(a) *Area of concern*

All students. (Those with special difficulties in literacy will be dealt with on a withdrawal basis.)

The problem areas are principally:

(a) students with ability but lack of interest in reading.

(b) students with low ability and too difficult books.

(c) students with no recognized need for reading in their lives.

(b) *General procedure*

All students will have reading tests on entering the school: at the beginning of the third year, and again at the beginning of the fifth year.

The tests used are:

(c) *Reading tests*

Test	Ability measured	Age range	Score
1. Daniels and Diack Graded Test of Reading Experience	Reading Experience Age	6–14+	In years and months
2. Holborn Reading Scale	Individual test of reading age	5 years 9 months – 13 years 9 months	In years and months
3. Neales Analysis Test	Reading Age Comprehension Level Speed and Fluency		In years and months

Non-verbal tests

1. Compound Series Test by Morrisby	I.Q.	
2. Standard Progressive Matrices by J. C. Raven	Intellectual Capacity (5 grades from 'intellectually superior' to 'intellectually defective'—with a very broad band for the 'intellectually average'	

The results of these tests are avilable to all staff so that the appropriate ability levels of any teaching group can be readily determined.

This information is *an indication of a particular situation* and must not be regarded as an end in itself.

The English and Remedial teachers provide all students with tuition in the basic reading skills (word recognition, basic vocabulary, spelling, appreciation of literature, comprehension, etc.) and through a School

Reading Programme it is hoped to develop these skills more fully and to encourage all aspects of reading.

(d) *Reading procedures across the curriculum*

Set out below is a check-list of some of the procedures which will help the teacher play an effective part in the successful practice of reading within his or her own subject group. This is not intended as a prescriptive list, nor as a 'reading course'; it is merely a list of activities which singularly or collectively aid reading development.

Text testing techniques

(1) *Initial informal testing* in each subject using a passage from a textbook or reference book. By timing the reading and testing the comprehension the teacher will learn much about how well students read the text used in his or her subject.

(Through the standardized tests the teacher already knows the range of reading ability represented in his teaching group.)

Tests of this kind can show:

    (a) the accuracy with which the student comprehends main points.

    (b) how well the student can draw inferences.

    (c) the student's ability to organize his own ideas as he reads.

Questions need to be designed to elicit such responses.

One basic test to check the suitability of a particular text for a group of students is the cloze procedure.

This requires the student to fill in a gap, usually a whole word, which has been left in the text. To do this the child must employ a number of criteria:

    (i) select a word which is grammatically correct.

    (ii) select a word with the correct meaning.

    (iii) choose a word which best fits the vocabulary employed by the author.

Implications for the teacher are

    (a) the production of the text with appropriate gaps from subject text books.

    (b) to choose texts from the beginning, middle and end of book so as to obtain passages that are representative of the whole book.

    (c) to decide whether to employ 'structural deletion' (omission of not more than one word in ten), or 'lexical deletion' (where certain parts of speech are omitted, e.g. nouns or verbs). Each method appears to have some merit and provides a quick and easy way of checking a student's comprehension of a chosen text.

    (d) the use of standardized 'cloze' tests would simplify the testing of reading suitability.

(The 'cloze' method has however, several aspects which still need answers:

(1) What is the appropriate number deletions for each age group?

(2) Will *deletion*, or *omission* affect the results?

(3) Will results vary according to whether the test is given orally or in writing?

(4) What variables affect performance (e.g. vocabulary, sentence completion, level of comprehension, intelligence and socio-economic status)?

(5) What is the particular effect of heavy 'lexical deletion' (parts of speech)?

(6) Can a percentage score be equated with individual reading levels or even individual frustration level?

(2) Make a careful choice of textbooks, taking into account the vocabulary; illustrations; simplicity of reference sections (glossaries, indexes, footnotes, marginal headings); general layout of main ideas; clear expression of author's

ideas; level of previous knowledge required by student in order to find the book useful; the aims and achievements of the book (are they consistent with those of the teacher)? Even the most well-produced books need teacher assistance. The generous provisions of suitable reading material is essential. *Implication*—Familiarity with the variety of material available in any one subject may involve time spent by the teacher in bookshops, at publishers' exhibitions and at teachers' centres. Further capitation may also be necessary.

Pupil testing techniques

Before the teacher decides to use a particular textbook it is necessary to determine a student's level of ability *informally* using the following technique:

(i) at the *independent level* the student is able to read aloud fluently with 99 per cent accuracy. If he has more than one error in every 100 words then he has not reached this level with this material.

(ii) If however, the student has not more than 5 errors in every 100 words and can answer 75 per cent of the questions asked by the teacher, then the student is at the *instructional level* with the material.

(iii) With 10 or more errors in every 190 words and a literal comprehension rate of 50 per cent or below, the student is at *frustration level* and the material is too difficult for him.

This is an indication of a student's reading level on a particular text and the value of such information lies in the future action that the teacher takes. *Implications*—Thoughtful recording of this information is necessary if it is to be turned to advantage, and provision of a large selection of texts for differing abilities may be costly in time and money.

It must be stressed that there is no *one* reading activity which is the panacea for all. Any of the methods suggested above may be modified and used according to the purpose and material. To attempt the use of a single technique may well be a handicap to the teacher and the student.

Study techniques

1. Use of Survey Q3R

This system can be used on textbooks in many subjects, but is most successful with material which is organized in a logical pattern. Five stages are involved:

Step 1—Survey:

Look through the passage to be read and note the information given by

(a) Boldface type, (b) Pictures and captions, (c) Charts,
(d) Drawings with captions, (e) Maps and diagrams, (f) Summaries,
(g) Questions.

Step 2—Question:

Questions can be formulated by the student and teachers. (Use of the information contained in the headings and sub-headings is adequate for this purpose). Questions can be written down one side of a piece of exercise paper folded lengthwise and answers need only be represented by *key words*; there is no need to write long answers.

Step 3—Read:

Read to find the main points which answer the questions. (There are usually one or two main points in each section). Remember the important facts.

Step 4—Recite:

Return to the question sheet. Cover the answers and attempt to answer the questions—reference to the key words and/or the book may be necessary. The immediate recall and then the practice until all the questions can be answered without reference to key words or text is very *important*.

Step 5—Review:

Answer the questions again some three or four weeks later and before examinations. Re-read only the passages which have been forgotten.

This is a basic study method and as such is capable of being modified.

2. The teacher may cater for the various reading abilities within a group by setting different reading tasks—simple factual work for those of low ability; more critical comments on content and style from those of high ability. Simpler texts or pamphlets on the same topic, ready-made or written by the teacher, will meet the requirements.

Critical reading (reading and selecting for the purpose of reaching a conclusion).

The demands on adults to read critically are greater today than ever before. A single textbook, considered to be authoritative, is not conducive to critical reading. Comparative reading should be attempted whenever possible. Questions that require only verbatim reproduction of the ideas read, deter critical reading.

Students must read slowly; subject teachers should plan to allocate adequate time for instruction in critical reading. (Less material may be covered but the quality of the student's reading should improve).

Implications—Considerable time needed to prepare the various pamphlets required by the group and the arrangement of the different tasks for students of varying abilities will demand careful organization and grouping in the classroom. The teacher may need help when determining the reading levels of the material he intends to create. Collection over the years of work from able students provides material which has been simplified from more difficult sources.

3. In every subject the student should be taught to glance through the book, chapter or passage to obtain an idea of the content, and then see how this fits in with his previous knowledge and his present and future needs.

Implications — Discussion of possible goals is important for greater understanding.

Anticipation of what the author is going to say sharpens interpretation and usually increases concentration.

'Literal' comprehension is important and though the techniques might be learned in an English lesson, the amount of practice required must come in other subjects 'Inferential' comprehension is time consuming but must be made part of the reading in every subject if a student is ever to realize the implications of what he reads.

4. The use of various reading aids must be pointed out; pictures, charts diagrams; indexes; tables of contents; footnotes; glossaries; chapter, section and marginal headings; and questions.

In each subject an understanding of these aids makes the difference between true comprehension and a vague impression.

Implications—Subject time must include this specific instruction.

5. Speed of reading and what to look for in any reading task needs to be indicated by the teacher.

If a student is to study a basic book in a subject then he needs to read slowly in order to grasp the main points and supporting details of each paragraph.

Implications—When to 'skim' and when to 'study' a text must be pointed out to the student so that he may make more economic use of his time.

6. For the student in any subject the setting of specific goals which are

attainable through reading is an important factor in creating a 'felt need' for the reading experience. Having a purpose creates 'readiness to read'.

Implications—Use of blackboards and/or printed sheets for thought-provoking questions related to the reading, greatly aid the student's success with these goals. The problem-solving method with answers attainable through reading needs similar preparation.

7. Time to discuss what they have been reading is necessary for the students' understanding; this sharing of reading-experiences with others is important.

Implications—The Bullock Report stresses the need for group discussion on any reading material attempted by a class and time must be available for this activity within any 'reading' allocation. The ability to read critically can be fostered by discussion.

8. The student can be helped to acquire the particular vocabulary for each subject—through lists and glossaries specially prepared by subject teachers and students, and kept for reference in exercise books or notebooks. The preparation of a glossary by the student is a much more impressive experience than the ready-made glossary in front of him (there is a glossary of 300 words peculiar to Music).

Implications—Initial tests are useful to determine the extent of a student's identification of particular terms used in a subject. (In mathematics where sentences are stripped to the minimum there is little to suggest the meaning of a particular term in a sentence; its meaning must be taught.)

9. Students should be encouraged to use school and public libraries to supplement subject reading—specific references must be given to the student.

Implications—The teacher's own knowledge of specific references available in public and school library is essential for any real encouragement of pupils' reading.

10. The student's previous familiarization, through some other medium (television, film-strips, tape-recording, records, illustrations, models, etc.), with the material to be taught is often an aid to more effective reading in a subject. The poor reader who turns to the 'practical' subjects because he does not have to read about them, is disillusioned when he is confronted *immediately* by a textbook or a worksheet that teems with technical vocabulary.

Implications—Pre-viewing of films, television programmes and similar material, and the organization of its presentation to the students must become part of the 'reading' preparation. The Resources Department has facilities for aiding all subject teachers with this preparation.

11. The student should be able to plan his reading, to know what can be read for a general impression and what needs detailed consideration. He must be taught to read selectively and to summarize the information gained not merely by copying but by making his own notes. Students who are too dependent upon the teacher for what they should read become unable to make their own choice.

Implications—When the student plans his own reading activity, he becomes an 'active' not a 'passive' reader and can take advantage of the opportunities that the printed words offers for exercising reason, existing knowledge and imagination:

(a) the time, extent and place of the reading can often be chosen.
(b) past or future parts of the text are always readily available for re-reading.
(c) the reading process can be halted at any moment to allow time for

thought, for note-making or for making comparisons with other sources of information.

Section 3: Criteria for success

(a) *The success of reading improvement* across the curriculum depends on the following conditions:

    (a) All the teachers must recognize the need for such a scheme.

    (b) That this is not seen as a short-term measure.

    (c) Financial support for materials must be available where necessary (it may be necessary to limit the scheme to a small area of the curriculum at first).

    (d) Senior staff need to be sincerely and actively in favour of reading improvement on a school-wide basis.

(b) *Some questions and answers*

Q. Does a teacher need specialized training to help any student to improve his reading?

A. It depends upon the level of proficiency, but a good teacher who is friendly and understanding will help students improve their reading.

Q. Do I neglect the teaching of my subject for the teaching of reading?

A. Unless the teaching of reading is part of a student's instruction it is probable that he is a less-efficient student. The teacher becomes frustrated; he/she feels teaching is impossible if the students are unable to read satisfactorily. The check list provided will help subject teachers with a basic approach.

Q. With a limited number of periods for my subject how am I expected to do the job of an English teacher as well as my own?

A. The teaching and practice of reading is the concern of all staff and all students. Helping students to read more efficiently is part of the teacher's professional role and is not an extra task or the task of one department.

Q. What can I do in a cla. of varied ability when I have to use the same textbook for all students?

A. By recognizing that there is no one method which will improve all students' reading and by employing a variety of the activities suggested, some satisfaction should arise for students and teacher.

(c) Conclusion

If reading is understood to encompass all those activities listed in the opening part of this booklet, and more, then any evaluation of a reading scheme across the curriculum is extremely complex. Subject teachers need (a) to state their specific objectives when attempting any reading with their students, (b) to consider carefully the material they are using and, (c) to choose the reading activities most likely to achieve the stated objectives and which are most appropriate for the subject content.

When the reading has been completed the evaluation takes place and must include an assessment of the success or failure of the objectives. In the light of this knowledge there must then be a review of (a) *materials* and (b) *reading activities* in order to determine whether future policy will be a repetition or a modification of these.

The aim of evaluation is to promote growth not merely measure it.

The evaluation of the total reading programme across the curriculum is a major undertaking requiring separate consideration with representatives from many areas of the school.

> The aim of all developmental reading programmes is to produce effective readers who like to read, who are not deterred by any reasonable difficulty, who are independent and analytical in their reading, who are capable of literary appreciation, and who are interested in the possibility of a better life and a better world. (*The Improvement of Reading*, Strang, McCullough and Traxler, McGraw-Hill, p. 198.)

Appendix Six

Television

Any policy concerned with language must include reference to the dominant entertainment and art form of our age, television. The Report firmly recommends:

> Television is now part of our culture and therefore a legitimate study for schools. The school has an important part to play in promoting a discriminating approach to it, but it is equally important that children should learn to appreciate the positive values and variety of experiences the medium can provide. (C & R 295)

I hope that once and for all its recommendations have pulled television out of 'audio-visual aids' and placed it in a position analogous to the books, cassettes, or pictures in a resource centre. Unfortunately even the report, for all its strong encouragement, places its discussion towards the end of the chapter (22) entitled 'Technological Aids and Broadcasting'. It should rather be in the continuum of talk, reading, and literature, for the approach to television is analogous to the approach to literature.

The emphasis should not be on criticism—that is, the 'Reading and Discrimination' approach. It should certainly not be heavily influenced by concentration on what is judged to be meretricious in an attempt to drive that enjoyment out of the pupils' lives. The sharing of enthusiasm is more educative than the attempt to persuade to see the faults in certain programmes.

There is now a substantial body of books and articles to help the teacher, but it is sad that although the Committee declared: 'We were impressed by such work as we did see' it also registered concern at how little was being done.

The question the school has to ask is where the approach will come. Some schools respond to this recognition of a curriculum need by putting a new subject on the timetable, and thus there are schools that study separately the mass media or screen appreciation. I do not regard this as an adequate approach to television, which is, after all, a medium not a subject. The Report recommends three complementary approaches:

> (a) the group study of television programmes, extracts, and scripts alongside other media dealing with the same theme;
> (b) the study of a full-length television work in its own right, with associated discussion and writing;
> (c) the study of television as a medium, with some exploration of production methods, comparison with other media, and analysis of the output of programmes.

Although (c) is necessarily limited to one subject area, (a) certainly and (b) to some extent should be used in a number of subject areas. (a) could be thought of as a thematic approach, and simply suggests that the material, normally on video recordings, should be used as often as possible as one of the elements in the range of learning resources assembled for a particular topic. This is fairly easy in the Humanities. (b) is likely to be especially the province of English, when plays or dramatizations will be the main fare. However, documentaries and other presentations must not be overlooked across the curriculum.

All work is probably helped if there is a specialist option in the fourth and fifth years, for not only does that permit the pupil whose interests have been aroused to pursue the topic more methodically, but also it helps a teacher develop a special expertise, skill in presentation, and range of material which will help the work elsewhere. Obviously, however, this special patch is not so important to the school as a whole as the contextualized approach. This will be helped by a proper stocking of books in the library, displays in various parts of the school, references in assemblies, and the like, but above all the use of television material in a variety of subject areas, with teacher-led responses and questions about the nature of the medium as evidence.

A Language Policy Reading List

This is a short list of further reading that Heads and Deputies would find useful and realistic. All quotations and references have been credited in footnotes with full bibliographical details.

Titles have been grouped into sections, and alphabetically by author within sections.

The key books, such as might make the initial reading for a Working Party, are asterisked.

Bullock Committee

*A Language for Life, HMSO, 1975.

Language

*Britton, James, *Language and Learning*, Penguin, 1970.

Bruner, J. S., *Language as an Instrument of Thought*, in Davies, A. (ed.), *Problems in Language and Learning*, Heinemann Educational Books, 1975.

Creber, Patrick, *Lost for Words: Language and Educational Failure*, Penguin, 1972.

Gleason, H. A. Jr, *Linguistics and English Grammar*, Holt, Rinehart and Winston, 1965.

Lawton, Dennis, *Social Class, Language and Education*, Routledge and Kegan Paul, 1968.

Open University, *Language in Education*, Routledge and Kegan Paul, 1972.

Pride, J. B., and Holmes, Janet (eds.), *Sociolinguistics, selected readings*, Penguin, 1972.

Quirk, R., *The Use of English*, Longman, 1962.

Trudgill, P., *Sociolinguistics*, Penguin, 1975.

*Wilkinson, Andrew, *The Foundations of Language*, OUP, 1971.

Wilkinson, Andrew, *Language and Education*, OUP, 1975.

Williamson, A. (ed.), *The State of Language*, University of Birmingham, 1969.

Talking

*Barnes, Douglas, *From Communication to Curriculum*, Penguin, 1976.

*Barnes, D., Britton, J. and Rosen, H., *Language, the Learner, and the School*, Penguin, revised edition, 1971.

Reading

Cashdan, A. (ed.), *The Content of Reading*, Proceedings of the 1975 UKRA Conference, Ward Lock Educational, 1976.

Fader, Daniel N. and McNeil, Elton B., *Hooked on Books*, Pergamon Press, 1969.

Harris, Albert J. and Sipay, Edward R. (eds), *Readings on Reading Instruction*, David McKay and Company, N.Y., second edition, 1972.

*Herber, Harold L., *Teaching Reading in Content Areas*, Prentice-Hall, 1970.

Mackay, D., Thompson, B., and Schaub, P., *Breakthrough to Literacy*, Teachers' Manual, Longman, 1970.

Melnik, Amelia and Merritt, John (eds), *The Reading Curriculum*, University of London Press, 1972.

*Melnik, Amelia and Merritt, John (eds), *Reading: Today and Tomorrow*, University of London Press, 1972.

Moyle, D. (ed.), *Reading/What of the Future?* Proceedings of the 1974 UKRA Conference, Ward Lock Educational, 1975.

Pumfrey, Peter, *Reading: Tests and Assessment Techniques*, Hodder and Stoughton, for UKRA, 1976.

Robinson, H. Alan, *Teaching Reading and Study Strategies*, Allyn and Bacon,

Robinson, H. Alan and Thomas, Ellen Lamar (eds), *Fusing Reading Skills and Content*, International Reading Association, 1969.

Schools Council, *Children's Reading Interests*, being Working Paper 52, Evans/Methuen Educational, 1974.

Smith, Frank, *Understanding Reading*, Holt, Rinehart and Winston, 1971.

Turner, J., *The Assessment of Reading Skills*, UKRA bibliography No 2, UKRA, 1972.

Walker, C., *Reading Development and Extension*, Ward Lock Educational, 1974.

Writing

*Britton, James *et al.*, *The Development of Writing Abilities (11–18)*, Macmillan for the Schools Council, 1975.

Martin, Nancy; D'Arcy, Pat; Newton, Bryan; and Parker, Robert, *Writing and Learning Across the Curriculum, 11–16*, Ward Lock Educational, 1976.

Peters, Margaret L., *Diagnostic and Remedial Spelling Manual*, Macmillan, 1975.

Peters, Margaret L., *Spelling: Caught or Taught?* Routledge and Kegan Paul, 1967.

Writing Across the Curriculum Project, *From Information to Understanding, Why Write?, From Talking to Writing, Keeping Options Open, Writing in Science, Language and Learning in the Humanities, Language Policies in Schools*, Ward Lock Educational, 1976–7.

Listening

Wilkinson, Andrew; Stratta, Leslie; and Dudley, Peter, *The Quality of Listening*, a Schools Council Research Study, Macmillan Education, 1974.

Organizing Resources

Beswick, Norman, *Organizing Resources*, Heinemann Organization in Schools Series, 1975.

Beswick, Norman, *Resource-Based Learning*, Heinemann Organization in Schools Series, 1977.

Library Association, *School Library Resource Centre: Recommended Standards for Policy and Provision*, The Library Association, 1975.

Schools Council, *School Resource Centres*, being Working Paper 43, Evans, 1972.

Teaching of English (General)

Central Committee on English (Scottish), *The Teaching of English Language* (Bulletin No. 5), HMSO, 1972.

Currie, W. B., *New Directions in Teaching English Language*, Longman, 1973.

Dixon, John, *Growth Through English*, OUP, revised edition, 1975.

Dixon, John and Stratta, Leslie, *Patterns of Language*, Heinemann Educational Books, 1975.

Owens, Graham and Marland, Michael, *The Practice of English Teaching*, Blackie, 1970.

Whitehead, Frank, *The Disappearing Dais*, Chatto and Windus, 1966.

Index

1. The word 'Report' means the Bullock Report, details of which will be found in the footnote at the bottom of the first page of the preface.
2. The letter 'n' indicates footnotes at the bottom of the page given.